ART ON SIGHT

Christophe Fratin:
Eagles and Prey,
1850, Central Park,
New York, NY

ART
ON
SIGHT

Discovering the Best Museums, Galleries,

Sculpture Parks, Auction Houses,

Monuments, Stained Glass, and More,

in NYC and Its Surroundings

LUCY D. ROSENFELD AND MARINA HARRISON

The Countryman Press
Woodstock, Vermont

Book design and composition by Susan Livingston
Maps by Lucy D. Rosenfeld

Library of Congress Cataloging-in-Publication Data are available
Art on Sight
978-0-88150-996-0

Published by The Countryman Press,
P.O. Box 748, Woodstock, VT 05091
Distributed by W. W. Norton & Company, Inc.,
500 Fifth Avenue, New York, NY 10110
Printed in the United States of America

10 9 8 7 6 5 4 3 2 1

ART ON SIGHT

CONTENTS

The Shimmering of Heated Air, Japanese basket, Asia Society Museum, New York, NY

Edward Hopper's boyhood home

Bridge of Sighs
at Yale University,
New Haven, CT

Geleda-Yoruba
mask, Nigeria,
SMA Museum,
Tenafly, NJ

ART ON SGHIT

COLOR KEY

The margins have color-coded listings to serve as a quick guide for visiting the sites. While some of the categories overlap—all museums are cultural centers—the colors should give you a good general idea of the sorts of places and sites you'll encounter.

Museums

Churches

Parks & Cemeteries

Building exteriors, lobbies

Complex of buildings, grounds, etc.

Artwork

Auction Houses & Galleries; Restaurants with artwork

Cultural Institutions: Art Spaces, Colleges, etc.

PREFACE

Welcome to *Art on Sight*! In the following pages we will take you on a fascinating variety of explorations to the world of visual art. We hope that if you have a taste for beauty and enjoy walking, you will discover many wonderful new sites to pique your fancy in our city and the nearby tristate region. We have brought together eclectic outings that will introduce you to the rich and diverse treasures of the metropolitan area. New York has amazed us with its wealth of art and natural beauty—not only in Manhattan, but in the outer boroughs as well. Parks, plazas, gardens, atria, as well as the city's great museums, are all home to the visual pleasures of public art. The nearby suburbs and countryside also have their share of amazing art to see. Join us in discovering these exciting venues. Our book includes as large a variety as possible of styles and eras of art. Whether you are a fancier of the latest contemporary works, ethnic artifacts, or arts of the past, we think you will find outings that will inspire you.

For these outings, we have used a broad definition of *art*. The lines separating art from craft have long ago blurred, and environmental and landscape art have touched the boundaries of architecture. We have similarly tried to include a wide variety of artistic styles, and to give fair representation to younger, lesser-known artists, as well as to the great names of past and present.

What do we mean by *public art*? It is art that is available to be seen on a regular basis (with or without charge of suggested donation—see listed websites for current information). To us the phrase *public art* includes the many forms of the visual arts to be enjoyed in outdoor or indoor public spaces. Our walks include everything from traditional paintings to performance art and auctions, from works in progress to outdoor sculptures, from tapestries to stained-glass windows, from WPA murals to contemporary installations.

This book is for those of you who have a taste for art and architecture, as well as curiosity for exploring unusual places of artistic interest. You need not be a connoisseur to appreciate the aesthetic pleasures of *Art on Sight*.

We do not pretend that this is a comprehensive guide to the region's many artistic treats. From the numerous places we visited we have selected these outings because they captured our imagination. In your wanderings you might well discover additional places that we would be happy to know about.

This book represents our tenth collaboration, and we are grateful to our many readers who have told us how much they have enjoyed our introductions into the worlds of art and gardens and architecture. We wish to acknowledge the photographic contribution to this book of Robert L. Harrison, whose fine photographs have been an essential element.

We hope you will get as much pleasure from these adventures as we have.

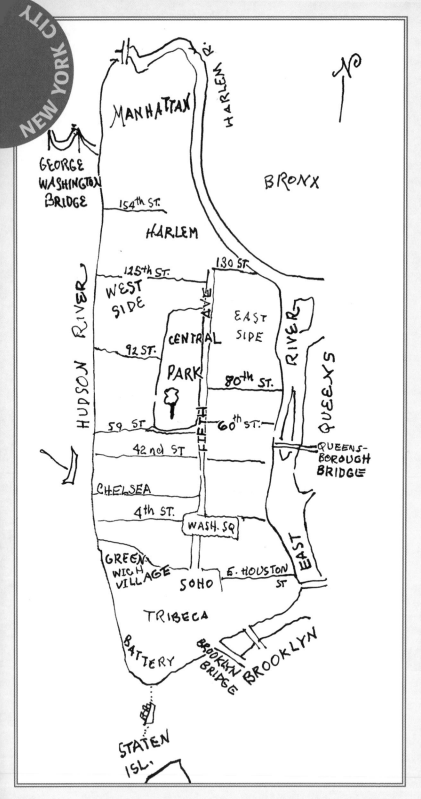

I. NEW YORK CITY
MANHATTAN

1 **From the Museum of Arts and Design to Lincoln Center: Six Blocks Celebrating the Arts**

DIRECTIONS » By subway, take the A, B, C, D, or 1 line to Columbus Circle.

In its new (2002) expanded space, our first stop is a terrific addition to the city's art sites: the **Museum of Arts and Design**, 2 Columbus Circle at 59th Street (212-299-7777; www.madmuseum.org). 🕒 Tuesday, Wednesday, Friday–Sunday 11 AM–6 PM; Thursday 11 AM–9 PM. (Closed Monday.) Admission fee; free admission for children under age 12; tours and open studios. Occupying a vertical museum building originally designed by Edward Durell Stone, and beautifully redone by Brad Cloepfil of Allied Works Architecture, this is a rare treasure.

Museum of Arts and Design
2 Columbus Circle at 59th Street
212-299-7777
www.madmuseum.org

Originally called the American Craft Museum, it has expanded both in a spatial sense and in its understanding and definition of crafts and design—or what this museum calls "the blur between art, design and craft today."

One gallery on each floor displays a tremendous variety of frequently changing exhibits that range from pottery to baskets, fiberworks to wood creations, jewelry to glassworks, painting to illustrations. There is an ongoing emphasis on process and the media used by these worldwide, multifaceted artists and artisans. Their creations are original—to say the least—and the spacious settings allow you to study, for example, art using dirt, chairs made of grown reeds, and baskets and wall hangings of the oddest of shapes.

Recent shows include the provocative *Swept Away: Dust, Ash, and Dirt as Media*, *Glasstress New York*, *Art of Scent*, and *Beauty in All Things: Japanese Art and Design*. One show was devoted to art from the Venice Biennale. There is also an ongoing interest in craft as it relates to jewelry; this is the only museum in the nation with a permanent collection of contemporary art jewelry.

The museum offers talks and curator-led tours, as well as workshops. Don't miss this museum visit.

On leaving Columbus Circle, walk up Broadway to

Museum of Biblical Art (MOBIA)
1865 Broadway
at 61st Street
212-408-1500
www.mobia.org

Church of St. Paul the Apostle
405 West 59th Street
212-265-3495

Fordham University Law School
140 West 62nd Street

the unusual and provocative **Museum of Biblical Art (MOBIA)**, 1865 Broadway at 61st Street (212-408-1500; www.mobia.org). ♿ Tuesday, Wednesday, Friday–Sunday 10 AM–6 PM; Thursday 10 AM–8 PM. (Closed Monday.) Free admission; tours are available free of charge.

This upstairs gallery hosts many different shows, many from other sources. A recent exhibit of contemporary stained glass was outstanding. Other shows have included *The Book of Life: Family Bibles in America* and *Jerusalem and the Holy Land: Paintings of Ludwig Blum*.

From MOBIA, walk to Columbus Avenue (west) and 59th Street. Here you'll see the Late Gothic–style **Church of St. Paul the Apostle** at 405 West 59th Street (212-265-3495). This imposing building was put up in 1885 and has recently undergone a successful renovation. Designed by Jeremiah O'Rourke, it employed some notable artists and architects of its time, including John La Farge, Stanford White, and Augustus Saint-Gaudens.

There are many wonderful surprises within, so enter and walk around. Note, for example, the mosaic-like patterns on the floors that are made of various colors of marble; they represent the buildings of the Acropolis that the apostle Paul saw before him. The ceiling is a beautiful blue and is an artistic symbol of the constellations on the day the church was dedicated. There are several murals in the church (including one high up on the south wall). While they are somewhat dark and hard to see, note the *Angel of the Moon* (the high one); it was designed by John La Farge. He also created the design for the columns and the narthex. Philip Martiny created the altar. As for the windows, they are some of the church's most appealing elements. The most notable are also John La Farge designs (the East Window over the entrance and the blue windows near the altar are particularly deep-toned and luminous). Pick up a pamphlet, which will describe all of the artistic aspects.

On leaving the church, head north on Columbus Avenue to **Fordham University Law School** at 140 West 62nd Street. There are two large buildings here, but it is the outdoor campus that draws our attention, featuring a number of interesting works. The street-level sculpture (some of which are permanent) and the sculpture garden (up a flight of steps) show mostly contemporary works (only some of them are identi-fied) amid pleasant gardens.

Next, you will come to one of the city's premier attractions: **Lincoln Center**, on Columbus Avenue (212-875-5350 for guided tours and hours; www.lincolncenter.org/tours). No art tour of New York can claim to be complete without a visit to this major part of the city's cultural life. Following are some ideas of what you might see within the buildings of Lincoln Center. Please note that to visit some areas of the inte-riors without actually having a ticket to a performance, you will need to sign up for a tour. The information booth is located across Columbus Avenue from Lincoln Center Plaza, at the David Rubinstein Atrium. Tours of major buildings and their artworks last approximately 75 minutes and vary as to subject matter.

Lincoln Center
Columbus Avenue from 62nd to 65th Streets
212-875-5350
www.lincolncenter.org/tours

Even if you do not choose to attend the world-class events that take place here, you should definitely walk around to see the art and architecture. Within the complex of the opera house and concert halls and theaters—all set within much-loved plazas—are many works of art, both inside and out. These range from the spectacular Chagall murals (Metropolitan Opera House) to dramatic mobiles (Avery Fisher Hall) to a dramatic Henry Moore sculpture reclining outdoors.

Even though many of the artworks are modern in design (in keeping with the architectural styles of the building by Eero Saarinen and Philip Johnson), there are some more realistic works to be seen, too.

If you choose to walk around without a tour, begin at Avery Fisher Hall (65th Street); the lobby is open to the public. Among the eye-catching art in the lobby is Richard Lippold's giant mobile hanging from above. Called *Orpheus and Apollo*, it dates to 1961 and is made of 190 strips of shining metal. (It stretches a very long way, suspended by steel wires!) You can see it move slightly. Dimitri Hadzi's abstract sculpture called *K. 458—The Hunt* is a tribute to a Mozart string quartet. (You'll find it to the left in the lobby.) There is a small café; just behind it is Seymour Lipton's *Archangel* of 1964.

If you go up to the grand Promenade level, you'll see Antoine Bourdelle's *Tragic Mask of Beethoven* (1901), and Auguste Rodin's head of Gustav Mahler, made in 1901.

Note, as you leave the building, the "Illumination Lawn," (accessible in season). This is a slanted, geo-

metric area of grass and dividers where visitors rest and enjoy the plaza. In summer, the Philip Johnson–designed fountain features five-minute light shows (noon–8 PM, weather permitting.) Additional recently renovated amenities include plantings and walkways.

The Vivian Beaumont Theater is to the right, just behind the reflecting pool. You can't miss the typical Henry Moore *Reclining Figure* (1965) that graces this spot.

And inside the front lobby of the building is *Zig IV* (1961) by David Smith. (This abstract bronze work can be seen through the windows when the theater is not open.)

Adjacent to the theater is the New York Public Library at Lincoln Center—a treasure trove of material relating to the performing arts. Here you'll see a great Alexander Calder stabile, made in 1965. A painted black steel structure, it resembles a giant creature with tentacles; it is 14 feet high and called *Le Guichet* (which means "ticket window" in French). (There is also a variety of exhibits relating to the arts in the library.)

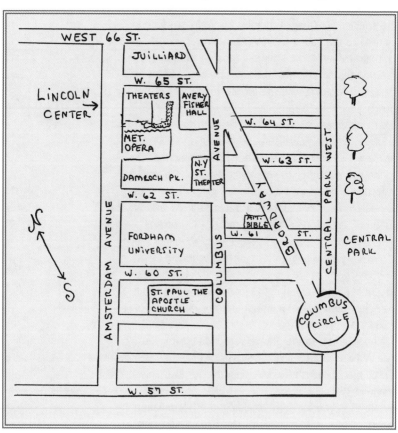

Next we take you to the centerpiece of Lincoln Center: the Metropolitan Opera House. Even if you don't see it at night when it is lit up and as dramatic as you can imagine, it is nonetheless a don't miss attraction for New York. If you want to see its vast collection relating to opera, history, great singers, and so on, you should take a tour, or better yet, attend a performance. But you can still see several sights of interest. Of major importance, of course, are the Chagall murals that picture singers, dancers, musicians; scenes of opera, jazz, folk music; portraits of the artist and his wife—all in the inimitable, brilliantly colored Chagall style. (Keep in mind that on sunny days the murals are covered for protection, so you won't be able to see them from outdoors.) These wonderful 1966 works include *Le Triomphe de la Musique* (the predominately red mural depicting 13 different themes) and *Les Sources de la Musique* (mostly yellow) on the north wall, where you might recognize Bach, Wagner, Verdi, and Beethoven, as well as King David and Orpheus. Several operas are also included, and floating down a river is the Tree of Life. Even if you see these murals over and over, you'll find new images and ideas each time.

The sculptor Aristide Maillol is represented here by *Venus Without Arms* (1920) and *Summer* (1910)—both works are on the Grand Tier—while *Kneeling Woman: Monument to Debussy* (1931) is on the level above.

On the ground floor (below the lobby) you will enjoy paintings of opera stars and composers; you may recognize Enrico Caruso, Maria Callas, or Lily Pons, for example.

The David H. Koch Theater, between 62nd and 63rd Streets, is the final major building on our tour of Lincoln Center's artworks. While it has many wonderful works of art within, it is, as of this writing, mostly visitable only on a tour. If you can get in to explore, look for works by Jasper Johns, Lee Bontecou, Yashide Kobashi, Reuben Nakian, and Elie Nadelman.

Although your visit to Lincoln Center is now more or less complete, don't miss the tiny park at the intersection of Broadway and Columbus Avenue at 63rd Street. Here is **Dante Alighieri** on a tall granite pedestal. The work of Ettore Ximenes (1921), this portrait of the great writer shows him with a copy of *The Divine Comedy* in his hand, and a laurel wreath on his

Dante Alighieri
Broadway and Columbus Avenue at 63rd Street

5

head. It was commissioned to observe the 600th anniversary of the poet's death.

Walk north one block to the east side of Columbus at 66th Street to the **American Folk Art Museum**, 2 Lincoln Square across from Lincoln Center (212-595-9533). ⓗ Tuesday–Saturday noon–7:30 PM, Sunday noon–6 PM. (Closed Monday.) Free admission. This intimate space features quilts, sculptures, handcrafted objects, and fabric designs made by American folk artists.

American
Folk Art
Museum
2 Lincoln Square across
from Lincoln Center
212-595-9533
www.folkartmuseum.org

2 The Thirties in New York: An Art Deco Walk

DIRECTIONS » By subway, take the 6 line to 33rd Street.

The art deco period in America (which followed close on the style's emergence in Europe) was particularly popular in New York. As the city became more and more sophisticated in the late 1920s and '30s, the glamorous new style was ubiquitous in theaters, skyscrapers, lobbies, the interior design of restaurants, and all kinds of public buildings. A great deal of this emphasis on deco design is still in evidence today, and this outing will take you to see some of New York's most prominent examples.

First, a word or two about what *art deco* means, and what to look for in a site described as "deco."

The Exposition des Arts Decoratifs et Industriels opened in Paris 1925. Its emphasis on the fashionable design was quickly brought to the United States. Its new look was seen as forward thinking, streamlined, and above all, appropriate to the new age of innovation.

Deco design had a heady combination of straight lines and swirls, with hard-edged geometry beautifully intertwined with curves. Strongly influenced by art nouveau, it avoided symmetry and picked up many stylish elements from the burgeoning modern art movements in Europe, as well as idioms of Egyptian, Aztec, and other exotic cultures. From cubism's emphasis on straight lines; art nouveau's use of decorative, curving forms; and the stepped designs of exotic civilizations (some recently discovered by Westerners), it encompassed a vast and new sense of exuberant, and often symbolic, design. And as it came to this country, another element was added—the "Machine Age": the sense of endless possibility; of the streamlined, the speedy, and the images that reflected movement;

René Chambellan:
fountainhead figure
at Channel Gardens

excitement—in fact, optimism became central to American art deco.

Those disparate elements affected everything from architecture to fabric design, to such interior details as grilles and windows, to lighting fixtures, wall design, and furniture.

A visit to a few of New York's deco sites will introduce you to a city of deco delights.

Our first stop is at Park Avenue and 32nd Street. Here at **2 Park Avenue** is a 1927 building designed by Albert Buchanan and Ely Jacques Kahn; Kahn was known as the major art deco architect of his time. Look at the front of the building; here is glazed terra-cotta cladding in brilliant color. Inside, in the lobby, are mosaics—a favorite medium of the deco era, in a typical zigzag design.

2 Park Avenue
at 32nd Street

Two blocks north is the **Cheney Building** at 34th Street and Madison Avenue (southeast corner). Note the ironwork grilles and gates, particularly indicative of deco iron use and imagery. The artist was a Frenchman, Edgar Brandt. Note the emphasis on burgeoning flowers, a typical deco image.

Cheney Building
34th Street and
Madison Avenue

Also on Madison Avenue, six blocks north, at 275 Madison Avenue at 40th Street is the **Farmer's Trust Building**. The elevators and lobby are of special interest, as are the floor design and fluted columns within, all part of an integrated design.

Farmer's Trust Building
275 Madison Avenue
at 40th Street

The **Chanin Building** at 122 East 42nd Street occupies an entire block between 41st and 42nd Streets on Lexington Avenue. This building typifies the deco era in New York; built between 1927 and 1930 by Sloan and Robertson, it features a number of iconic deco ornaments and design elements. Note the terra-cotta

Chanin Building
122 East 42nd Street
between 41st and
42nd Streets

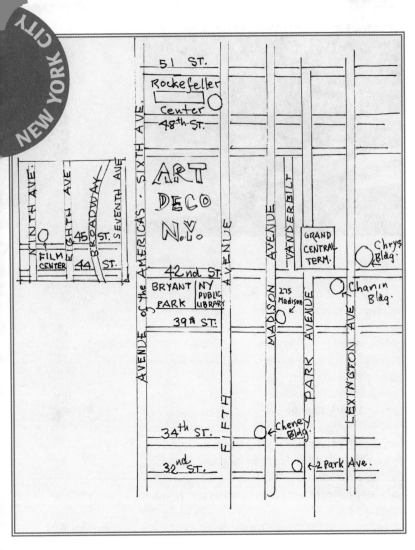

The map shows:

51 ST.
Rockefeller Center
48th ST.

ART DECO N.Y.C.

42nd ST.
BRYANT PARK | NY PUBLIC LIBRARY
39th ST.

34th ST.
32nd ST.

NINTH AVE.
EIGHTH AVE.
BROADWAY
45 ST.
SEVENTH AVE.
44 ST.
FILM CENTER

AVENIDE of the AMERICAS · SIXTH AVE.

FIFTH AVENUE

MADISON AVENUE
275 Madison
Cheney Bldg.
2 Park Ave.

VANDERBILT AVENUE
GRAND CENTRAL TERM.

PARK AVENUE

LEXINGTON AVE.
Chrys. Bldg.
Chanin Bldg.

ornamentation on the front (again, growing forms) and in the lobby, a true treasure trove of symbolic and abstract patterns. The small sculptured panels are by Rene Chambellan (they represent human and natural energy) in allegorical forms. The brass radiator grilles, decorative columns with fan-shaped designs (suggesting antiquity), the mix of swirling forms and straight lines all suggest the deco sense of exuberance.

Perhaps New York's favorite building is just a block north at 405 Lexington Avenue between 42nd and 43rd Streets: the **Chrysler Building**. Built in 1930 by William Van Alen, it was the tallest building in the world. Its soaring height, machine symbolism, and magnificent design all suggested the promise of the age. Before entering, we suggest a view from a block

Chrysler Building
405 Lexington Avenue between 42nd and 43rd Streets

8

or two away, so that you can see its silhouette reaching so elegantly into New York's skyline. As you approach you will spot its destructive use of automobile symbolism (it was, of course, constructed for Walter Chrysler); there are winged radiator-cap-gargoyles, basketweave designs (another deco pattern), and a banded area of abstract designs. On the west side of the building, by the entrance, you'll spot a steel and glass design of zigzags and geometric shapes set against black glass.

In the lobby, which is triangular, the lighting is by cathode rays, and on the ceiling is a mural by Edward Trumbull called *Transport and Human Endeavor*. Needless to say, it represents speed, travel, and nature's forces in an airy design. Note the deco-style grillework, lighting fixtures, and wood-veneered walls. The elevator doors and interiors—among the best known in the nation—have geometric patterns, much like collages, and feature wood veneers. The Chrysler Building is a must-see on any tour of New York.

Make your way to **Rockefeller Center**. Here, at Fifth Avenue and 50th Street, is the city's best known tourist attraction (tours are offered); it is also a site of several deco venues. First, of course, is the great statue *Atlas*, created by Lee Lawrie and René Chambellan and installed in 1937. Just behind the muscled statue at 636 Fifth Avenue are several artworks of interest, such as the polychrome limestone cartouches by Attilio Piccirilli and some carved glass by the Corning Company.

Rockefeller Center
Fifth Avenue
and 50th Street

At **630 Fifth Avenue**, there is a spectacular lobby with copper-lined walls, and steel beams covered by green marble. Nearby, at **25 West 50th Street**, is another Lee Lawrie piece, a sculptural relief made of polychrome limestone. Like many deco reliefs, these panels represent internationalism, and are both stylized and symbolic in design.

Other works by Lee Lawrie can be seen at **30 Rockefeller Plaza** (once the RCA Building): Here, sculptures by Lawrie are outside the entrance, where you'll find *Wisdom* (1950), with light and sound waves as a subject; sculptural relief above the doorways; and the well-known Paul Manship work atop a fountain, *Prometheus* (1934), representing the mythical figure who steals fire from the gods. Manship's sleek lines and gold-leafed bronze surface became typical of 1930s taste in the United States.

A striking series of murals by José Maria Sert, *Amer-*

Atlas, 1937,
**Lee Lawrie and
René Chambellan.**
Rockefeller Center

ican *Progress and Time* and *Man's Intellectual Mastery of the Universe* are at 30 Rockefeller Plaza (they are a replacement for Diego Rivera's original works, which were considered to have "communist imagery" and were strongly opposed by Rockefeller himself). Sert's murals portray an upbeat view of progress and the future.

Nearby is one of the most beloved deco interiors of all: **Radio City Music Hall**, at 1260 Avenue of the Americas at 50th Street. (You have to take a tour to see the designs of the master decorator Donald Deskey, from wallpapers to the staircase to furniture. The hall itself can be seen if you attend a show, of course.)

Radio City Music Hall
1260 Avenue of the
Americas at 50th Street

Our final stop after leaving the Music Hall is at 45th Street, west to Ninth Avenue. Here, at 630 Ninth Avenue is one more lobby that is a striking example of art deco. This is the **Film Center Building**, designed by Ely Jacques Kahn between 1928 and 1929—when the business of films was a new and exciting aspect of New York's cultural life. The lobby features bright colors, molded plaster and stone, brass radiator grills, and an Aztec sensibility from walls to ceiling.

Film Center Building
630 Ninth Avenue
at 45th Street

AND IN ADDITION . . .

Other prime midtown art deco sites, perhaps for a longer walk, include the following:

The **Daily News Building**, 220 East 42nd Street, was designed by Raymond Hood. Note the entrance relief and the ceiling globe and design.

The **Fuller Building**, 41 East 57th Street at Madison Avenue, has an entrance with statues by Elie Nadelman (there are many galleries in the building, too).

The **McGraw-Hill Building**, 330 West 42nd Street, is a giant of a building with horizontal bands of blue-green terra cotta. Inside, note the lobby with its original detailing, elevators, and entrance.

The elegant building farther downtown at **60 Hudson Street**, between Hudson, Thomas, and Worth Streets and West Broadway, will give you another taste of a lobby of the deco era, from its complex brickwork to its lighting fixtures to its grand proportions.

At **745 Fifth Avenue** (formerly the Squibb Building), between 57th and 58th Streets, is an unusual painted lobby ceiling from the deco era. Painted by Arthur Covey, it is a brightly colored mosaic-style, semi-abstract picture of Manhattan Island.

Petrossian, 182 West 58th Street, is a well-known deco-style restaurant.

The **Beekman Tower Hotel**, 3 Mitchell Place, at First Avenue and 49th Street, was built in 1928 and has been renovated recently. Its design includes deco details, proportions, and other design elements.

3 **Discovering Central Park and Its Environs**

DIRECTIONS» By subway, take the N or R line to Fifth Avenue (59th Street).

Central Park is in the very heart of Manhattan, and in many ways it captures the spirit of our bustling city, its energetic and creative people, its interest in nature and art. Since its founding in the 1860s, it has provided a wonderful space of beauty and tranquility to millions who love its pathways and fields and reservoir—all laid out by Frederick Law Olmsted in 843 leafy acres.

While you may be familiar with its bicycle paths, soccer fields, or birding adventures, or its many outdoor performances, you may not realize that the park also functions as an outdoor sculpture gallery. For here,

MANHATTAN

Daily News Building
220 East 42nd Street

Fuller Building
41 East 57th Street at Madison Avenue

McGraw-Hill Building
330 West 42nd Street

60 Hudson Street
between Hudson, Thomas, and Worth Streets and West Broadway

745 Fifth Avenue
between 57th and 58th Streets

Petrossian
182 West 58th Street

Beekman Tower Hotel
3 Mitchell Place, at First Avenue and 49th Street

Central Park
from Central Park South (59th Street) to Central Park North (110th Street), between Central Park West (Eighth Avenue) and Fifth Avenue

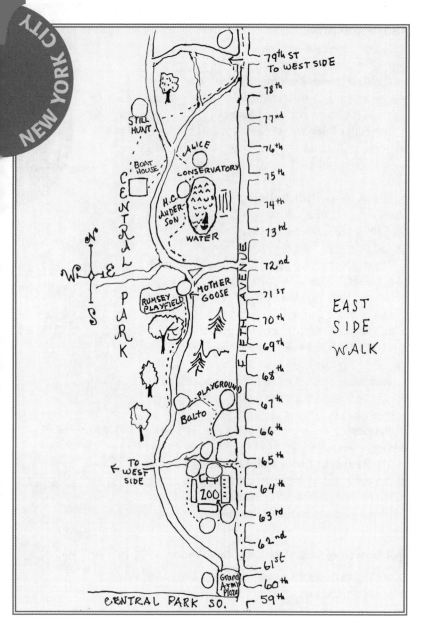

scattered throughout the park, are all kinds of sculptures that will be off interest to anyone who enjoys discovering art in beautiful surroundings.

We recommend this trip as a family outing, and so we have divided it into two parts: the east side of the park from the Central Park Zoo at Fifth Avenue and 64th Street north to 76th Street; and the west side portion from Central Park West and 81st Street to 91st Street and Amsterdam Avenue.

A map of the park is available at the information

center at the entrance to the zoo. So with the following list in hand, and a map to guide you, try to find to find the following (perhaps as a form of treasure hunt for kids).

EAST SIDE

1. Clock with animal musicians: (bear, monkeys, kangaroo, hippo, goat, and elephant)
2. Tigress and her cubs
3. Dancing goat and frogs
4. Dancing bear with five small frogs
5. Animal gate
6. Arched bridge
7. Heroic Siberian husky dog
8. Mother Goose with her friends: Mother Hubbard, Old King Cole, Humpty Dumpty, Little Bo-Peep
9. Hans Christian Andersen with the ugly duckling
10. Alice in Wonderland
11. Rowboat
12. Stalking panther
13. Three bears

We begin our walk with the East Side, entering Central Park at the Zoo at 64th Street and Fifth Avenue.

Your first sighting will be the delightful *Delacorte Clock* (1964–65), by Andrea Spadini. The philanthropist George Delacorte loved the animated clocks he had come upon in Europe; this one has a hippo who plays the violin, a bear playing the tambourine, and two bronze monkeys striking a bell—among other treats. On the hour you'll be entranced by these animals playing familiar tunes (and on the half hour, there is a shorter version).

Within the zoo itself are three works of art: near the (real) monkey display you'll find the first of them: *Tigress and Cubs* (1866), a bold work by Auguste Cain, with a larger-than-life tiger holding a dead peacock in her teeth.

Dancing Goat is a fanciful 6-foot-tall goat that balances on its back legs as water from the fountain sprays from the mouths of little frogs. This is one of two fountain sculptures by Frederick George Roth.

The counterpart of this fountain statue is *Honey Bear* (ca. 1937), which you'll find near the *Delacorte*

Frederick George Richard Roth: *Honey Bear*, circa 1937, Central Park

Clock as you exit the zoo. It also has frogs spewing water.

As you leave the zoo, walk under the overpass (to the 65th Street Transverse), where on your right is a special zoo for small children. Called the Lehman Children's Zoo, its gates (1960–61) were designed by a leading American sculptor of his time, Paul Manship. The gates feature humans and animals dancing while a variety of birds look on, and two boys play the pipes of Pan—a truly charming celebration of music, dance, and childhood.

Adjacent to Fifth Avenue (at 67th Street) is the children's playground. Among its pretty plantings and natural boulders is a Japanese-style arched bridge.

From the playground, bearing left at the fork, walk to one of the city's favorite statues. This is *Balto* (1925), the city's commemoration of a heroic dog. The Siberian husky led a team through Arctic blizzards to carry diphtheria vaccine to epidemic-stricken Nome, Alaska, in 1925. His exploits are thought to have saved the city (though the dog died from his exertion). Here he appears in a sculpture by Frederick George Roth as a larger-than-life figure in bronze, atop a natural boulder. (You will find children climbing on this statue—while their elders read a plaque describing his amazing exploits.)

From here, head north (along the road) to a 1938 statue by the same artist. Mother Goose sits amid the greenery, surrounding by the old favorites of every toddler—Old King Cole, Little Bo-Peep, Humpty Dumpty, and Old Mother Hubbard. But it is Mother Goose herself, with a witch's hat, flying cape, and giant basket, who will grab your children's attention.

At 72nd Street and Fifth Avenue is the Conservatory, a much-loved part of the park where children sail toy boats, and where you'll find two well-known pieces of art.

The first is a legendary statue of the father of so many adored tales: Hans Christian Andersen. Here he sits with an open book in his lap and a sculpted duckling at his feet. This 8-foot-tall work of bronze was made by Georg John Lober and installed in 1956. On Saturdays, from May to September, is storytelling here at Andersen's feet. Bring the family!

On the other side of the same little pond (in an alcove near 75th Street and Fifth Avenue) is another New York City favorite: *Alice in Wonderland* with her friends, made by sculptor José de Creeft. She is surrounded by Lewis Carroll's unforgettable characters: the Cheshire cat, the Dormouse, and the March Hare— all bearing a resemblance to John Tenniel's original illustrations of the book.

José de Creeft: *Alice in Wonderland*, 1959, Central Park

Near the boathouse (walk west) is the sculpted *Rowboat* by Irwin Glusker.

At 76th Street and East Drive is a bold panther sculpture; this stalking beast is the work of Edward Kemeys. Called *Still Hunt*, it is a dramatic, somewhat exaggerated portrait of a feline about to pounce.

Our last East Side statue is of three friendly-looking bears. They are the centerpiece of the playground at 79th Street and Fifth Avenue, and are by Paul Manship. Here, too, you'll find children climbing on the sculptures.

WEST SIDE

1. 15th-century Polish king on a horse
2. Four characters from Shakespeare
3. Herbs and flowers descended from Shakespeare's own garden
4. Six wild creatures and Teddy Roosevelt with his guides, decorating a museum
5. Stone squirrel eating an acorn
6. Hands-on museum just for children
7. Stone family on a bench
8. Flock of sheep

There are only a few West Side sculptures within the park (as well as a few nearby outside the park). While you are in the park itself, you can continue westward to find these treasures—or begin a separate outing by entering the park from Central Park West at 81st Street. Not far from *Still Hunt*, and also near Belvedere Lake, is a sculpture called *King Jagiello* (1939), depicting a Polish warrior and king, by Stanislaw Ostrowski. First shown at the Polish Pavilion of the World's Fair in New York in 1939, it represented Polish patriotism during the war years in Europe.

On the main path, bearing left is the well-known Delacorte Theater, home to Shakespeare in the Park—one of the city's favorite festivals each year. In this beautiful and romantic setting, with the castle in the background, are the Shakespeare garden, and two relevant statues. Here are *Romeo and Juliet* (1977) and *Prospero and Miranda* from *The Tempest*, both by sculptor Milton Hebold. Romeo and Juliet, as you might expect, appear in a romantic, lyrical pose, while the characters from *The Tempest* seem appropriately turbulent.

If you exit Central Park at 77th Street, you'll be across the street from the **American Museum of Natural History**, an imposing and important cultural institution (212-769-5100; www.amh.org/museum). Ⓗ daily 10 AM–5:45 PM. (Closed Thanksgiving Day and Christmas Day.) Admission fee. A visit to this museum is a must-see for anyone who is visiting from out of town; New Yorkers visit frequently. The building is a grand edifice that is decorated with animals and carvings galore. Near the entrance you can spot granite bas-relief with a moose, rams, bison, bears, and lions, among other beasts; don't miss the giant eagle over the portico. There is a memorial to Theodore Roosevelt, a "father of conservation" and an avid naturalist. The statue (ca. 1940) depicts him as an explorer

MANHATTAN

American
Museum
of Natural
History
Central Park West
at 79th Street
212-769-5100
www.amnh.org/museum

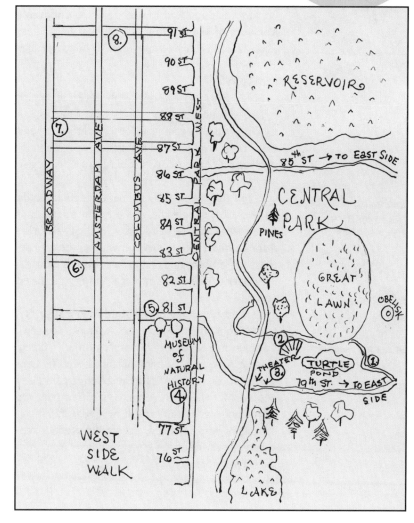

with one African and one Native American guide. The sculpture was made by James Earl Fraser. (He also designed the nickel with its buffalo and Indian images.)

While in this area, you might wish to visit this fantastic museum—but leave plenty of time. This is not a place to duck in and out of, but one where you will be anxious to see all kinds of art and natural treasures. Among the numerous displays of an artistic nature are ethic artifacts from all over the world, primitive art, African masks, re-created villages—all in addition to the spectacular dinosaurs and the wonderful Rose Center for Earth and Space.

Just north of the museum, on the front of the building at 25 West 81st Street, look up to the third floor. Here your treasure hunters can spot a carved squirrel eating an acorn. And not far away, between Broadway and Amsterdam Avenue, is the **Children's Museum of Manhattan**, at 212 West 83rd Street (212-721-1234; www.cmom.org). ❿ Sunday–Friday 10 AM–5 PM; Saturday 10 AM–7 PM. (Closed Monday.) Admission fee.

This is a favorite location for the kids of this area; it is filled with innovative and hands-on experiences and exhibits. Patterns, games, videos, an art studio, and many other child-oriented features make this an outstanding museum-laboratory for inspiring school-age—and even younger—children.

If you and the small fry still have the energy to do more exploring, note the statue in the courtyard of the Montana Building at 247 West 87th Street. Called **Park Bench** (1985), this is a work by Bruno Lucchesi; the family seated on the park bench is astonishingly lifelike, particularly when real families are seated nearby!

Our last stop is the **playground** at 91st Street between Columbus and Amsterdam Avenues. Here you'll discover one of those rare settings on an ordinary block: a wonderful collection of stone sheep, by Constantin Nivola, who specializes in sculpture particularly designed for children to enjoy. His aim to populate playgrounds with approachable sculpture—his sheep are colorful, rough-textured, and just the size for climbing on—show why he is a leading exponent of environmental playground art.

Children's Museum of Manhattan
212 West 83rd Street
212-721-1234
www.cmom.org

Park Bench
247 West 87th Street

Playground
91st Street between Columbus and Amsterdam Avenues

4 **An Artwalk Around a University Campus and Nearby Cathedral: Art Pleasures at Columbia and St. John the Divine**

Daniel Chester French: *Alma Mater*, 1904, Columbia University Library

DIRECTIONS » By subway, take the 1 or 9 line to 116th Street/Columbia University.

The campus of **Columbia University**, a leafy oasis in the heart of uptown Manhattan, has a wonderful collection of outdoor sculpture. Set amid walkways and greenery are a number of artworks, each carefully placed to enhance its surroundings. A walk around this lovely campus to view the art and experience the lively college scene is a real pleasure.

Columbia University
2960 Broadway
at 116th Street

The following walking tour touches upon some highlights of Columbia's outdoor art only; on campus there are obviously galleries and other indoor sites that exhibit the work of students and others, but we leave it to you to discover them on your own.

Begin your walk at the imposing gates that mark the entrance to the campus at 116th Street. The two giant granite statues that form the gates are allegories that represent *Letters* and *Science* in the classical style. *Letters* is depicted as a draped female figure, appropriately holding a book, while *Science*, her male counterpart, holds a globe and a compass. The works

19

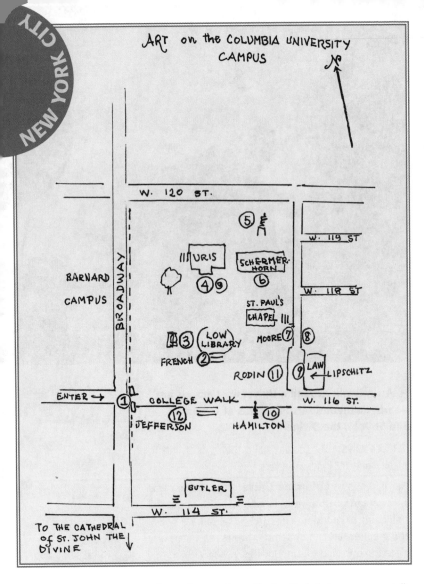

ART on the COLUMBIA UNIVERSITY CAMPUS

of American sculptor Charles Keck (who was especially known for his monuments and architectural sculpture), they date to the early 20th century.

Once through the gates, you've reached the center of the university's main campus. On your left is Low Library (now used for exhibits and other events), with its wide steps. There you can't miss the iconic *Alma Mater*, perhaps Columbia's best-known sculpture. The work of the master Daniel Chester French, it was installed in 1904 and became a symbol of the university. *Alma Mater* is a representation of the goddess Athena, with her laurel wreath, an owl in the fold of her robe (French was intrigued by taxidermy and often included owls in his works), and a scepter in one hand. She is a graceful, seated bronze figure with an open book on her lap and outstretched arms in a welcoming gesture. *Alma Mater* has been at the center of campus life for years, surrounded by the coming and goings of students, demonstrations, and even bombing (in the 1960s).

Walk up the steps for a quick look inside Low's elegant rotunda (you might chance upon an exhibit of interest). As you exit, head west of the library. Here, on the Lewisohn Lawn, is one of the more amusing (and once even controversial) works: *The Great God Pan*. This very large bronze statue (considered to be the largest ever cast in the country at the time it was made in the 1890s) appears as a half-man, half-goat figure, lying on a rock and playing his pipe, a sardonic expression on his face. This is not your usual campus sculpture—and in fact, the work had been commissioned for another site, but ended up here after much discussion (the university trustees were worried about placing a nude pagan deity in front of the chapel), and it is has since become very much a part of the campus.

Our next site, located in front of Columbia's School of Business, is a distinctly different type of sculpture. This colossal work of black-painted steel, *Curl* (1968), is by the sculptor Clement Meadmore. Twelve feet high, it consists of a hollow square tube twisted into a series of curved forms. Meadmore, a native of Australia, made mostly monumental pieces that combined elements of abstract expressionism with minimalism. *Curl*, a striking work, makes its own strong statement.

We now walk toward the large plaza near Mudd Hall (School of Engineering). Here you'll find *Le Marteleur*, a bold, bronze piece made in 1886 by the Belgian artist Constantin Émile Meunier. This is a strong, quite realistic statue that celebrates the modern laborer. *Le Marteleur* (The Hammerman) is one of Meunier's sculptures that calls attention to the world's workers as noble, proud, and powerful. The figure here carries pincers for pouring molten metal; he wears a leather apron, a worker's cap, and enormous protective footwear. He is an impressive man, confident and capable.

Continue walking south to an overpass crossing Amsterdam Avenue at 117th Street. You'll see Henry Moore's (1967) *Three-Way Piece*. This is a large bronze sculpture comprising a group of abstract, curvaceous, and pointed forms that rest on three "feet" atop

a cylindrical pedestal. The surface appears smooth (typical of Moore's works), but if you inspect it up close you will see small scratch marks. This fascinating form reflects the straight edges and round walls of nearby structures.

At Revson Plaza, across the nearby overpass, is the more realistic *Tightrope Walker* (1973–79), by Dutch sculptor Keese Verkade. This very tall (14-foot-high) bronze work depicts two acrobats, one balancing upon the shoulders of the other, as the two cross a tightrope. These are elongated, ultrathin figures, somewhat reminiscent of Giacometti's people (through on a larger scale). This engaging piece was given to the university to honor the intrepid war hero Major General "Wild Bill" Donovan, an alumnus of Columbia.

Walk over to Jerome Greene Hall, the Law School's building, where *Bellerophon Taming Pegasus* (1967) by Jacques Lipchitz towers above the entrance. This giant sculpture is 40 feet tall and therefore perhaps better viewed from a distance. It depicts an event in Greek mythology in which Bellerophon captures Pegasus (the winged horse of the gods), then triumphs after having tamed the horse. The horse is shown with bulging eyes and contorted shape—typical of Lipchitz's style.

For a more traditional campus sculpture, walk back onto College Walk toward Broadway. A 1908 bronze statue of Alexander Hamilton by William Ordway Partridge graces the front of Hamilton Hall. (Hamilton was one of the most illustrious students at Columbia.)

Hamilton is shown making a speech, his hand on his heart, his gaze intense. Partridge was a prominent American sculptor whose commissions were largely for portrait busts and public works. Unlike many of his fellow late 19th- and early 20th-century sculptors, he worked in a style at tended toward impressionism.

And now for something you might not have expected to see here: Auguste Rodin's *The Thinker*. This iconic work, sculpted in 1880, has been cast and recast again and again; what you see here, in front of the philosophy building, is one of the many copies. What could be a more appropriate site for this sculpture? Whatever the statue represents—whether a "poet-artist" brooding over the human condition or "a social symbol" (terms used by the master himself in describing his work), it still has a strong impact on a college campus and invites further interpretation.

The last outdoor sculpture we visit on our walk could be said to celebrate the "thinker." You'll find a fine statue of Thomas Jefferson (another work by William Ordway Partridge) in front of the Graduate School of Journalism. This fairly traditional 1914 piece depicts Jefferson as a man of intellect, with a serious expression and deep in thought.

The second part of this outing takes you to visit America's largest Gothic cathedral and definitely a major attraction here in New York. From the Columbia University campus it's an easy walk to the **Cathedral Church of St. John the Divine**, located at Amsterdam Avenue and 112th Street. Begun in 1982, this magnificent structure is a work in progress, as it is still not completed—but, after all, during the Middle Ages it took at least as long or even longer to build such churches, and some were never finished (we hope this won't be the case with St. John the Divine!). You'll find this a stimulating place to visit—as it is a bustling community unto itself. The St. John the Divine "compound" is filled with artists and artisans, construction workers, church people, all coming and going, moving about in its vast spaces, and engaged in many different activities. As an art lover, you will certainly appreciate the stained-glass windows, lovely rose window, stone carvings, individual chapels, tapestries, bronze doors, arches, columns, and many other details.

The cathedral's stained-glass windows are very decorative, with their deep, intense color. They vary from traditional to contemporary styles and their subjects might surprise you. Not only do you see the expected Biblical scenes, but also some celebrating everyday activities in ordinary people's lives: sports (bowling, auto racing, swimming, etc.), the arts, medicine, the press, motherhood, and more. But the most beautiful window of all is the magnificent rose window at the end, in a more traditional mode.

There are seven chapels, each a tribute to a specific ethnic group, all filled with art objects of interest. The noted sculptor Gutzon Borglum is well represented in a couple of them: in St. Columbia's Chapel (dedicated to people of Celtic descent) you'll see Borglum's figures of noteworthy personages in the English Church, and in St. Savior's Chapel (dedicated to Russian Orthodoxy) are some 50 carvings by him—in addition to some ancient icons of great beauty. In yet another chapel, St. Ambrose's, are Renaissance paintings by

MANHATTAN

Cathedral
Church of
St. John the Divine
Amsterdam Avenue
and 112th Street

Simone Martini, Giovanni di Paolo, and the School of Paolo Veronese.

St. John the Divine also has a great collection of rare tapestries. (If you wish to have more details about these, as well as other treasures found within this church, you might want to take a guided tour or pick up a guidebook available in the gift shop just outside the church.) For now, suffice it to say that there are basically two sets of tapestries, both from the 17th century and both illustrating scenes from the New Testament. Those hanging in the nave were based on designs by Raphael and made in England; the others, known as the Barberini Tapestries, were woven in Rome under the aegis of Cardinal Barberini.

Everywhere in the church you'll discover stone and wood carvings, statues, altars, pulpits, columns, and niches—some still empty, awaiting future works of art.

Outside the church you'll find a small but delightful Biblical garden, consisting of plants mentioned in Scripture and a pretty courtyard with a fountain. Don't miss the nearby Children's Sculpture Garden. Within it is a Peace Fountain, designed by sculptor Greg Wyatt in 1985 (more about him below). Unlike most sculpture parks, children here are actually encouraged to touch the artworks and splash around the fountain. Note, too, the more than 100 small bronze sculpture surrounding the fountain. Actually designed by children (who participated in contests over the years), they are the refreshing expressions of young artists.

Another interesting part of this visit is the crypt of the cathedral, where Greg Wyatt has been sculptor-in-residence for many years. Here in a grand space, his giant sculptures take form, while undergoing the various stages that must happen before their casting in bronze. Mr. Wyatt uses the space for both cathedral projects and his own commissions—many of them monuments for corporate and public buildings.

After visiting the inside of the cathedral, be sure to see the stone-carving workshop on the north side of the building. Here, for many years, stone carvings for various parts of the cathedral—pediments, cornices, and other architectural structures—have been cut from limestone and other stones. Although much of the work on the façade has slowed down in the last few years due to a lack of funds, the stonework does continue for other projects around the country.

St. John the Divine is also known for its wonderful

24

series of concerts (its magnificent organ has recently been refurbished) and other special events.

AND IN ADDITION . . .

Riverside Church, 490 Riverside Drive at 120th Street (212-870-6700), has some wonderful stone carvings, stained-glass windows, paintings, and a cloister, as well as a 392-foot bell tower. Don't miss Jacob Epstein's *Christ in Majesty* in the nave on the second-floor gallery (the gilded plaster mold for his 1954–55 casting housed in Llandruff Cathedral in Cardiff, Wales) and his 1927 *Madonna and Child* in the court next to the cloister.

The nearby **Interchurch Center**, at 475 Riverside Drive between 119th and 120th Streets (212-870-2200), is quite active in the area's arts scene. In addition to sponsoring events, such as concerts (on Wednesdays at noon), film screenings, and special art demonstrations, the center also houses inviting exhibition spaces on the main floor: the Treasure Room Gallery, with changing displays of paintings, sculpture, drawings, photographs, and textiles; and some 20 display windows along the surrounding corridors for additional fine-arts viewing.

The **Nicholas Roerich Museum**, 319 West 107th Street at Riverside Drive (212-864-7752), is a one-of-a-kind small museum in an elegant townhouse devoted to the works of Nicholas Roerich, an eclectic Russian artist, anthropologist, philosopher, traveler to the Far East, and nominee for the Nobel Peace Prize. Among his unusual collections are paintings evoking Russia's ancient past and others celebrating nature's mystical powers. Particularly striking are the costume and set designs he created for opera and ballet. (His collaboration with Igor Stravinsky on *The Rite of Spring* is legendary.) 🕐 Tuesday–Friday noon–5 PM, Saturday and Sunday 2 PM–5 PM. (Closed Monday.) Free admission.

Grant's Tomb, Riverside Drive at West 122nd Street. This imposing memorial, now shiningly refurbished, is a dignified tribute to a beloved American hero. (It also happens to be the largest mausoleum in the country.) Reminiscent of the grand tombs of the emperors Hadrian and Napoleon, its marble interior includes a massive dome, allegorical bas-reliefs and sculptures, and matching polished-wood sarcophagi of Grant and his wife, Julia. There are also interesting

MANHATTAN

Riverside Church
490 Riverside Drive at 120th Street
212-870-6700

Interchurch Center
475 Riverside Drive between 119th and 120th Streets
212-870-2200

Nicholas Roerich Museum
319 West 107th Street at Riverside Drive
212-864-7752

Grant's Tomb
Riverside Drive at West 122nd Street

Sakura Park
122nd Street
between Riverside Drive
and Claremont Avenue

displays concerning Grant's life. Outside, surrounding the building, is an unusual artistic feature: A series of benches, adorned with bright mosaic-tile designs, surround the monument and depict myriad images of city life. They were made by residents of the community and are filled with cheerful energy and good humor. Just across the street (on 122nd Street, between Riverside Drive and Claremont Avenue) is a little gem of a park called **Sakura Park**. Designed by Frederick Law Olmsted's architectural firm, it is a lovely oasis.

5 An Island of Art in New York's Harbor: Governors Island

DIRECTIONS» There is free weekend ferry service to the island (a 10-minute trip) from Manhattan. By subway, take the 1, N, or R line to South Ferry–Whitehall Street and walk to the Battery Maritime Building at 10 South Street, near the Staten Island Ferry Terminal. There is also ferry service from Brooklyn.

To depart from Governors Island, ferries leave from the Battery Maritime Building and run Friday–Sunday and holiday Mondays. Friday, ferries leave on the hour from 10 AM–3 PM and return from Governors Island on the half-hour 10:30 AM–4:30 PM, with a final ferry departing at 5 PM. Saturday, Sunday, and holiday Mondays, ferries leave at 10 AM and 11 AM, then every half-hour until 5:30 PM; and return from Governors Island every half-hour 10:30 AM–7 PM. One of the pleasures of visiting this island is that you can rent a bike reasonably right near the ramp from the ferry. (There are no cars on the island.)

Governors Island
212-440-2200
www.govisland.com

Governors Island (212-440-2200; www.govisland. com) is open from the end of May until the end of September. Guided tours are available.

You won't find a more enjoyable art outing than this one—a recent addition to the bustling art scene of New York. Here you can combine a delightful ferry ride (with spectacular views of lower Manhattan and Brooklyn) with a lovely flat walk or bike ride through an old-fashioned village-style community with art all around you. Don't miss this one!

The story is another example of imaginative reuse—in which a derelict but inviting site gets a complete makeover as an artistic venue. Just as many industrial neighborhoods were revitalized by the studios and galleries of artists, Governors Island has a brave new cultural identity—without losing its historic and pictur-esque past.

About two years ago the state handed over the is-land to New York City. (Today its 150 acres are man-aged by a trust, with 22 additional acres owned by the National Park Service.)

From 1783 to 1966, Governors Island was a United States Army post; and until 1996, a US Coast Guard installation. When you stroll through the grounds you'll notice the lovely 19th-century houses surrounding a vast town green (the Parade Ground of the past); the finest of these homes were lived in by military brass; there are also a charming chapel, a round 1811 fort called Castle Williams, and walkways and promenades with views of the water all around.

(You will enjoy reading up on the history of Gover-nors Island, which played a role in so many of Amer-ica's wars, as well as in peacetime. For a full write-up, see the Trust for Governors Island website, as noted above, or pick up material at the visitor's center.)

Today, a visit here is an entirely different experience from its military past. When you get off the ferry you are almost immediately confronted by sculpture set magnificently throughout the site. A variety of chang-ing exhibitions of contemporary art appear here; our visit was to a terrific outdoor show by sculptor Mark di Suvero. In addition, there is a gallery space (which hosts such groups as the Sculptors Guild) and a large variety of events—fairs, art workshops, cultural exhibits, kite flying—and artists' studios to visit. You can picnic, visit a working farm, and find food and drink available at Water Taxi Beach (near your arrival spot).

All of these amenities and artistic pleasures are free and accessible to families with children in tow. We recommend this outing to both native New York-ers and tourists; and as a lot of people seem to agree, we suggest you aim for a Friday, when it is much less crowded.

6 The Unexpected at New York's Art Auctions

DIRECTIONS » **Sotheby's:** By subway, take the 6 line to 68th Street. Walk east to York Avenue.

» **Christie's:** By subway, take the B, D, F or M line to 47th–50th Streets/Rockefeller Center.

» **Swann Auction Galleries:** By subway, take the 6 line to 23rd Street.

» Bonhams: By subway, take the 4, 5, or 6 line to 59th Street.

» Doyle Galleries: By subway, take the 4, 5, or 6 line to 86th Street.

Visiting an art auction is an unusual and rather fascinating experience. If you've never done so, this will introduce you to an aspect of the art world generally known only to collectors, dealers, curators and—like us—art lovers with curiosity about this melding of great art and commerce. Much like a performance, auctions of fine art follow a script in which an (often prime) work of art is displayed and an audience, both in attendance and on the telephone or Internet, bids for it in a hushed and almost silent atmosphere. Great collectors all over the world know what is coming up for sale, its estimated value, and whether they can meet the bids of other avid buyers.

You will see anything from million-dollar paintings to fine ceramics, to iconic sculptures, to—at some auctions—lesser-known works of great beauty or unusual provenance. We have found art auctions mesmerizing, not only for the vast amount of money being exchanged for art, but for the oddity of seeing a Picasso or a Monet or a Ming vase close at hand on its way to a new museum or perhaps an anonymous collector in a foreign land. The pace is dizzying. (Many buyers come some days before to see the art being displayed, which is also an enjoyable outing, by the way, so that when the work comes up for auction they are well prepared.)

Keep in mind that not everything sold at art auctions is terrifically expensive; often art items appear that are less well known, and bargains can still be found, which is, of course, part of the fun.

We take you in this chapter to several of New York's most prominent art auction houses (there are several others in the city as well), and each venue can give you advance information about what will be auctioned and when. (Most of the material comes from collectors' thinning out their holdings or museums' deaccessioning works, etc.) If your interest is in a particular style or era or medium, check with the auction house for a particularly appropriate sale; they often link together similar pieces of an era, or country, or style. Catalogs are usually available free of charge. In many auction houses you are expected to register if you plan to bid on anything, and are given a paddle with a number on it, which you raise during bidding.

One of the world's premier auction houses is **Sotheby's** at 1334 York Avenue at 72nd Street (212-606-7000; www.sothebys.com). Here is the art auction of elegance, high finance, and important art. From the uniformed guards to the plush surroundings to the well-dressed customers, you will sense the rarified world of art collectors at the highest level. Enjoy a taste of this glamorous environment as great examples of the world's paintings, jewelry, sculpture, objets d'art, prints, and more are auctioned off. Sotheby's is at the center of the world's art market; it has auction houses in Tokyo, Madrid, Beverly Hills, St. Moritz, and London, as well as here in New York, and many of the people you see are international dealers.

Before the auction you can wander through the galleries, consulting your catalog for items to be sold and their estimated value. The auction itself takes place at a great speed; there is an auctioneer and a long row of bid-takers in front of you, keeping the action moving either electronically or by pointing out raised paddles. Vast amounts of money are announced quickly and each work of art has a brief appearance onstage. Don't miss this experience!

Sotheby's
1334 York Avenue
at 72nd Street
212-606-7000
www.sothebys.com

But Sotheby's is not only a haven for the highest-priced art. One of the surprises of a visit here is Sotheby's Arcade. Here, for those of us to whom a Sotheby's auction is only a form of entertainment, there is another option: a gallery of less expensive art in the same building. If you really wish to purchase art—some of it quite terrific, if by lesser-known artists—visit the Arcade. These auctions are at 2 PM, and you might find a genuine, affordable piece of art that you must have!

Another notable auction house is the internationally acclaimed **Christie's**, 20 Rockefeller Plaza (212-636-2000; www.christies.com). Christie's has an inviting space with display galleries showing art, furniture, objects, rugs—everything relating to art and design. Choose the subjects that interest you by looking up in advance what auctions are coming up.

Christie's
20 Rockefeller Plaza
212-636-2000
www.christies.com

When you walk in, the first thing you'll notice is Sol LeWitt's brightly colored mural in the lobby. Pick up a catalog at the desk and proceed upstairs, which houses both galleries and auctions. We found this an inviting and entertaining place to visit; many estates were being sold on our last stop here. There were examples of

deco furniture, watercolors, sculpture, and so on, for very reasonable prices (some under $1,000). Among recent auctions at Christie's were animation art, old master paintings, and 20th-century Indian art. Viewing of items to be auctioned takes place several days in advance of the auction.

Another international auction house is **Bonhams**, 580 Madison Avenue near 55th Street (212-644-9001; www.bonhams.com/newyork), where sales range from Asian art, to fine jewelry, from snuff bottles to the best in Japanese prints.

Recent sales at this international auction house included "Chinese Works of Art from Hong Kong and San Francisco," "Modern Contemporary South Asian Art," and "Twentieth-Century Decorative Arts."

Describing itself as the preeminent auction house for work on paper, **Swann Auction Galleries**, 104 East 25th Street (212-254-4710; www.swanngalleries.com), is less exalted than the international auction houses, but relaxed and fun to visit. These galleries auction a variety of things, ranging from rare books to prints, posters, drawings, photographs, and oddities. Prices are lower than at the international houses, and you can walk around days in advance of the auction to look at the upcoming materials. Recent sales included "Atelier 17, Abstract Expression and the New York School" and "African American Fine Art."

Doyle Galleries at 175 East 87th Street (212-427-2730; www.doylenewyork.com) offers a somewhat different auction experience. There is a cluttered and appealing atmosphere here, with people wandering about examining the art and objects, with less of the hushed elegance of Sotheby's, for example. Many of the visitors here are interior designers seeking a bargain or something unusual and affordable. You will feel comfortable here as you examine oddities like old silver, art nouveau, posters of long-ago events, and belle époque decorative arts. Exhibition hours are Saturday 10 AM–5 PM, Sunday noon–5 PM, Monday 9 AM–7:30 PM, and Tuesday 9 AM–2 PM. Auctions take place several times a month, usually on Wednesdays and Thursdays and occasional evenings.

AND IN ADDITION . . .

Sotheby's has a series of lectures and seminars that are of very high quality. Recent examples included a series on Georgia O'Keeffe and Alfred Stieglitz, a fine-

Bonhams
580 Madison Avenue
near 55th Street
212-644-9001
www.bonhams.com
/newyork

Swann Auction Galleries
104 East 25th Street
212-254-4710
www.swanngalleries.com

Doyle Galleries
175 East 87th Street
212-427-2730
www.doylenewyork.com

arts conservation seminar, and a travel seminar to Italy on futurism. For information, call 212-894-1111.

Sotheby's "S2," on the second floor of its York Avenue headquarters, focuses on less-famous artists' work, which are both on exhibit and for sale.

Christie's has special events and seminars in a variety of art-related topics; they are open to the public and free of charge on a first-come, first-served basis; call 212-636-2687.

Clarke Auction Gallery, 2372 Boston Post Road, Larchmont, NY (914-833-8336; www.clarkeny.com). This auction house is Westchester's best-known auction house dealing in antiques, Chinese art, and so on.

MANHATTAN

7 Exploring the City Hall Area: A Downtown Adventure

DIRECTIONS » By subway, take the 4 or 5 line to Fulton Street; the 2 or 3 line to Park Place; or the N or R line to City Hall.

The City Hall area may not be the first place one would look for public art. People rush around from one building to the next and official business is conducted everywhere in busy municipal offices. But it is these very buildings that have a treasure trove of "official art," much of it commissioned by the city as early as the 18th century. There are allegorical sculptures, statues in plazas, and the occasional contemporary work. Much of what you'll see is symbolic of civic pride.

We begin our outing at Broadway and Park Place, opposite City Hall Park. This is an icon of New York buildings: the **Woolworth Building** at 233 Broadway. When it was constructed in 1913, it was the tallest building in the world, at 700 feet. Designed by Cass Gilbert, it is an elegant example of Gothic Revival architecture. On the south side of City Hall Park are changing exhibitions of sculpture. A statue of Nathan Hale, by Frederick MacMonnies, stands near City Hall.

City Hall itself, at 260 Broadway between Broadway, Park Row, and Chambers Street, is a small, intimate building (almost dwarfed by its high-rise neighbors) but a gem to see. Built in 1803–1811 in a refined Georgian Renaissance style, it offers both architectural and artistic pleasures.

As you walk toward the building, note the figure atop the cupola. A statue called *Justice*, it is made of painted copper (it replaced two wooden figures of the

Woolworth Building
233 Broadway
at Park Place

City Hall
260 Broadway
between Broadway,
Park Row, and
Chambers Street

**Statue of
Benjamin Franklin**
Printing House Square

**Statue of
Horace Greeley**
Park Row

Surrogate's Court
31 Chambers Street

past) in 1878. In her hands are a scale, and at her side, a sword (her designer is unknown.) Like many civic statues of the time, *Justice* is vaguely classical in style.

On the far side of the park is Park Row, and here you'll find another New York educational institutional: Pace University, at 1 Park Plaza. In front, on Printing House Square, is a well-loved bronze **statue of Benjamin Franklin**, by Ernest Plassman (1872), a German-born sculptor. Franklin, a diplomat and printer, appears with a newspaper (the *Pennsylvania Gazette*) in hand. The unveiling of the sculpture was a big event, at which Horace Greeley, editor of the *Tribune*, made the address, and Samuel F. B. Morse swept off a "star-spangled" covering. Also at Pace's plaza is a much more recent work, *Setting the Pace*, by Mike Melville. It is a tribute to police dogs.

Across Park Row is the more northern section of City Hall Park, where you can see a **statue of Greeley** himself. Made by John Quincy Adams Ward in 1890, the famous journalist is a realistically rumpled, whiskered figure, and was considered an excellent likeness.

Cross nearby Chambers Street to no. 31. This is **Surrogate's Court** (also known as the Hall of Records). In keeping with 19th- and early 20th-century emphasis on symbolic art for civic buildings, the statuary here is allegorical and elaborate in design.

There are 42 statues decorating the façade here, all meant to inspire civic pride. The main ones, flanking the entrance, are made of granite; they are by Philip Martiny, a French protégé of Augustus Saint-Gaudens. On the right, representing *New York in Its Infancy* (1907,) is a woman clutching a book and wearing a feathered headdress. On the left, a female figure holds a globe and a torch. She wears a helmet, and she is called *New York in Revolutionary Times* (1907). (You can see additional Martiny works in Foley Square, where you'll find his *Justice* and *Authority* of 1906.)

The 24 cornice figures (high up on the façade) are either portraits of notable New Yorkers, including Peter Stuyvesant and DeWitt Clinton, and various early mayors (whose names appear on many downtown streets), or allegories. The Chambers Street façade has the recognizable images, while the Centre Street side has eight female figures of allegory, such as *Medicine*, *Commerce*, and *Industry*. On the Reade Street side are *Justice* and *Tradition*, and symbolic representations of *Printing* and *Electricity* and *Painting* and *Sculpture*, among others.

Sculptor Henry Kirke Bush-Browne is represented by *Maternity*, *Philosophy*, and *Poetry*, as well as by *The Four Seasons* (seen high up on the building). This is perhaps the most decorated of city buildings, a testament to the 19th century's interests and pre-occupations with grandeur and growth and American enterprise.

You can go inside this court building, which you'll find as ornate and decorative as the exterior. Sculptured reliefs by Albert Weinert decorate the marble foyer, depicting New York's past. Even the windows have wrought-iron designs. A fabulous mosaic (ca. 1905) decorates the ceiling; it is by the artist William Leftwich Dodge and it, too, shows allegorical figures in ancient garb. Note particularly the grand marble staircase rising to the colonnaded rotunda (which suggested a Piranesi drawing to us).

Directly across the street is the huge, impressive **Manhattan Municipal Building**. Numerous statues decorate its exterior, too. Most well known is *Civic Fame* (1913–14), by Adolph Alexander Weinman; it sits atop the tower, and is the largest statue in Manhattan. It appears golden but is, in fact, copper covered with gold leaf. This graceful figure balances on the globe and holds a crown with five turrets, each representing a borough of New York City. (Rising 582 feet above the city, the work is hard to see from close by; back up into the park for a good view!) Also on the exterior are a variety of medallions, coats of arms, and groups of allegories of civic virtues (including *Executive Power* and *Guidance*).

Not far away is **Police Plaza**, a brick-faced, more modern setting for a much more recent work: Tony Rosenthal's *Five in One* (1974), which is a 30-foot-tall, 75-ton COR-TEN steel sculpture. Its composition is of five disks in an abstract design. (Unfortunately, plans to add more art to the area have not materialized; we found the plaza awash in trash).

The **New York County Courthouse** is next on our tour. If you walk along Pearl Street, you'll come to Foley Square, where you'll see this elegant building, at 60 Centre Street. Great stone steps to a colonnaded entrance are flanked by two statues of note: Philip

Municipal Building
1 Centre Street

Police Plaza
Park Row

New York County Courthouse
60 Centre Street at Foley Square

African Burial Ground
Duane Street

Clyde Lynds:
America Song **(1995)**
Ted Weiss
Federal Office Building
290 Broadway

Jacob K. Javits Federal Building
26 Federal Plaza

Martiny's *Justice* and *Authority* (1906). These seated figures are large and curiously impressive with their allegorical items in hand, suggesting more modern images of the future.

A contemporary work, Lorenzo Pace's black steel ***Triumph of the Human Spirit*** (2000), sits in the center of Foley Square. This is an evocative memorial to the history of America's slaves. It is just across the street from the quite recently discovered **African Burial Ground** (on Duane Street). Don't miss this site. The plain grassy space is partly where the burial ground was located, as well as just next door, at 290 Broadway. Here is the huge **Ted Weiss Federal Office Building**. On the exterior wall is Clyde Lynds' *America Song* (1995), which combines stainless steel, granite, and concrete with electronics.

Within the building are some provocative artworks relating to the burial ground. Of particular interest is Barbara Chase Riboud's 1998 sculpture *Africa Rising*. A silkscreen collage work by Tomie Arai (1998) commemorates the discovery of the site. And at the Duane Street entrance to the building you'll find a mosaic high up on the wall. This shows dozens of faces, some skeletal, and is the work of Roger Brown. A nearby installation called *The New Ring Shout* (1994) features a 40-foot round lighted terrazzo-and-brass dance floor. It is a tribute to Africans, Indians, and European buried beneath the building. (In the lobby, pick up fliers describing these artworks.)

Across Duane Street is the **Jacob K. Javits Federal Building** whose plaza is dotted with art. You'll recognize an Alexander Calder work: *Object in Five Planes* (1965) is a large red steel piece in his inimitable style. A rough-textured iron columnar work is by Beverly Pepper on the opposite corner of the plaza.

If you walk around this building, you'll come back to 1 Centre Street, the **Municipal Building**. On the Centre Street side is a sculpted relief by William Zorach. Called *Law* (1960), it depicts a judge surrounded by a family in the artist's rather stylized manner, executed with his traditional block of granite and a chisel.

Our last stop is to see a bas-relief on the Lafayette Street side of the building. (There is a small park there, good for resting, at the end of this tour!) Here, too, is a portrayal of *Justice*. This work, a counterpart to Zorach's, is also a bas-relief. By Joseph Kiselewski, it is an allegory from the pre–World War II era, depicting a floating female figure bearing scales and hovering above a baby and a snake.

To return uptown, walk north to the subway stations at Canal Street and Broadway (6, J, N, Q, and R lines), or to the Tribeca art sites.

8 A Walk down Medieval Garden Paths at the Cloisters

DIRECTIONS» By subway, take the A line to 190th Street to Overlook Terrace. Exit by elevator and walk through Fort Tryon Park. By car, take the Henry Hudson Parkway north to first exit after George Washington Bridge; follow the signs; parking on premises.

A visit to the **Cloisters** (the Metropolitan Museum's medieval-style museum in northern Manhattan), 99 Margaret Corbin Drive, Fort Tryon Park (212-923-3700; www.metmuseum.org/visit/visit-the/cloisters) is a beautiful experience, for walking through this reconstructed medieval building filled with some 5,000 medieval artworks and exquisite gardens is like no other experience in New York. **🕐** 10 AM to 5:15 PM (March to October) and 10 AM to 4:45 PM (November to February). Suggested admission fee; tours available.

Cloisters
99 Corbin Drive,
Fort Tryon Park
212-923-3700
www.metmuseum.org
/visit/visit-the/cloisters

Constructed from the remains of several cloistered abbeys (one from the year 878, and another from 1206), you are transported to a distant time and place, with the marvelous collection of medieval sculpture, stained-glass artifacts, tapestries, and metalwork all around you. Here you'll find the Unicorn Tapestries in all their splendor, extraordinary sculpture of kings and queens and religious figures, depictions of medieval life and lore—in all, a must-see visit in New York.

In addition to the tapestries, don't miss the stained-glass in the Boppard Room, the wonderful altarpiece by the 15th-century painter Robert Campin, and our particular favorites, the medieval wood sculptures. Children, by the way, will enjoy this walk; there are numerous crenellated walls, dark staircases, and impressive and picturesque statues that they'll love, and there are even medieval playing cards on display.

Among the particularly magical parts of the Cloisters are the gardens. While the pleasures of visiting the museum's medieval architecture and seeing its exquisite collection of fine art from the Middle Ages may be well known to museum-goers, its gardens are perhaps less so—and they are definitely worth a special

trip. Great care has been taken to reconstruct the arcades of five cloisters with the original stones; and integrated into the museum's architecture, four cloisters surround their own gardens. The intimate gardens are so rich with sculptural, architectural, and botanical interest that you will be tempted to spend hours walking about, perhaps in a dreamy state, imagining you are in 13th-century France. In the background you might barely hear the sounds of Gregorian chant, which add a sense of mystery to this experience.

Two of the cloisters (square-columned walkways that once were parts of monasteries) are enjoyable to visit even out of garden season, for they are in cov-

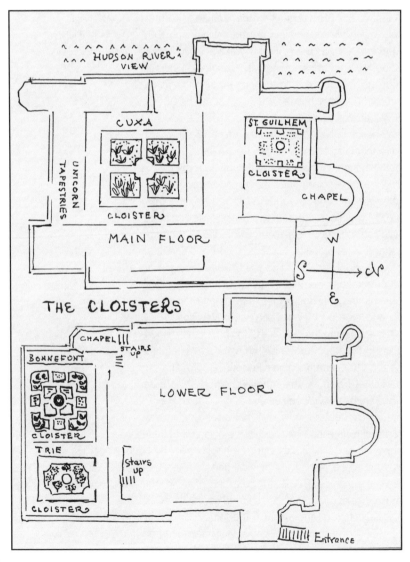

ered areas and their flowers are kept blooming. But, of course, all four of the cloister gardens are at their best in late spring and early summer.

Saint-Guilhem-le-Desert, the earliest of the cloisters, was once part of a French abbey dating back to a Benedictine order in 804 b.c. Built in 1206, its stone pillars are topped by capitals with designs based on plant motifs. But many other decorations are carved on these columns: a series of faces, flowers, entwined vines, and elegant foliage. Some of the sculptural decoration was influenced by ancient Roman design. Inside this cloister is an indoor garden that is planted fully in early spring (in winter, the flowers are kept in neatly arranged pots).

Across the central room from the Saint-Guilhem-le-Desert Cloister is the wonderful Saint-Michel-de-Cuxa Cloister, the central part of the framework of the Cloisters Museum. This cloister was in a Benedictine abbey first built in 878, though the cloister itself dates to the 12th century. Its original function—as a communal place for monks to walk, meditate, or read—can be imagined. The stone walks are surrounded by archways and columns and lead to a sunlit garden of flowers and plants in individual beds. The columns are decorated with gargoyles, two-headed animals, and other images typical of medieval times. You'll find this a truly inviting spot both in winter and spring and summer, while it is ablaze with flowers.

The Bonnefont Cloister, a purely outdoor garden walkway, is on the lower level of the museum. Its origins are in the region of Toulouse, in the south of France. The cloister, dating from the late 13th or early 14th century, is graced with slender columns in rows of two. Years ago, Cistercian monks walked solemnly through these cloisters, and their asceticism is reflected in the simple design of the architecture and sculptural pattern. (Decoration was meant not to draw attention away from devotion to duty and God.)

A favorite attraction here is the delightful garden, with its more than 250 species of plants grown in the Middle Ages. The herbs are planted in raised beds, enclosed with fences; in the center is a little wall. We especially liked the image of the espaliers growing against lattices in the sunlight.

Finally, the fourth cloister, also on the lower level, is the Trie Cloister. Originally from a Carmelite building in the Bigorre region of southern France, it was

reassembled with parts of several other cloisters. This small outdoor garden arcade is of particular interest if you first take a look at the Unicorn Tapestries in the museum. You'll discover that the garden contains samples of the same plants woven into the design of the tapestries some five centuries ago. (Information at the Cloisters will identify them for you.)

Although obviously you will get more pleasure from this medieval garden walk in the growing season, even in wintertime it is nice to wander about the unkempt cloisters outdoors, to see the view of the Hudson, and to contemplate the beauty of the architecture and sculptural designs in the indoor gardens.

A visit to the Cloisters is perhaps the closest you can get to being in France while in Manhattan. We found the combination of art history and flowering plants an irresistible delight.

AND IN ADDITION . . .

The Cloisters also offers gallery talks (on such subjects as tapestries, gardens of the Middle Ages, and medieval imagery); concerts of medieval music played on early instruments; and demonstrations on ancient techniques, such as miniature painting and enameling. Available as well is a guide to the gardens in which each plant is carefully labeled.

Fort Tryon Park
between Riverside Drive and Broadway, and 192nd and Dyckman Streets

If you wish to take a lovely walk in the area, we recommend a walk through **Fort Tryon Park**, a very pleasant nearby site, where you will enjoy terrific views of the Hudson. (Leave the Cloisters and follow the signs for the park, which is located from Riverside Drive to Broadway, and 192nd and Dyckman Streets.)

9 Sampling Manhattan's International Art Scene: Galleries, Embassies, and Cultural Centers

DIRECTIONS » By subway, take the N, R, or 4, 5, or 6 line to Lexington Avenue and 59th Street.

» Korean Cultural Service Gallery: 460 Park Avenue (212-759-9550; www.koreanculture.org). ⊕ Monday–Friday 10 AM–5 PM.

» À La Vieille Russie: 781 Fifth Avenue (212-752-1727). ⊕ Monday–Friday 10 AM–5 PM.

» French Institute (Alliance Française): 22 East 60th Street (212-355-6100; www.fiaf.org). ⊕ Monday–

Thursday 9 AM–9 PM, Friday 9 AM–6 PM, Saturday 9 AM–5 PM. (Closed Sunday.)

» **China Institute:** 125 East 65th Street (212-744-8181; www.chinainstitute.org). 🄷 Monday, Wednesday, Friday, and Saturday 10 AM–5 PM; Tuesday and Thursday 10 AM–8 PM. (Closed Sunday.)

» **Herbert and Eileen Bernard Museum of Judaica:** 1 East 65th Street (212-744-1400; www.emanuelnyc.org). 🄷 Sunday–Thursday 10 AM–4:30 PM. (Closed Friday and Saturday.) Free.

» **Americas Society:** 680 Park Avenue at 68th Street (212-249-8950; www.americas-society.org). 🄷 Wednesday-Sunday, noon–6. Free.

» **Italian Cultural Institute (part of the Italian Consulate):** 686 Park Avenue at 68th Street (212-879-4242; www.iicnewyork.esteri.it). 🄷 Monday–Friday 10 AM–4:30 PM.

» **Asia Society and Museum:** 725 Park Avenue at 70th Street (212-288-6400; www.asiasociety.org). 🄷 Tuesday–Thursday, Saturday, and Sunday 11 AM–6 PM; Friday 11 AM–9 PM. (Closed Monday.)

» **Ukrainian Institute of America:** 2 East 79th Street (212-288-8660; www.ukrainianinstitute.org). 🄷 Tuesday–Sunday noon–6 PM. (Closed Monday.)

» **Goethe-Institute (also known as Goethe House):** 1014 Fifth Avenue at 83rd Street (212-228-6848; www.goethe.de/newyork). 🄷 Monday 9 AM–5:30 PM, Tuesday–Friday 9 AM–4:15 PM.

» **Czech Center New York:** 321 East 73rd Street (646-422-3399; www.czechcenter.com). Gallery 🄷 Monday–Friday 10 AM–6 PM, Tuesday 10 AM–7 PM.

On this walk you'll be "going around the world" while actually staying put in Manhattan. We all know that New York is among the most international cities on the planet—and also that it is considered by many to be the capital of the art world. Combine the two—international and art—and you are in for a fascinating experience.

This artwalk covers some 20 blocks on the east side of Manhattan (not counting additional sites), where you can visit cultural centers, foreign institutes, consulates, galleries, and even specialty shops focusing on the arts of other lands. You will be exposed to a wide variety of artistic works—from ethnic collections to the latest art being done abroad to antiquities and native art. And all of this in just a few blocks!

Korean Cultural Service Agency
460 Park Avenue
at 57th Street
212-759-9550
www.koreanculture.org

À La Vieille Russie
781 Fifth Avenue
at 59th Street
212-752-1727
http://www.alvr.com

French Institute (Alliance Française)
22 East 60th Street
212-355-6100
www.fiaf.org

China Institute
125 East 65th Street
Between Lexington
and Park
212-744-8181
www.chinainstitute.org

Herbert and Eileen Bernard Museum of Judaica
1 East 65th Street
at Fifth Avenues
212-744-1400
www.emanuelnyc.org

Our walk starts with the **Korean Cultural Service Gallery**, at 460 Park Avenue at 57th Street. This elegant gallery, located on the 6th floor, has stunning exhibits of Korean art, including contemporary works drawing on ancient traditions. Perhaps not as familiar to most of us as Japanese or Chinese art, the arts of Korea have their own forms going back at least 5,000 years, and there is much to see—from tomb murals of centuries ago, to ceramic objects, to wood or stone sculpture, to decorative arts in bamboo, jade, or weaving and embroidery. A recent show at the gallery, *Take Old Road New Way*, featured seven contemporary artists whose personal interpretations of traditional Korean arts and materials linked the past with the present.

From Korea we take you to Russia. At 781 Fifth Avenue at 59th Street, you'll see **À La Vieille Russie**, an elegant shop that has graced this spot since 1961. A family enterprise dating from the mid-19th century (there are additional shops abroad), it includes gallery space where you can look at dazzling pre-Soviet jewelry, Fabergé eggs, and other antiques of interest. Among the art collection (some on display, some for sale) are sculpture, silverware, porcelain, paintings, and—of special interest to us—beautiful icons (some dating to the Middle Ages). Altogether, this site speaks eloquently of Russia's past.

The **French Institute (Alliance Française)** at 22 East 60th Street, between Madison and Fifth Avenues, is just around the corner but worlds apart, with its focus on stylish contemporary French culture. Aside from French language classes, for which it is especially known, the Alliance offers art exhibitions, cinema festivals, concerts, and other cultural happenings. The Alliance also houses the Haskell Library, considered to be among the best French libraries in the country.

A short walk away you'll find the **China Institute**, at 125 East 65th Street. Its mission is to introduce Chinese culture, language, and literature to Americans. A 2009 photo exhibit, *Humanism in China*, was of great interest.

Our next stop is the **Herbert and Eileen Bernard Museum of Judaica** at 1 East 65th Street at Fifth Avenue. This small museum, part of the imposing Congregation of Temple Emanu-El (the largest Jewish temple in the world) has a collection of religious and cultural memorabilia of note. Among its many treasures are antique silver, enamel, jewelry, and a very old (14th-century) Hanukkah lamp. While you are there, be sure to go inside the temple to see its remarkable mosaics and stained-glass windows.

At 680 Park Avenue at 68th Street is the **Americas Society Art Gallery**, where the work of artists from Central and South America, the Caribbean, and Canada is displayed. This splendid, landmark mansion dating to 1912 (and designed by McKim, Mead & White) is a work of art in itself, with its high ceilings, elegant chandeliers, and polished wood floors. The gallery offers workshops, concerts, stage reading, and, of course, art exhibitions—which have included both historic and contemporary subjects.

Next door, at 686 Park Avenue, is the **Italian Cultural Institute**, a part of the Italian consulate. Although exhibition space is somewhat limited here, there are shows of Italian art now and again (check the small display board, which lists what is going on) and these are usually of high quality. A recent show highlighted the Venice Biennale 2013.

We now take you back to Asia, to the magnificent

Americas Society Art Gallery
680 Park Avenue
at 68th Street
212-249-8950
www.americas-society.org

Italian Cultural Institute
686 Park Avenue at 68th Street
212-879-4242
www.iicnewyork.esteri.it

Japanese flower basket with wooden handle (20th century), Asia Society

Asia Society and Museum at 725 Park Avenue at 70th Street. The museum, housed in a striking building designed by Edward Larrabee Barnes and elegantly renovated a few years ago, has a stellar collection of Asian art—from the famed Mr. and Mrs. John D. Rockefeller collection to the cutting-edge society's Contemporary Arts collection. The exhibits are always first rate. Recent shows have included *The Artful Recluse: Painting, Poetry, and Politics in 17th-Century China* and *Revolutionary Ink: The Paintings of Wu Guanzhong*.

Our next stop is the **Ukrainian Institute of America**, housed in an almost forbidding, castlelike mansion with iron gates, at 2 East 79th Street. The inside of this imposing site is quite the opposite: filled with colorful folk art, bright posters, and many paintings. On display is the permanent collection, including such luminaries as Alexander Archipenko and Alexis Gritchenko; upstairs are traditionally painted Easter eggs, regional costumes, and other decorative arts from the Ukraine. The institute present film screenings, poetry readings, lectures, symposia, events for children, and more.

Walk a few more blocks up Fifth Avenue to a site well worth the slight detour: the **Goethe House** at 1014 Fifth Avenue (opposite the Metropolitan Museum). Housed in a recently renovated Beaux-Arts townhouse, this impressive institute (it has several other sites throughout Europe) is devoted to promoting German arts and culture. In this capacity it hosts exhibitions of all types (especially contemporary art), film screening, performances, and literary events.

Note that you are now very near the great museums within New York's famous Museum Mile (see chapter 11); we think that those deserve their separate visit and therefore we are purposefully turning east to several smaller galleries on Madison Avenue that specialize in art from distant lands. Among them are the following:

Scholten Japanese Art Gallery, 145 West 58th Street, is the largest gallery devoted to Japanese screens, prints, and ceramics in New York. For an appointment, call 212-585-0474; www.scholten-japanese -art.com.

Mary-Anne Martin/Fine Art at 23 East 73rd Street (212-288-2313; www.mamfa.com), specializes in Modern Mexican and Latin American paintings, drawings, and sculpture, includes works by Tamayo, Rivera, and Orozco.

Asia Society and Museum
725 Park Avenue at 70th Street
212-288-6400
www.asiasociety.org

Ukrainian Institute of America
2 East 79th Street
212-288-8660
www.ukrainian institute.org

Goethe House
1014 Fifth Avenue at 83rd Street
212-228-6848
www.goethe.de/newyork

Scholten Japanese Art Gallery
145 West 58th Street, Suite 6D
212-585-0474
www.scholten-japanese -art.com

Mary-Anne Martin/ Fine Art
23 East 73rd Street
212-288-2313
www.mamfa.com

Walk farther east to 321 East 73rd Street and you'll come to another not-to-be-missed cultural center. **Czech Center New York**, located in the Grand Bohemian National Hall (a landmark building dating to the 1890s). It features Czech culture, business, and tourism. In includes an unusually attractive gallery committed to presenting the latest works of Czech artists to the American public. (The building also houses the Consulate General of the Czech Republic and the Bohemia Benevolent and Literary Association.)

The stylish gallery, recently restored in a glamorous minimalist mode and accessed by an almost transparent circular staircase, is certainly worth a visit for anyone interested in the contemporary arts of a different culture. Here you will have a taste of innovative works by today's Czech painters, sculptors, photographers, and conceptual artists, and the provocative issues that they raise. A recent exhibit featured the well regarded conceptual artist Karel Miler, along with four lesser-known artists, in an exhibition called *There Is Nothing Here*, where the abstract ideas of belonging and identity were explored.

The Bohemian National Hall, by the way, is an architectural gem in its own right. Built in the Renaissance Revival style, it is one of the surviving social halls for New York's immigrant ethnic communities and was designated as a landmark building in 1994. If possible, take a look at the beautiful ballroom (which holds some 300 people), a truly grand hall, now used for concerts, plays, and other cultural events.

MANHATTAN

Czech Center New York
321 East 73rd Street
646-422-3399
www.czech center.com

AND IN ADDITION . . .

Much farther uptown, on the west side of Manhattan, is the **Hispanic Society of America**, 613 West 155th Street at Broadway (212-926-2334), within a vast courtyard that also includes the Numismatic Society and the American Academy of Arts of Letters.

At the center of the courtyard is a collection of dramatic sculptures, by Anna Hyatt Huntington, representing El Cid and a variety of animals. The Hispanic Society of America is now the centerpiece of the courtyard. This surprisingly rich collection was created through the efforts of Archer M. Huntington (Anna's husband), who, from an early age, was fascinated by Iberian culture. Inside this lovely Renaissance-style Spanish mansion are beautiful galleries, and riches of carved wood, terra-cotta archways, and brightly colored

Hispanic Society of America
613 West 155th Street at Broadway
212-926-2334
www.hispanicsociety.org

43

wall tiles. The rooms are filled with art treasures—a surprising number of fine paintings, drawings, sculpture, as well as decorative arts (rugs, furniture, ceramics, textiles, etc.). The paintings—from the earliest, intensely religious 14th-century works of the Catalan, Aragonese, Valencian, and Castillian schools to modern works—include an exceptionally rich collection of masterworks by El Greco, Zurbaran, Velásquez, Riberas, and Morales. And not surprisingly, the society has several splendid Goyas (five paintings and ten drawings), including the very large painting *Duchess of Alba* (1797), as well as many works by the more recent Spanish artist, Joaquin Sonolla y Bastida, a great friend of Huntington's.

We hope you will also visit on another day—the following ethnic collections: the **National Museum of the American Indian** (see page 95), the **Chinatown History Museum** (70 Mulberry Street), the **Caribbean Cultural Center** (see page 55), **El Museo del Barrio** (see page 51), the **Swiss Institute** (495 Broadway at Broome Street), the **Galeria Venezuela** (7 East 51st Street), and **Scandinavia House** (58 Park Avenue at 38th Street).

Also of note:

At the **Asian American Arts Center**, 26 Bowery between Bayard and Pell Streets (212-233-2154), you can see changing exhibits related to Asian and Asian American arts and culture.

The **Ukrainian Museum**, 222 East 6th Street (212-228-0110), features painted Easter eggs, photos, folk arts, jewelry, paintings, and sculpture (including works by Archipenko).

The **Latin Collector Art Center**, 153 Hudson Street (212-334-7814), shows contemporary Latin American artists.

The **Japan Society**, 333 East 47th Street (212-832-1155), displays Japanese prints, sculptures, and paintings of centuries.

The extraordinary **MEGU Restaurants**, at two locations—62 Thomas Street and 845 United Nations Plaza at 47th Street and First Avenue (212-964-7777)—are so filled with unusual art and artifacts that they are worth a visit, whether you eat there or not. Stacked bolts of antique kimono fabric, an enormous temple bell, a Buddha ice sculpture, columns of interlocking rice bowls, hand-drawn tiger murals—these are a few of the surprising visual effects.

Asian American Arts Center
26 Bowery between Bayard and Pell Streets
212-233-2154

Ukrainian Museum
222 East 6th Street
212-228-0110

Latin Collector Art Center
153 Hudson Street
212-334-7814

Japan Society
333 East 47th Street
212-832-1155

MEGU Restaurants
62 Thomas Street
845 United Nations Plaza at 47th Street and First Avenue
212-964-7777

In Brooklyn you can visit the **Kurdish Library**, 114 Underhill Avenue at Park Place (718-987-3500). This is North America's only cultural center devoted to the history and arts of the Kurdish people.

Almost every one of these institutions has extensive series of lectures, concerts, symposia, films, language classes, art discussion, and so on. Pick up fliers and listings when you visit or phone ahead to see what is being offered and when.

Kurdish Library
114 Underhill Avenue at Park Place
Brooklyn
718-987-3500

10 An Aerial Park Overlooking the Cityscape: The High Line

DIRECTIONS» By subway, take the A, C, E, or L line to 14th Street (8th Avenue); the C or E line to 23rd Street (8th Avenue); the 1, 2, or 3 line to 14th Street (7th Avenue); the 1 line to 18th Street (7th Avenue); or the 1 line to 23rd Street (7th Avenue).

» Section 1 starts at Gansevoort Street (near 12th Street, between 10th and 11th Avenues) and ends at West 20th Street;

» Section 2 starts at West 20th Street and goes to West 30th Street. The park's entrances are at: Gansevoort, 14th Street (elevator access), 16th Street (elevator access), 18th Street, 20th Street, 23rd Street (elevator access), 26th Street, 28th Street, and 30th Street (elevator access).

If you have not yet experienced the **High Line** (212-500-6035; www.thehighline.org)—that spectacular new greenway floating 30 feet above the city streets of the West Village and Chelsea—you are in for a rare treat. Ever since it opened (the first section in 2009, the second in 2011), this linear urban park has become a very popular destination with both out-of-towners and locals, as it offers a most welcome haven from the chaos of a high-energy city that never sleeps. It is open daily from 7 AM–10 PM (last entrance is at 9:45 PM).

High Line
Gansevoort Street (near West 12th Street, between 10th and 11th Avenues) to West 30th Street
212-500-6035
www.thehighline.org

Built atop a long-abandoned elevated railway, the High Line also offers the visitor a fascinating and surprisingly intimate glimpse of the city from a new and different vantage point. You are sure to be mesmerized by the combination of old brick warehouses, striking new buildings (some in progress), giant advertisements and bold graffiti, bustling residential neighborhoods, boat traffic along the nearby river, and distant

View of the High Line

skyscrapers—all coming together before you like a giant collage of different shapes, sizes, textures, and colors. In contrast, the much less frantic scene within the park (only pedestrians are allowed) has its own dynamic—depending on season, weather, time of day, people. There is always something interesting and new to see, no matter where you look.

The original railway, built in the 1930s, operated until about 1980. When the old structure was doomed for demolition, a group of active local citizens (the first was Peter Obletz) came together to preserve it. And so began the brilliant idea of converting the defunct railroad line into an elevated park. It took years, but eventually, in partnership with the City, the grassroots organization Friends of the High Line came up with a viable solution, and in the early millennium, work finally began.

The park stretches out a good mile and a half—from Gansevoort Street in the Village to West 30th Street, with a lot to see and savor from one end to the other. You can choose to walk however much of it you wish, as there are several entrances and exits along the route (see Directions for details). All you need to do is climb up a flight of steps from the street (there are a few elevators for wheelchairs, too) and you find yourself suddenly in another world.

The park's lovely landscape design is naturalistic and informal—inspired, we are told, by the wildflowers and grasses that appeared spontaneously around the old railroad tracks once they were no longer in use. During the growing season you see a wonderful and colorful variety of plants—feathery and light, well tended and artfully placed—as well as patches of dense vegetation interspersed with bits of lawn and ornamental grasses here and there. Restored art deco steel railings line the elegant walkways in places; large and stylish wooden chairs and teak benches are situated where people can rest and contemplate the world around them; and art installations are set up now and again to add a bit of spice. When we last visited we saw Sarah Sze's *Still Life with Landscape (Model for a Habitat)* displayed among the plantings and Julianne Swartz's *Digital Empathy*. You might also catch a glimpse of occasional artworks whimsically exhibited on nearby rooftops or billboards.

The idea of a suspended park built on old railroad tracks is not original with the High Line; we know of such a park in Paris, dating from the 1980s, and no doubt elsewhere too, as this clever idea for creating an inviting public space within a crowded urban setting takes hold. But each park is different, depending on its surroundings. New York's version reflects the vibrancy of its constantly changing environment in a compelling way. No wonder the High Line is often busy (even crowded, on beautiful holiday weekends). You'll find a visit here not only lively and entertaining (all that people watching!), but also inspiring and informative, as you discover new sites you might not have known even existed.

The last section of the High Line up to 34th Street has recently become assured with a generous gift, so that the three million annual visitors (10 times the expected attendance) will be able to walk a full mile and a half from one end of the park to the other.

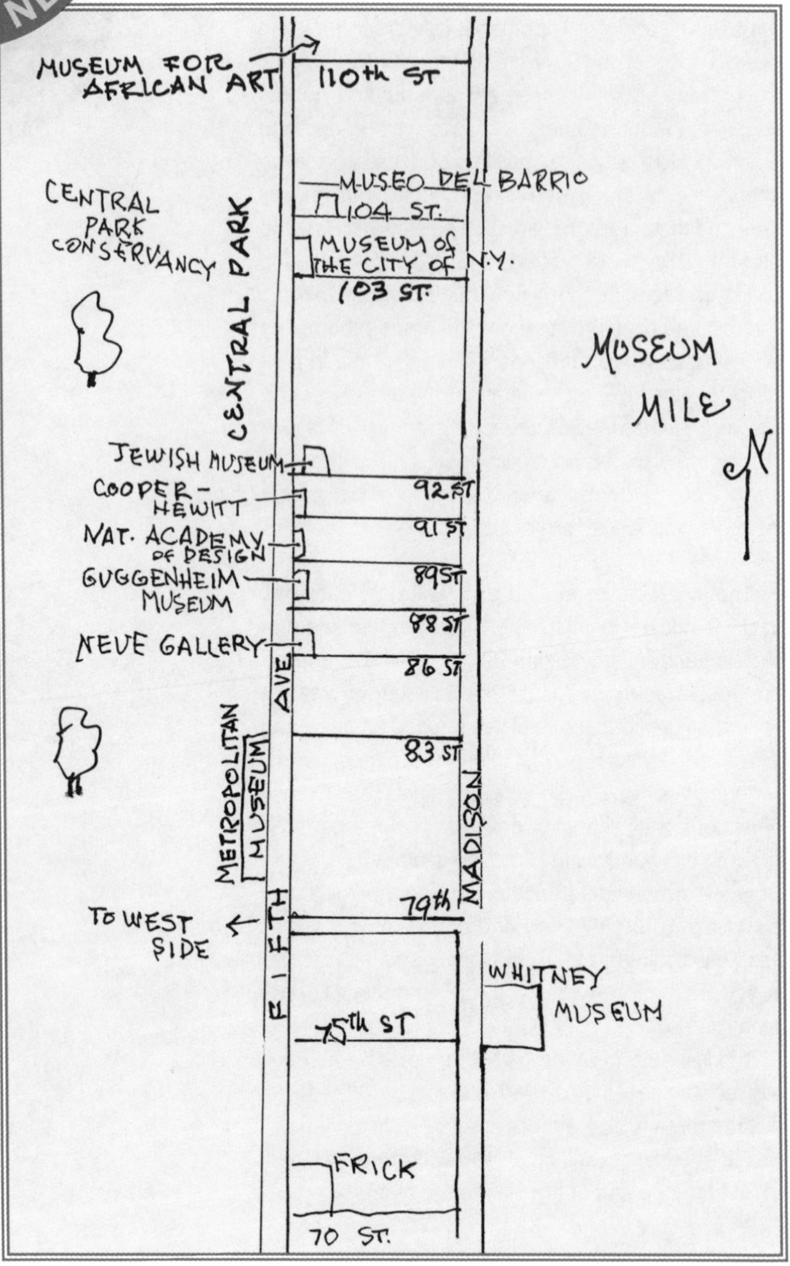

NEW YORK CITY

MUSEUM FOR AFRICAN ART   110th ST

CENTRAL PARK CONSERVANCY

CENTRAL PARK

MUSEO DEL BARRIO
104 ST.

MUSEUM OF THE CITY OF N.Y.
103 ST

MUSEUM MILE

N

JEWISH MUSEUM

COOPER-HEWITT   92 ST

NAT. ACADEMY of DESIGN   91 ST

GUGGENHEIM MUSEUM   89 ST

                            88 ST

NEUE GALLERY   86 ST

                            83 ST

METROPOLITAN MUSEUM
FIFTH AVE
MADISON

TO WEST SIDE ←   79th

WHITNEY MUSEUM

5th ST

FRICK
70 ST.

DIRECTIONS» By subway, take the 4, 5, or 6 line to 86th Street (Lexington Avenue); walk west to Fifth Avenue and south to 84th Street. Officially, the Mile runs along Fifth Avenue, between 82nd and 105th streets, but we are expanding that a bit.

Museum Mile is undoubtedly one of New York's most important attractions—whether you're a frequent museum-goer or a visitor from out of town. Some of the world's finest collections of art and artifacts can be found within walking distance of one another—though you will hardly be able to visit this abundance of treasures in one day! Not only are these permanent collections of the highest quality, but the museums feature constantly changing exhibitions as well. Our suggestion for how to handle this extraordinary embarrassment of riches is to plan for a full day or two at the Metropolitan Museum of Art (perhaps a mile's walk in of itself, if you see all of it), and then, according to your interests, plan additional time for the smaller collections we have listed below. Museum Mile is, in fact, a walkable, straight tour up Fifth Avenue from 81st to 110th Street. In this compact area, you will be able to see every kind of art you could wish for (and perhaps some art you never knew of, or imagined).

We begin at the **Metropolitan Museum of Art**, 1000 Fifth Avenue at 81st Street (212-535-7710; www.metmuseum.org). **ℍ** open every day, 10 AM–5:30 PM. Suggested admission fee. Tours and audio tours are available.

Metropolitan Museum of Art
1000 Fifth Avenue at 81st Street
212-535-7710
www.metmuseum.org

Before you enter, note Isamu Noguchi's *Unidentified Object* (1979), an abstract basalt sculpture just south of the museum at 80th Street.

The magnificent, comprehensive museum has one of the greatest collections of European painting in the world (some 2,000 works of art); massive collections of ancient art: Egyptian (don't miss the entire Temple of Dendur), Greek, and Roman sculptures and vases; Asian art of all kinds; an entire American wing; furniture, musical instruments, costumes, medieval armor, and manuscripts; and much, much more. (Pick up a map as you enter.) While all of these treasures are in separate sections, you can also enjoy changing exhibitions. Remember to visit the marvelous roof garden

with its large outdoor sculptures (Rodin, Gaston Lachaise, and David Smith—among many others), and the Charles Englehard Court (featuring works by other notable sculptors). The museum has all kinds of educational and artistic events, lectures, and concerts.

Just across the street is a much more recent addition to the city's appealing museums—one of our favorite sites. This is the **Neue Galerie**, 1048 Fifth Avenue at 86th Street (212-628-6200; www.neuegalerie.org). ⓗ Monday, Saturday, and Sunday 11 AM–6 PM; Friday 11 AM–9 PM. Admission fee.

The Neue Galerie is housed in a former mansion; its several stories are not too large, and its collection and shows are always interesting. There is a distinguished collection of art from early 20th-century Austria and Germany, with an emphasis on paintings (e.g., Egon Schiele, Gustav Klimt, and Oskar Kokoschka) and the wonderful decorative arts of the Wiener Werkstatte and other leading designers of the period. Don't miss the spectacular Viennese clocks, the Josef Hoffmann creations, or the fabric and wallpaper designs. There are changing exhibitions, as well. (Lunch here at the Café Sabarsky will make you think you are in 1920s Vienna.)

Just up Fifth Avenue is Frank Lloyd Wright's famous 1959 **Solomon R. Guggenheim Museum** building, 1071 Fifth Avenue at 89th Street (212-423-3500; www.guggenheim.org). ⓗ Friday–Wednesday 10 AM–5:45 PM, Saturday 10 AM–7:45 PM. (Closed Thursday.) Admission fee. Its amazing interior invites you to walk a great spiral pathway flanked with art. Guggenheim was an industrialist with an eye for early modern art; here you'll see one of the world's great collections of Kandinskys, Mondrians, Mirós, and Braques—many of the great of European modern art. We recommend taking the elevator to the top, and following the gentle ramp downward. This will be a memorable museum experience (whether you come to see the art or the building).

On a different note, our next stop is the **National Academy**, 1083 Fifth Avenue at 89th Street (212-369-4880; www.nationalacademy.org). ⓗ Wednesday–Sunday 11 AM–6 PM. (Closed Monday and Tuesday.) Admission fee. This is a very old institution, founded in 1825 to show American art in the new nation. It has a rather conservative taste, but a series of

Neue Galerie
1048 Fifth Avenue
at 86th Street
212-628-6200
www.neuegalerie.org

Solomon R. Guggenheim Museum
1071 Fifth Avenue
at 89th Street
212-423-3500
www.guggenheim.org

National Academy
1083 Fifth Avenue
at 89th Street
212-369-4880
www.national
academy.org

changing shows has moved away from pure tradition-alism; its watercolor shows are particularly fine.

A few blocks north, you'll find the **Cooper-Hewitt National Design Museum** at 2 East 91st Street (212-849-8351; www.cooperhewitt.org). (Currently undergoing renovation, the museum is scheduled to reopen in 2014.) This museum is actually part of the Smithsonian Institution; it is the National Museum of Design. And it exhibits a top-notch collection of textiles, ceramic figurines, salad bowls, architectural drawings, glass work, 19th-century jewelry—anything and everything relating to the history of design—all shown in the glamorous former Andrew Carnegie mansion.

From here we continue north to the newly reno-vated **Jewish Museum**, 1109 Fifth Avenue at 92nd Street (212-423-3200; www.jewishmuseum.org). ⓗ Saturday–Tuesday 11 AM–5:45 PM, Thursday 11 AM–8 PM, Friday 11 AM–4 PM. (Closed Wednesday.) Admission fee; free admission Saturday and for children under age 12. Devoted to Jewish art and history, this museum shows works from ancient times to the present, and offers some of the most interesting exhibitions around. From the ancient Jewish ceremonial items to medieval manuscripts to photos, paintings and prints, this collection is filled with rarities. This is one of the city's must-see museums.

Our next walk up Fifth Avenue brings us to the **Museum of the City of New York** at 1220 Fifth Avenue and 103rd Street (212-534-1672; www.mcny.org). ⓗ Wednesday–Saturday 10 AM–5 PM, Sunday noon–5 PM. (Closed Monday and Tuesday.) Suggested admission fee; free admission for children ages 12 and under.

In front of the building is a 1941 statue of Alexander Hamilton by Adolph Weinman. Inside is a panoply of images (paintings, artifacts, dioramas, costumes, etc.) representing New York's ongoing history. A series of changing exhibitions, events—many designed for children, and lectures bring this city's past to life.

If you continue up Fifth Avenue, you'll come to our next stop: **El Museo del Barrio** in an inviting building, 1230 Fifth Avenue at 107th Street (212-831-7272; www.elmuseo.org). ⓗ Tuesday–Saturday 11 AM–6 PM, Sunday 1 PM–5 PM. Suggested admission fee; free admission for children under age 12. Devoted to Hispanic culture, it features prints, paintings, and ar-

MANHATTAN

Cooper-Hewitt National Design Museum
2 East 91st Street
212-849-8351
www.cooperhewitt.org

Jewish Museum
1109 Fifth Avenue
at 92nd Street
212-423-3200
www.jewishmuseum.org

Museum of the City of New York
1220 Fifth Avenue
and 103rd Street
212-534-1672
www.mcny.org

El Museo del Barrio
1230 Fifth Avenue
at 107th Street
212-831-7272
www.elmuseo.org

51

tifacts from the Spanish Western Hemisphere. Ranging from historic Hispanic art to works by contemporary Latin American painters and sculptors, this is a large, rare, and interesting collection.

You can continue north to 110th Street and Fifth Avenue to see the new **Museum for African Art**, but be sure it is open (see chapter 12.) As of this writing, the new building was still closed to the public.

AND IN ADDITION . . .

Museum of Modern Art
11 West 53rd Street
212-708-9400
www.moma.org

Museum of Modern Art, 11 West 53rd Street (212-708-9400; www.moma.org). Ⓗ Thursday–Tuesday 10:30 AM–5:45 PM; Friday 10:30 AM–8:15 PM. Admission fee. While New York's major modern art museum is geographically not part of Museum Mile, no description of the city's greatest museum would be complete with its inclusion. From cubism to futurism, Fauvism to surrealism, abstract expressionism to today's many contemporary styles of art—this museum has it all. One of the world's great collections of art (and design, too), the MOMA, as it is called in New York, is a must-see for any art lover. You will be nearby overwhelmed by the treasures in this collection, as well as by the sense of excitement that pervades its shows and events. The future is here—as are the beginnings of modern art and some of its most iconic works, from Van Gogh to Matisse to Rauschenberg to the most avant-garde of today's art. Following are other museums, galleries, and art sites of interest in the neighborhood, but not considered to be a part of the Museum Mile.

Whitney Museum of American Art
945 Madison Avenue
at 75th Street
212-570-3676
www.whitney.org

Whitney Museum of American Art, 945 Madison Avenue at 75th Street (212-570-3676; www.whitney.org). Ⓗ Tuesday–Thursday 11 AM–6 PM; Friday 1 PM –9 PM; Saturday–Sunday 11 AM–6 PM. Admission fee. This major collection of American Art with a specialty in 20th-century contemporary art is a must-see in the city. It is expected to move to a new building near the High Line in 2015.

Frick Collection
1 East 70th Street
at Fifth Avenue
212-288-0700
www.frick.org

Once the grand home of Henry Clay Frick, today the **Frick Collection**, 1 East 70th Street (212-288-0700), houses in exquisite surroundings a fabulous collection of European art from the 14th through 19th centuries. Ⓗ Tuesday–Saturday 10 AM–6 PM, Sunday 11 AM–5 PM. (Closed Monday.) Admission fee. Children under 10 are not admitted.

Arsenal Gallery
830 Fifth Avenue
at 64th Street
212-360-8111

The giant **Arsenal Gallery**, 830 Fifth Avenue at 64th Street (212-360-8111), offers a variety of exhibitions, including community arts, antique shows, and other events. The New York City Department of Parks administers the gallery. Ⓗ Monday–Friday, 9 AM–5 PM. Free admission.

Alice Aycock's grand construction **East River Roundabout** (1995) is at 60th Street off FDR Drive. An amusement park–like aluminum work in looping spirals, it faces the East River.

Galeria Taller Boricua, 1680 Lexington Avenue between 105th and 106th Streets (212-831-4333; www.tallerboricua.org). Ⓗ Tuesday–Saturday noon–6 PM, Thursday 1 PM–7 PM (Closed Sunday and Monday.) Here today's Hispanic artists have their own exhibition space. There are numerous lectures and cultural events—all of which are aimed at the general public, as well as the Hispanic community.

12 Harlem's Artistic Heritage

DIRECTIONS» Museum for African Art: By subway, take the 6 line to 110th Street.

» Studio Museum of Harlem and nearby points: By subway, take the 2 or 3 line, or the A, B, C, or D line to 125th Street.

New York has one of the largest and most exciting collections of African American art—as well as art from the Caribbean and Africa. Art made by contemporary African American artists is enjoying a cultural boom, as is more traditional black art: African masks, three-dimensional sculpture, Haitian painting, and folk arts from many centuries. The following will introduce you to the black diaspora—the widespread dissemination of black visual culture.

We had hoped you could begin this walk at the brand-new **Museum for African Art**, 1280 Fifth Avenue at 110th Street (718-784-7000). However, as of this writing, the museum is expected to open by 2014, its galleries in a temporary location in Long Island City having been closed for some years.

The museum's sparkling new home—within a larger residential tower with extraordinary views of Central Park—faces Duke Ellington Circle, where stands a heroic 25-foot-high equestrian-style statue of Ellington; but instead of being on a horse, the famed musician is shown with his grand piano, atop a group of nine muses. (Unveiled in 1997, this work is by Robert Graham.) The museum itself, designed by the noted firm

MANHATTAN

East River Roundabout
60th Street
off FDR Drive

Galeria Taller Boricua
1680 Lexington Avenue
between 105th and
106th Streets
212-831-4333
www.tallerboricua.org

Museum for African Art
1280 Fifth Avenue
at 110th Street
718-784-7000
www.africanart.org

Robert A. M. Stern Architects, is unusually stunning. Its dynamic façade features one-of-a-kind "trapezoidal" windows with vibrant, colored patterns reminiscent of African textiles. Inside is a spacious lobby with high ceiling, curving walls, a grand staircase surrounding a giant perforated metal drum with reflecting lights, and gallery space galore.

The museum has a rich permanent collection, which includes magnificent masks, figure sculptures, and other arts of various tribal origins. Here you can explore African art at its purest form and find many references to these traditional shapes and styles as you journey into contemporary black art.

One of the major exhibition spaces in New York for art of African heritage is surely the **Studio Museum of Harlem**, 144 West 125th Street (212-864-4500; www.studiomuseum.org). **H** Thursday and Friday noon–9 PM, Saturday 10 AM–6 PM, Sunday noon–6 PM. Admission fee; free admission for children under age 12. This facility is a lively place with frequently changing exhibitions. The recent *Studio Museum in Harlem: The Bearden Project*, celebrating the centennial of Romare Bearden, was especially impressive. Featuring not only superb works by the noted artist himself, the show also included tributes to him by 100 contemporary artists of all ages. Among these new images was Kira Lynn Harris's reinterpretation of Bearden's 1971 *The Block*, an 18-foot collage showing life in Harlem; Harris's version used video, photography, drawing, and painting. Another interesting homage to the Harlem tradition has been an ongoing project called *Harlem Postcards*, in which contemporary artists depict this iconic site as a center of culture. (Postcards of these works are available at the museum.)

In the same building as the exhibition space are studios where artists can work and then have their output exhibited. This supportive setup encourages a number of black visual artists to work within the community. Among the museum's many other offerings are seminars and classes, both in art itself and in collecting, art history, and other aspects of the field. The museum sponsors tours and workshops.

Our next stop is the **Schomburg Center for Research in Black Culture**, 515 Malcolm X Boulevard at 135th Street (212-491-2200; www.nypl.org). **H** Tuesday–Thursday noon–8 PM, Friday and Saturday 10 AM–6 PM. (Closed Sunday and Monday.) Free ad-

**Studio Museum
of Harlem**
144 West 125th Street
212-864-4500
www.studiomuseum.org

**Schomburg Center
for Research in
Black Culture**
515 Malcolm X
Boulevard
at 135th Street
212-491-2200
www.nypl.org

mission. There are various types of art here, as well as material—both historic and contemporary—about black life and culture, history, and African American experiences. A permanent collection of African carving and metal work is augmented by special exhibitions by black artists.

Not far away on 135th Street is the **Harlem YMCA**, 180 West 135th Street (212-912-2100), where you'll find a WPA mural by the well-known Harlem Renaissance artist Aaron Douglas, titled *Evolution of Negro Dance*. (Finding an important work of art in a sports facility might come as a surprise!) This recently restored 1933 painting, depicting a lively scene of outdoor dancers, was actually commissioned by the Harlem YMCA, where it is on display in the lobby.

You'll find additional WPA murals at our next site, **Harlem Hospital**, 506 Malcolm X Boulevard at 137th Street (212-939-3548 for art program). Here, on display at the New Patient Pavilion, is an impressive group that represents the first major commission offered to African American artists by the US government. The five murals, whose subjects deal with both ritualistic and modern medicine, were recently restored after years in storage. They include *Pursuit of Happiness* (1937), by Vertis Hayes; *Recreation in Harlem* (1937), by Georgette Seabrooke; *Magic in Medicine* and *Modern Medicine* (1940), by Charles Alston; and *Modern Surgery and Anesthesia* (1936) by Alfred Crimi (the only non–African American represented in this group). In addition, three panels from these murals will be rendered on the façade of the New Pavilion.

At 144th Street is the well-known **Harlem School of the Arts**, 645 St. Nicholas Avenue at 141st Street (212-926-4100). This institution sponsors a number of art exhibits each year—both by its students and by outside professional artists, and is also noted for teaching the performing and visual arts. This is a good place to discover up-and-coming young artists in a supportive and enthusiastic atmosphere. (Phone before you go, to see where visitors are welcome).

AND IN ADDITION . . .
The **Caribbean Cultural Center**, 1825 Park Avenue, Suite 602; Entrance: 103 East 125 Street (212-307-7420), is a good place to enjoy art, films, and other cultural events.

MANHATTAN

Harlem
YMCA
180 West
135th Street
212-912-2100

Harlem Hospital
506 Malcolm X
Boulevard at 137th
Street
212-939-3548

Harlem School
of the Arts
645 St. Nicholas Avenue
at 141st Street
212-926-4100

Caribbean Cultural
Center
1825 Park Avenue
Suite 602. Entrance:
103 East 125 Street
212-307-7420
www.cccadi.org

13 Asian Art: A Sampling of Himalayan, Chinese, Japanese, and Korean Sites Around the City

DIRECTIONS?» **Rubin Museum of Art:** 150 West 17th Street at Seventh Avenue (212-620-5000; www.rmanyc.org). **ⓗ** Monday and Thursday 11 AM–5 PM, Wednesday 11 AM–7 PM, Friday 11 AM–10 PM, Saturday and Sunday 11 AM–6 PM. (Closed Tuesday.) Admission fee; free admission for children ages 12 and under.

» **Jacques Marchais Museum of Tibetan Arts:** 338 Lighthouse Avenue, Staten Island (718-987-3500; www.tibetanmuseum.com). **ⓗ** Wednesday–Sunday 1 PM–5 PM. (Closed Monday and Tuesday.) Admission fee.

» **Tibet House Gallery:** 22 West 15th Street (212-807-0563; www.tibethouse.us). **ⓗ** Monday–Friday noon–5 PM. Free admission.

» **Asia Society and Museum:** 725 Park Avenue and 70th Street (212-288-6400; www.asiasociety.org). **ⓗ** Tuesday–Thursday, Saturday, and Sunday 11 AM–6 PM; Friday 11 AM–9 PM. (Closed Monday.) Admission fee.

If Asian art is your special interest and you would like to explore more sites, in addition to those already mentioned in our "international" outing (chapter 9), following are some suggestions. We continue to be amazed by the city's many galleries, museums, shops, neighborhoods, and cultural centers. In fact, one can say that outside Asia, few places equal New York City for its wealth of Eastern art.

Rubin Museum of Art
150 West 17th Street
at Seventh Avenue
212-620-5000
www.rmanyc.org

Our first site, at 150 West 17th Street at Seventh Avenue, is the impressive **Rubin Museum of Art**, which boasts one of the largest Western collections of religious art from the Himalayan region. Housed in an elegant space, this vast gallery includes five floors surrounding a glamorous spiral staircase, preserved from the previous interior. Here you will see a remarkable collection of tangkas—the lively Himalayan scroll paintings in brilliant red, gold, and green cloth, which illustrate Buddhist landscapes and iconography—from the 12th through the 19th centuries. In addition, you'll find statuary, masks, woodblocks, textiles, murals, and illuminated manuscripts. Himalayan art is fascinating for its symbolic imagery expressing such universal themes

Vairapani, Tibet (12th century), Rubin Museum of Art

as human suffering, our connection with nature, and life after death.

Recent shows at the Rubin Museum have included *Living Shrines of Uyghur China*, photographs of sacred landscapes of Northwest China by photographer Lisa Ross; *Radical Terrain*, part of a series on modernist art from India since its independence; and *The Place of Provenance: Regional Styles in Tibetan Painting*.

The museum offers visiting exhibits, cultural programs, and special events relating to Tibet, Nepal, Bhutan, India, Mongolia, and China.

For a more intimate taste of Tibetan art, we recommend a visit to the **Jacques Marchais Museum of Tibetan Art** (see Chapter 30). In the most unlikely setting imaginable—on a suburban Staten Island street—you'll find this very unusual center devoted to the arts of Tibet. The center includes a small garden in Tibetan style, artifacts, musical instruments, and many, many works of art—all housed in two stone buildings built to resemble a Tibetan monastery.

A special exhibit there (which has been on display

Jacques Marchais Museum of Tibetan Art
338 Lighthouse Avenue, Staten Island
718-987-3500
www.tibetan museum.com

Tibet House Gallery
22 West 15th Street
212-807-0563
www.tibethouse.us

Asia Society and Museum
725 Park Avenue and 70th Street
212-288-6400
www.asiasociety.org

since 2005) has been the Bhutanese Sand Mandala, created by three Buddhist monks. Like other mandalas, these are traditional images made of sand and crushed stone dyed in a variety of colors, ritualistically created and destroyed to symbolize the transitory nature of life.

Also worth a visit, for works inspired by Tibetan and other Buddhist cultures, is the **Tibet House Gallery**, 22 West 15th Street (212-807-0563; www.tibethouse. us). 🕒 Monday–Friday noon–5 PM. Free admission. An exhibit we enjoyed was *Tibetan Contemporary Art: Tantric Vision of Modern Self Expression*, a new interpretation of classical Tibetan aesthetic that combines individual expression with traditional archetypal vision.

The **Asia Society and Museum**, at 725 Park Avenue and 70th Street, has one of the most outstanding collections of Asian art in the city (see chapter 9). Here, in this elegant building, you can take your time savoring the remarkable Rockefeller Collection—which includes examples from ancient to 19th-century Asia: statuary, ceramics, ink paintings, and more. You can also acquaint yourself with contemporary Asian works in video, animation, and new media. In fact, in creating the Contemporary Art Collection in 2007, the museum was one of the first in the country to establish a collection focused exclusively on the latest art coming from Asia, with such artists as Nam June Paik, Yoko Ono, Xu Bing, and Wang Gong Xin.

The Asia Society has become yet more inviting since its successful renovation of a few years ago. The works from the permanent collection, as well as changing shows are beautifully displayed in its luminous interior and sleek décor. We thought it was the perfect place for Yoshi Waterhouse's curving shoji screens of glass, wood, and metal screening and Heri Dono's *Flying in a Cocoon*, hanging from the ceiling in the Garden Court.

It goes without saying that the **Metropolitan Museum of Art** is in a category by itself in most categories, including Asian art. Here you will find the galleries devoted to art from all of Asia. If your interest is more in Chinese art, visit the **China Institute Gallery**, at 125 East 65th Street (see chapter 9). The intimate space offers worthwhile rotating exhibits and also sponsors symposia of interest, sometimes relating to Chinese art.

AND IN ADDITION . . .

The **New York Chinese Scholar's Garden** at Snug Harbor (Staten Island) is another site not to be missed; see chapter 30.

At **St. John's University** at 8000 Utopia Parkway in Queens, visit the (formerly the Chung-Cheng Art Gallery) in Sun Yat Sen Hall, where works by local and Chinese artists are shown. ⊕ Tuesday–Friday 10 AM–5 PM, Saturday noon–5 PM. (Closed Sunday and Monday.) Free admission.

A visit to Manhattan's **Chinatown** will also add to your Chinese experience in New York. Chinatown is located on the Lower East Side, east of Broadway, south of Delancy Street.

For a taste of Japanese art, visit the **Japan Society**, 333 East 47th Street (212-832-1155; www.japan society.org). ⊕ Tuesday–Thursday 11 AM–6 PM, Friday 11 AM–9 PM, Saturday and Sunday 11 AM–5 PM. (Closed Monday.) Free admission. Its gallery displays Japanese prints, sculpture, and decorations of many centuries. The society also sponsors programs of interest, open to the public.

Tenri Cultural Institute of New York, 43A West 13th Street (212-645-2800); www.tenri.org), is an organization devoted to Japanese cultural enrichment. In an unusually attractive environment, it includes an arts gallery featuring shows of contemporary art each year (a recent one featured the fascinating light installations of Han Ho, using Korean hanji paper), as well as classes, symposia, and concerts. ⊕ Monday–Thursday noon–6 PM, Saturday noon–5 PM. (Closed Friday and Sunday.) Free admission.

Two venues for viewing Korean art are the **Korean Cultural Service Gallery**, 460 Park Avenue at 57th Street, sixth floor (212-759-9550; www.koreanculture .org), ⊕ Monday–Friday 10 AM–5 PM; free admission; and the **Brooklyn Museum** (see page 110), which contains one of the most significant collections of Korean art in the country. (The museum is also noted for its Persian Qajar Dynasty art.)

MANHATTAN

Japan Society
333 East 47th Street
212-832-1155
www.japansociety.org

Tenri Cultural Institute of New York
43A West 13th Street
212-645-2800)
www.tenri.org

Korean Cultural Service Gallery
460 Park Avenue
at 57th Street, sixth floor
212-759-9550
www.koreanculture.org

14 The Best of Manhattan's Art-Featuring Restaurants and Hotels

In our explorations around the city, we have discovered that some of the most interesting art is sometimes found in restaurants and hotels. You won't see these pieces elsewhere, as they could be original work given or loaned to the restaurant or hotel by artist, or part of a personal art collection, or odd pieces found here and there. Obviously paintings, photographs, sculptures, and other forms of art can greatly enhance an interior décor, creating an inviting—and simulating—ambience for guests and visitors.

Our research took us to many different places throughout Manhattan, from which we selected the following. (They were chosen for their art, not their food.) All were hospitable—whether or not we ate in the restaurants. However, we think that you should decide what is best for you in terms of seeing their artworks—whether over a nice meal, or just by popping in and out for a quick look (preferably during off hours). We hope that you will enjoy this outing.

Carlyle Hotel
35 East 76th Street
at Madison Avenue
212-744-1600

In the elegant East Side **Carlyle Hotel**, 35 East 76th Street at Madison Avenue (212-744-1600), are two cafés especially noted for their décor. The Bemelmans Bar is named for Ludwig Bemelmans, creator of the beloved children's storybook character "Madeleine." Years ago, he was asked to paint a mural to decorate the walls of the bar, and the result was *Central Park*, a fanciful panorama filled with whimsical creatures carrying on in the greenery. In delightfully topsy-turvy scenes, dressed-up animals run free (while people are in cages) in a magical world of fun and games. Fans of "Madeleine" will love to stop for a drink here (if you have children with you, check first whether you can bring them for a quick look).

Mandarin Hotel
60 Columbus Circle
Entrance at
60th Street

The **Mandarin Hotel**, at 60 Columbus Circle (the entrance is at 60th Street), is a relatively new stylish and glamorous hotel with an Asian touch. We particularly liked the glass chandeliers and sculptures of Dale Chihuli. Look for pieces of art on the ground floor lobby and the Sky Lobby, way up on the 35th floor (and enjoy the fabulous view, while you're at it!); there are paintings, sculpture, and photography by Dirk Debruyker, Babs Amour, Victor Pasamor, Suk Ja Kang-Engles, Nancy Lawrence, and Valerio Adami, as well as other contemporary artists. You'll identify Asian motifs in the rich gold, silver, and copper Mandarin robes by Richard Mafong, as well as antique embroidered Mandarin robes, lotus designs, calligraphy, and curlicues.

The venerable restaurant **Petrossian**, 182 West 58th Street at Seventh Avenue (whose specialties are caviar with vodka and champagne) has an elegant art deco interior.

Petrossian
182 West 58th Street at Seventh Avenue

The popular Italian bistro **Trattoria dell'Arte**, 900 Seventh Avenue at 57th Street, near Carnegie Hall, has one of the most original and unusual décors we know of. Throughout the restaurant you'll find anatomical sculptures by Milton Steckel: giant plaster ears, noses (of many shapes and sizes), and torsos. The nose theme continues in the upstairs dining room, where there are pictures of famous noses from the time of Caesar to the present (including the comedian Jimmy Durante, whose prominent nose was legendary).

Trattoria dell'Arte
900 Seventh Avenue at 57th Street

Michael's, at 24 West 55th Street, is one of our favorite restaurants for viewing art and enjoying a meal. Both the food (California-style) and art (modern art, mostly late 20th century), are absolutely terrific, as is the welcoming ambience. Here you'll see works by David Hockney, Marcel Duchamp, Richard Diebenkorn, Frank Stella, Helen Frankenthaler, and Jasper Johns; there are even some pieces by the late composer John Cage. The owner of the restaurant, Michael McCarthy, is clearly a serious art collector (the other half of his collection is in his California restaurant). If you are dining here, take your time and view the art tranquilly either before or after your meal.

Michael's
24 West 55th Street

Old King Cole (1894), at the **St. Regis Hotel**, 2 East 55th Street, is a Maxfield Parrish fan's delight. You'll enjoy his great mural (28 feet long) illustrating the old nursery rhyme of the restaurant's namesake.

St. Regis Hotel
2 East 55th Street

Casa Lever, 390 Park Avenue at 53rd Street, is decorated with works by Andy Warhol. At **Patroon**, 160 East 46th Street between Lexington and Third Avenues, you can enjoy a wonderful collection of vintage photos while dining.

Casa Lever
390 Park Avenue at 53rd Street

Patroon
160 East 46th Street between Lexington and Third Avenues

An elegant townhouse at 3 East 52nd Street is the setting or the stylish French restaurant known as **La Grenouille**, going strong since 1962. Everything about this restaurant is pleasing: its extraordinary cuisine, its décor and dining room filled with freshly cut flowers, and its impeccable service. Of special interest to us is the upstairs private dining room, an enchanting surprise with its many works of art. In the 1940s it

La Grenouille
3 East 52nd Street

The Four Seasons
99 East 52nd Street

'21' Club
21 West 52nd Street

Firebird
365 West 46th Street between Eighth and Ninth Avenues

Sardi's
234 West 44th Street between Broadway and Eighth Avenue

was the working studio of Bernard Lamotte, a French painter and illustrator, and soon became a meeting place for artists, actors, writers, and musicians. (Antoine de Saint-Exupéry was one who apparently wrote here.) The impressionist-style paintings you see, gracing the walls before you, speak of life in Paris. You will enjoy spending a moment in this intimate room—or, if you're lucky, dining in this gracious ambience.

The beloved celebrity restaurant **The Four Seasons**, at 99 East 52nd Street, needs no introduction. Situated in the Seagram Building (built by Mies van der Rohe in 1969), it was designed by architects Philip Johnson and William Pahlmann and awarded landmark status several years later. The artworks inside have been moved around, and some removed altogether; but there are still things worth seeing. Among them is a major work by Richard Lippold hanging from the ceiling of the deep brown Bar Room and Grill. Its shiny brass rods catch the surrounding light, making it appear like a vision from another planet. (Note: If you wish to see the art, you must eat here.)

The **'21' Club**, at 21 West 52nd Street, is a posh night spot and one of the most famous restaurants in the city. Dating to the '20s, it has received many, many celebrities over these years, including most presidents since FDR. It is also well known for its impressive collection of Frederick Remington works. Remington, an Easterner, went out West as a young man and literally adopted the cowboy culture, which was the focus of his art. Here, in the comfortable living room on the ground floor of this townhouse, you can view the more than 30 paintings and drawings of dynamic Wild West scenes by him: cowboys and Indians in action, rodeos, and other such subjects. There is something somewhat nostalgic about these works, as they represent a romantic America that is no more.

Also note a curious row of painted cast-iron lawn jockey statues, which decorate the outside terrace. They are unique to the club, as far as we know.

Described as a "feast for the eyes," the well-known dining spot **Firebird**, 365 West 46th Street between Eighth and Ninth Avenues, is filled with Russian art and artifacts.

Sardi's, 234 West 44th Street between Broadway and Eighth Avenue, is a must for fans of theatrical art and memorabilia, with its amusing array of caricatures on the walls.

The West Chelsea restaurant **B.E.S.**, at 559 West 22nd Street at 11th Avenue, functions as a gallery as well as an eatery. Some of the artwork you'll see is actually for sale.

Ilili, at 236 Fifth Avenue between 27th and 28th Streets, is in a different style: its spare, modernist décor suggests Frank Lloyd Wright's midcentury architecture, with squares and lighted rectangles; low, rectangular groups of tables and chairs; lots of glass; and a spectacular modernist lighted ceiling.

The **Gershwin Hotel**, 7 East 27th Street off Fifth Avenue, has certainly one of the most eclectic and original hotel lobbies. Its large pop art–filled lobby will surely catch your eye, and you'll enjoy the scene— including celebrities and hipsters—as well. Art is everywhere, from the huge hanging beehivelike structures outdoors to the constructions and paintings and Andy Warhol images on four large black-and-white silkscreen flags within.

SD 26, 19 East 26th Street between Fifth and Madison Avenues, a new version of the former San Domenico restaurant (originally on Central Park South), has maintained its art-filled décor, with added yarn art on the walls by Sheila Hicks. In addition, there are a number of prints by the Greek-born, Italian surrealist painter Giorgio de Chirico, many sculptures, and a glamorous, contemporary décor.

At **Bistro Lamazou**, 344 Third Avenue between 25th and 26th Streets, a charming, warm décor of stripes and colored glass lighting suggests a combination of the Middle East and the contemporary.

Union Square Cafe, at 21 East 16th Street, is one of New York's more recent favorites. This busy, bustling, and trendy restaurant is known for its highly rated cuisine and vast contemporary art collection. Well displayed on the walls are works by such noted artists as Claes Oldenburg, Frank Stella, Judy Rifka, Gail Staar, and many more. You are welcome to look around, but do be careful not to bump into the busy waiters! A list of the art on display is available.

Café Loup is a charming and intimate West Village bistro located at 105 West 13th Street at Sixth Avenue. You'll find this a pleasant and cozy place, filled with art of the highest quality literally taking up every inch of wall space. There are wonderful photographs by such masters as Henri Cartier-Bresson, Irving Penn, Berenice Abbott, and Joel Meyerowitz; lithographs by George

MANHATTAN

Ilili
236 Fifth Avenue between 27th and 28th Streets

Gershwin Hotel
7 East 27th Street off Fifth Avenue

SD 26
19 East 26th Street between Fifth and Madison Avenues

Union Square Cafe
21 East 16th Street

Café Loup
105 West 13th Street at Sixth Avenue

Tooker, Adolph Gottlieb, and Dorothy Dehner; and a great collage by Nancy Grossman. (The friendly staff is happy to show you a list of the works on display.) You are welcome to walk around and view the art at your leisure.

The trendy Southeast Asian restaurant **Spice Market**, 403 West 13th Street at Ninth Avenue, presided over by the well-known chef Jean-Georges Vongerichten, boasts a movie-style setting.

The quiet, elegant Austrian restaurant **Wallsé**, 344 West 11th Street at Washington Street, has paintings by Julian Schnabel.

AND IN ADDITION . . .
Alison Eighteen, 15 West 18th Street, a recently opened restaurant in the Flatiron District, has a charming, hand-screened décor depicting New York food scenes, by Payton Cosell Turner and Brian Kaspr.

See chapter 20 for three additional hotel sites of interest.

Spice Market
403 West
13th Street
at Ninth Avenue

Wallsé
344 West 11th Street
at Washington Street

Alison Eighteen
15 West 18th Street

15 The Museum at Eldridge Street: A Beautiful Past of Moorish and Romanesque Design, Carved Wood, and Fine Stained Glass

DIRECTIONS» By subway, take the F, M, J, or Z line to Delancey Street.

The **Eldridge Street Museum and Synagogue** are located at 12 Eldridge Street (212-219-0302; www.eldridgestreet.org). Ⓗ The museum is open to visitors Sunday–Thursday 10 AM–5 PM, Friday 10 AM–3 PM. (Closed Saturday.) Admission fee; free admission on Monday. Free guided tours are available.

This is truly an eye-opening experience; a visit here will introduce you to an architectural and artistic era in an intimate—but very fine—environment. From the Moorish and Romanesque exterior to its elegant, vibrant stained glass, this is a one-of-a-kind museum site. Built in 1887 (the first great synagogue built in the United States), it still functions as a temple, but is now also a museum that beautifully evokes the past and its Jewish faith. (Note the Star of David symbols, as well as the trompe l'oeil murals that represent windows looking out on views of Jerusalem.)

The main sanctuary has an impressive, 50-foot-high vaulted ceiling, decorated with Moorish symbols, gold-

Eldridge Street Museum and Synagogue
12 Eldridge Street
212-219-0302
www.eldridgestreet.org

leaf stars, and murals. Among the 57 stained-glass windows are antiques, including a rose window, as well as some contemporary designs by Kiki Smith and Deborah Gans. Note also the shiny brass light fixtures from the Victorian era, and the imposing central chandelier. The polished wood interior adds warmth and intimacy to this beautiful structure.

While the Eldridge Street Museum strongly evokes the past, the neighborhood surrounding it is bustling with a new version of the Lower East Side. Among the boutiques and chic restaurants are over 60 new galleries, primarily showing new and emerging artists; they have a variety of outlooks, styles, and media to exhibit.

If you enjoy seeing less established artists' work, look in on these busy streets: Eldridge, Hester, Kenmare, Orchard, Forsyth, and Stanton (among others). We recommend that you stop at 54 Orchard Street, where there is a L.E.S. (Lower East Side) office that hands out maps of galleries and other inviting sites.

Among the better-known art sites in the neighborhood are the **Henry Street Settlement's Miguel Abreu Gallery** (36 Orchard Street); the **Educational Alliance Gallery** (197 East Broadway near Clinton Street); and the **Storefront for Art and Architecture** (97 Kenmare Street.)

Eldridge Street Synagogue East Window

AND IN ADDITION . . .

The **Eldridge Street Museum** offers walking tours (for a fee) of the Lower East Side, as well as a variety of programs relating to history, architecture, and traditions of the neighborhood.

16 The Gallery Scene in Chelsea

DIRECTIONS » By subway, take the C or E line to 23rd Street (Eighth Avenue).

A visit to this gallery district is best done Wednesday–Saturday 11 AM–6 PM. Openings are usually late in the afternoon and welcome everyone. Pick up a Gallery Guide, free at most galleries, to plan your visit. There is also a regional guide available at all the galleries; called "Chelsea Art," this flier has a small map and the names of every single gallery.

Chelsea is the center of the art world in the city, these days (though other neighborhoods have galleries, too), but it is here between Ninth and Tenth Avenues and 20th to 25th Streets that dozens and dozens of galleries are active. Anyone who would like to experience the heady atmosphere of openings of new exhibitions (free and open to the public) should visit on an afternoon from about six o'clock on weekdays (except Mondays) and all day on Saturdays. You'll find people going from building to building, floor to floor, seeing the newest, the most unusual, the traditional, the computer-generated, the abstract, and the photographic—it's all in Chelsea.

Once an industrial neighborhood, Chelsea has put its large spaces to use, showing art on street level and throughout elevator buildings. (Some have as many as 20 galleries in them.) Such monumental spaces lead themselves to large canvases and huge sculptures and installations, so leave plenty of time to wander through this art lover's form of entertainment.

If you want to do a thorough job of seeing everything, you can go through major buildings listed in the gallery guide. If, on the other hand, your time is limited, you might want to follow our recommended route on 24th, 25th, and 26th Streets. (Use your gallery guide to determine specific shows of interest to you—e.g., multimedia art, or only sculpture, or computer art.)

As for gallery etiquette, it is acceptable to walk in and out at random, eat hors d'oeuvres at openings, and ask for prices at the desk if you wish.

Our suggested tour (which takes in all kinds of art, but all of it comparatively recent—no old master in sight) begins at 10th Avenue and 26th Street. Walk west toward 11th Avenue; in that one block alone you'll find a terrific mix of styles and media. A major building of galleries, the Chelsea Arts Building, is at **508–526 West 26th Street**; among them are those showing contemporary art (Greene Naftali), and prints (International Print Center). On the same block are a number of other interesting galleries (don't forget to notice the vast and evocative spaces that house the art, particularly in ground-floor galleries. At 542 West 26th Street is the **Stephen Haller Gallery** (one recent exhibition showed paintings from the 1960s); and at 521 West 26th Street is one of three **Pace** galleries.

Walk south one block on 11th Avenue to West 25th Street. Among the many galleries to see on this block are **Agora**, which recently featured contemporary art from France, and **New Century Artists**, which features multimedia art—both at 530 West 25th Street; and **Pace Wildenstein**, a noted gallery and one of the three Pace Galleries in the neighborhood each exhibiting different artworks, but all with an emphasis on the 20th century (545 West 22nd Street, 534 West 25th Street, and 510 West 25th Street). Also nearby is **Marlborough Chelsea Gallery**, at 545 West 25th Street—also a major gallery, showing such notable artists as Francis Bacon and Philip Gusto; and **Bertrand Delacroix Gallery** at 535 West 25th Street (212-627-4444), where an interesting recent four-person show featured minotaur-like statues in bright colors by Beth Carter and large, evocative canvasses of bulls and bullfighting, by Joseph Adolphe.

Back on 11th Avenue, walk south toward West 24th Street, stopping at **210 11th Avenue**, where a dozen galleries are located. Turn at the next corner, walking east on West 24th Street. At 555 West 24th Street you'll find the chic **Gagosian Gallery**, showing such notables as Richard Serra in a spectacular setting. At 541 West 24th Street is the cutting-edge **Mary Boone Gallery**; and at 531 West 24th Street, the **Luhring Augustine Gallery**. At 534 West 24th Street, is the **Andrea Meislin Gallery** (212-627-2552), where we enjoyed a series of extremely odd and amusing photographs of Russian museum interiors and their female guards, by Andy Freeberg.

MANHATTAN

Chelsea Arts Building
508–526 West 26th Street

Stephen Haller Gallery
542 West 26th Street

Pace PRINTS
521 West 26th Street

Agora and New Century Artists
530 West 25th Street

Pace Wildenstein
510 West 25th Street

Marlborough Chelsea Gallery
545 West 25th Street

Bertrand Delacroix Gallery
535 West 25th Street
212-627-4444

Gagosian Gallery
555 West 24th Street

Mary Boone Gallery
541 West 24th Street

Luhring Augustine Gallery
531 West 24th Street

Andrea Meislin Gallery
534 West 24th Street

Leo Koenig, Inc.
545 West 23rd Street

Sonnabend Gallery
536 West 22nd Street

Paula Cooper Gallery
534 West 21st Street

ACA Galleries
529 West 20th Street

Kitchen
512 West 19th Street
212-255-5793
www.thekitchen.org

Museum at FIT
(Fashion Institute of
Technology)
Seventh Avenue and
27th Street
212-217-4558
www.fitnyc.edu/museum

Poster Auctions
International
601 West 26th Street
Suite 1370
212-787-4000

The next block south is 23rd Street, where you will find several interesting galleries, including **Leo Koenig, Inc.**, at 545 West 23rd Street. A recent event was a Sigmar Polke show. Twenty-second Street is one of the major venues for art in the city.

At 536 West 22nd Street, the sophisticated **Sonnabend Gallery** shows contemporary art. There are several interesting galleries at **530 West 22nd Street**, too.

At 534 West 21st Street is the **Paula Cooper Gallery**, which shows important American art (Mark di Suvero and Sol LeWitt, for example).

Twentieth Street has many galleries, including **ACA Galleries**, 529 West 20th Street, in the same building where some 20 other galleries are housed. The ACA Gallery recently exhibited major collages by Romare Bearden, as well as works by Henri, Hopper, Burchfield, and Glackens.

A notable avant-garde gallery and cultural center is the **Kitchen** at 512 West 19th Street (212-255-5793). The Kitchen has eclectic offerings, such as its recent show *The View from a Volcano: The* Kitchen's *Soho Years 1971–1985*.

If you prefer a tour of the art gallery scene, contact **New York Gallery Tours** at 212-946-1548, which runs tours on Saturdays from September to June.

AND IN ADDITION . . .

At the **Museum at FIT** (Fashion Institute of Technology), Seventh Avenue and 27th Street (212-217-4558; www.fitnyc.edu/museum), some 50,000 items of clothing and accessories (both vintage and recent) from the 1700s to today are exhibited in a creative manner emphasizing textile history, design, and well-known artists and designers, such as Salvador Dalí, Raoul Dufy, and William Morris. **🕐** Tuesday–Friday noon–8 PM, Saturday 10 AM–5 PM. (Closed Sunday and Monday.) Free admission.

Poster Auctions International, 601 West 26th Street, Suite 1370 (212-787-4000), hosts auctions of vintage and other posters.

17 Walking Along the River: From Battery Park City to Battery Park

DIRECTIONS » By subway, take the 1, 2, 3, 9, A, or C line to Chambers Street.

When you are in the center of our bustling city, you may forget that Manhattan is an island, and that there is water all around. This walk takes you along the banks of the scenic Hudson River, where water views are part of the landscape and form a spectacular backdrop for lots of art.

We begin our mosey along the waterfront at Chambers Street and Hudson River Park. You will be amazed how close you are to the river's bank and how this has been incorporated into this fairly recent neighborhood of high-rises and adjacent esplanade. The Battery Park City Fine Arts Program has used this area as a form of laboratory for the combining of new architecture, contemporary art, and city planning at a truly beautiful site of faded piers and old boatslips in what was not so a long ago a neglected, unloved area.

At the entrance to the riverside's park at Warren Street, is a whimsical brick columned work facing the water. This 1992 structure, called **The Pavilion**, by Demetri Porphyrios, welcomes you into the park.

The Pavilion
Battery City Park
at Warren Street

Before entering the park, however, return to Warren Street's south side to see a most unusual playground/park called **Teardrop Park**, running through to Murray Street. Designed by Michael Van Valkenburgh Associates, it opened in 2004. With artwork designed by Ann Hamilton, this is a site devoted to huge rock formations, with play elements integrated into a landscape of tunnels (homage to Frederick Law Olmsted's Central Park design), precipice, rocky cliffs, huge sand pits—as well as an extremely long children's slide. This leafy enclave is more like an environmental artwork than a playground. (If this catches your fancy, be sure to visit **Opus 40** in Saugerties, New York; see page 165.)

Teardrop Park
Warren Street

Walk through the park to Murray Street. At 10 River Terrace (facing the river) is a chic home for **Poet's House**. In addition to its library and poetry events, there is an exhibition space with unusual and very fine works of art (some by poets). To find out about its interesting offerings, call 212-431-7920.

Poet's House
10 River Terrace
212-431-7920
www.poetshouse.org

Continue south along the river; don't miss the

Seamus Heaney and Mark Strand: *Inscribed Writings: The Lily Pool*, 1994
Battery Park City
West Street and Chambers Street

Irish Hunger Memorial
Vesey Street and North End Avenue

World Financial Center
200 Liberty Street

Ned Smythe: *The Upper Room*, 1987
The Esplanade at Albany Street

views! (Ellis Island, the Statue of Liberty, Jersey City across the river from here, and river boats).

Our next art site is about two blocks south at West Street and Chambers Street. Here, a charming small pond and waterfall (with ducks, goldfish, and some Asian-style paintings) are surrounded by a wall of marble, *Inscribed Writings: The Lily Pool*, 1994. The poetry on the wall is by artists Seamus Heaney and Mark Strand. We admired this quiet site so near to the hustle and bustle of downtown New York.

One of the city's most notable public monuments is next on our tour. The *Irish Hunger Memorial* on Vesey Street and North End Avenue is by Brian Tolle and Gail Wittwer; it was erected in 2002. This provocative and heartbreaking edifice is a memorial to the Irish famine of 1845–52, and to world hunger today. It is a large installation that re-creates an Irish rural landscape with a reconstructed cottage and rocks and ruins, surrounded by natural Irish plantings. There is a small theater and walls of quotations. Don't miss this site!

If you head south for another few blocks, you'll come to the **World Financial Center** at 200 Liberty Street—a rather shocking switch in mood from our last stop. Here, the elegant glass Winter Garden has an atrium open to the public (with many interesting events taking place) and towering indoor palms. The plaza itself is a popular outdoor meeting place, and is itself a kind of environmental art site. Designed by César Pelli, M. Paul Friedberg, Siah Armajani, and Scott Burton, there are several pieces of art as well. Among them are the Police Memorial with a sunken pool and granite walls, and two pylons by Martin Puryear (1995) near the water's edge. (They looked to us like giant fruits!) There is also a long fence with quotations by Walt Whitman and Frank O'Hara.

When you leave the plaza, continue south to see *The Upper Room* (1984–87), by Ned Smythe. This is a favorite New York outdoor sculpture; it is not just one form but a couple of shapes and symbols. Its media alone tell you a complicated story: stone, cut, glass, mosaics, and cast concrete. Its forms—mostly pink in tone—are ancient-seeming, part classical Roman perhaps, part Egyptian. Its arch seems Renaissance in style. There are columns, a seating area with inlaid chessboards, what might be an altar, and an arcade. There is a sense of postmodernism to this mélange, and it all fits together very expressively. You will find

R. M. Fischer: *Rector Gate*, 1988, Esplanade at Rector Place

it a good place to nest and enjoy the wonderful view, amid the ancient (but recent) architectural relics.

Next, you'll come to **Rector Gate**. This actually is a gate, but it is also sculpture. Designed by R. M. Fischer in 1988, it has curlicues and trapezoids and circles in an attractive pattern.

Not far away is Richard Artschwager's **Sitting/ Stance** (1988), which resembles two large chaise lounges made of wood and metal, set on granite platforms.

Richard Artschwager: *Sitting/Stance*, 1988 The Esplanade at West Thames Street

One of the city's major environmental art sites is next. In 1988, Mary Miss designed **South Cove**, a re-working of the riverbank into an environmental work of art. Commissioned by the city, she chose to use pilings that rose and fell with the tide, wisteria-covered wooden archways, blue lights, and Japanese-style landscaping. Working with architect Stanton Eckstut and landscape architect Susan Child, she was able to transform the area (You can see what it originally looked like just over the fence, where the Hudson's unruly banks survive as is). In fact, the design is an attempt to balance this coastline with the urban setting. There is a curving steel staircase, where you can get a great view of the art, as well as the river and New Jersey opposite.

Mary Miss: *South Cove*, 1988 The Esplanade at South Cove

Museum of Jewish
Heritage

**Museum of Jewish
Heritage**
36 Battery Place
646-437-4202
www.mjhnyc.org

There are several fairly recent museums to see as you continue south.

The entrance to the first is just to your left along the walkway, and is one of the newest: the **Museum of Jewish Heritage**, 36 Battery Place (212-968-1800). **ⓗ** The garden is open Sunday–Tuesday and Thursday 10 AM–5:45 PM, Wednesday 10 AM–8 PM, Friday 10 AM–3 PM. (Closed Saturday.) Admission fee; free admission Wednesday 4 PM–8 PM, and for children ages 12 and under. In addition to the museum's primary displays concerning Jewish culture and history, a mesmerizing new art site has also been added on its rooftop.

Perched on the rooftop of the newest wing is Andy Goldsworthy's *Garden of Stones*. It consists of 18 giant granite boulders (some weigh more than 13 tons), arranged so as to create narrow pathways. Surprisingly, from the top of each rock a tiny dwarf-oak has been planted. (They are expected eventually to reach 12 feet in height.) The garden was the artist's tribute to the struggles and tenacity of Holocaust survivors (the number 18 corresponds to "life" in Hebrew). This is an inspiring and imaginative spot, and you can easily spend some reflective time here (with the Statue of Liberty and Ellis Island forming an appropriate, if distant, backdrop).

Skyscraper Museum
39 Battery Place
212-968-1961
www.skyscraper.org

Just beyond this building is the recent **Skyscraper Museum** at 39 Battery Place (212-968-1961; www.skyscraper.org). **ⓗ** Wednesday–Sunday noon–6 PM. (Closed Monday and Tuesday.) Admission fee.

The next sculpture along the walkway is ***Ape and Cat (at the Dance)***, a 1993 work by Jim Dine. This fanciful piece will delight kids as well as grown-ups (and animal lovers). On the next corner of the walkway is a provocative sculpture by Louise Bourgeois, **Eyes**, whose two orbs were created in 1995 and bear little resemblance to her usual style.

As you near the tip of Manhattan, you'll come to a rather startling sculpture by Marisol called **American Merchant Mariners' Memorial** (1991). You have to look carefully to realize that the half-submerged figure reaching for help to three rescuing figures is, in fact, sculpture.

You will come now to the park itself. **Battery Park** has 12 permanently installed works of art. Wander about to see them, and many changing exhibitions. Among our favorites is Mac Adams's *Korean War Memorial* (1991), which has large cut-out figures and a bronze statue by Ettore Ximenes of Giovanni da Verrazzano (the first European to sail into this harbor), Wopo Holup's *River That Flows Two Ways* (2000), and the *US Coast Guard Memorial* (1947), by Norman M. Thomas (which is a heroic image of two guardsmen supporting an injured man).

Battery Park
Battery Place and State Street, at Broadway

Mac Adams: *Korean War Memorial* **(1991)**

Luis Sanguino: *The Immigrants* (1973)

Of particular interest is *The Immigrants* (1973), by Luis Sanguino, a sculpture showing Americans immigrants who came to Ellis Island at this very spot. (Once called the Immigrant Landing Depot, the building is now called Castle Clinton.) Sanguino's sculpture includes a variety of ethnic immigrants, including a mother and child, an African slave, a priest, an Eastern European, and so on—all seeking a new life in America. It is a touching sculpture focusing on real and ordinary people instead of heroes, and here, in view of the Statue of Liberty, is both naturalistic in style and symbolic of the nation's aspirations.

At the end of the short walkway (well lined with benches), you'll find a small museum of immigration and a reconstructed fortress. Walk through to the esplanade along the water and turn left.

You can also enjoy a variety of happenings and other events in Battery Park, one of the city's liveliest venues on a bright day. Here, too, you can get on the Staten Island Ferry for a beautiful ride (or to visit sites on the island; see chapter 30), and nearby is the ferry to Governors Island (see chapter 5). Or continue your exploration to Lower Manhattan.

18 A Beloved Neighborhood: Exploring the Village

DIRECTIONS?» The West Village is bounded to the north by 14th Street, to the east by the Bowery, to the west by the Hudson River, and to the south by Houston Street. The East Village is bounded by East 14th Street, East Houston Street, Third Avenue, and Avenue D.

Although this walk is primarily through the charming streets of Greenwich Village in downtown Manhattan, it also takes you to Cooper Square, a bit of lower Fifth Avenue, and several historic sites. It encompasses two nice churches, several galleries, a couple of universities, an art school, and a wonderful park. Within these settings you'll come upon quite a lot of art—particularly sculpture, as well as paintings, contemporary and historic, and even some 19th-century stained glass.

We begin our outing on the east side of the village at Cooper Square (East 7th Street and Third Avenue). You won't miss the grand building of **The Cooper Union for the Advancement of Science and Art**, 30 Cooper Square (212-353-4100). This massive 19th-century Italianate structure opened in 1859 to provide free education; it was founded by a philanthropist and industrialist named Peter Cooper. You'll see a fine Augustus Saint-Gardens statue of him in front of the building. Take a guided tour to see studios, classrooms, and exhibition areas, in addition to the Great Hall (where speakers included Abraham Lincoln, Andrew Carnegie, and Mark Twain, among numerous great figures in our history). Pick up material listing events here—all free and open to the public.

The Cooper Union for the Advancement of Science and Art
30 Cooper Square
212-353-4100
cooper.edu/about/galleries-auditoriums

One block away is Astor Place (Lafayette and Eighth Streets). The giant black rotating cube resting on one point is by Tony Rosenthal. Called **_Alamo_** (1967), it was one of the first abstract works installed on city land.

Alamo
Astor Place (Lafayette and Eighth Streets)

Walk went to 33 Washington Square East, where you'll find the **Grey Art Gallery** (212-998-6780). One of our favorite art sites, and part of New York University, it is a professional gallery showing a series of well-curated exhibitions with unusual and provoca-

Grey Art Gallery
33 Washington Square East
212-998-6780

Tony Rosenthal: *Alamo*
(1967)

tive themes. (A small donation is requested but not required.) In this not-too-big space, carefully designed and documented shows are presented. Among recent displays have been caricatures from the French Revolution, a retrospective of the work of Sonia Delaunay, contemporary Indian art, a mixed-media show by Jesús Soto, and works by David Hockney. Each year the gallery shows works from its own collection (some 4,000 pieces). Note its display windows, which are often striking.

Another NYU gallery is **80WSE Galleries**, 80 Washington Square East (212-998-5747), also open to the public Tuesday–Saturday after 11 AM. On either side of the entrance are medallions representing the Muses of art and music; made of terra cotta, they date to the late 19th century. Once a year, this gallery shows *Small Works*, an exhibition by artists from all over the world; the other exhibitions focus on works by the faculty and students.

80WSE Galleries
80 Washington Square
East, between
West 4th St. and
Washington Pl.
212-998-5747
steinhardt.nyu.
edu/80wse

You are now just opposite the famous park called Washington Square. Across from the park is a large, stainless-steel sculpture called, appropriately, *The University*, by Arthur Carter. It is directly in front of Bobst Library.

Turn left on LaGuardia Place. Here is, of course, a statue of the famous mayor of New York, ***Fiorello LaGuardia***, by Neil Estern (1994).

**Statue of Fiorello
LaGuardia**
LaGuardia Place

Continue on LaGuardia Place to Bleecker Street, where one of the city's major artworks sits in open space surrounded by the university's housing. This is Picasso's ***Bust of Sylvette***. A reproduction of Picasso's 2-foot-high cubist work of 1954, it is now a colossal statue showing both front and profile views of Sylvette simultaneously. It was the work of a Norwegian artist, Carl Nesjar, who turned 60 tons of sand-blasted concrete and black basalt into Picasso's forms with the help of architect I. M. Pei. Picasso, Nesjar, and Pei worked together to create this work.

Bust of Sylvette
Bleecker Street

Walk back (north) to Washington Square South and go left for one block to find the **Judson Memorial Church**, at no. 55. This is a turn-of-the-century Italian Romanesque-style building designed by Stanford White. Its amber-colored exterior with square bell tower features rounded arches and graceful moldings. Within you see an imposing John La Farge stained-glass window; he used techniques from Renaissance times, and helped make stained glass a central design element in American churches.

Judson
Memorial
Church
55 Washington
Square South

Giovanni Turini
Giuseppe Garibaldi,
(ca. 1888)

Now cross the street to see Washington Square Park, downtown New York's favorite oasis. Near the south entrance is the infamous **Hanging Tree**, where unfortunate New Yorkers met their doom; today it is carved into a rather grotesque totem pole.

On the eastern side of the park is Giovanni Turini's 1888 statue of the great revolutionary general of the Risorgimento, **Giuseppe Garibaldi**. (Reportedly, it took the artist only three weeks to make; it is a curiously unheroic view.) Also in the park is a work by John Quincy Adams Ward; it is a portrait of Alexander Holley, an engineer, and was made in 1890.

But **Washington Square Arch** is the major work of art here, the gateway and symbol of Greenwich Village. The inspiration of Stanford White (1892), it features sculpted images by major artists of the time. The winged figures above the arch's interior are by Frederick MacMonnies. On the east column is Hermon MacNeil's portrait of General Washington. On the west is Washington shown in front of two representatives of *Wisdom* and *Justice* (1897); this work was by A. Stirling Calder (father of Alexander, the mobile-maker).

From here, head to Fifth Avenue right before you; go to Eighth Street to stop in at the **New York Studio School of Drawing, Painting, and Sculpture** at 8 West Eighth Street (212-673-6466). Once the site of the Whitney Museum of American Art, it became an art school in 1964. Here you'll see more representational styles of paintings than at many spots; the school calls itself "an alternative to prevailing trends in American art schools." The atmosphere—you can walk around through its airy galleries and see its group shows and some studios—is uncommercial and friendly.

On the corner of 10th Street is the **Church of the Ascension**, 12 West 11th Street. This is the oldest church on Fifth Avenue (1840) and it has several notable artworks to see. (You must visit between noon and 2 PM, or 5–7 PM daily.) Although it was designed by Richard Upjohn, it was redecorated by Stanford White. Inside you can see two notable works of art: two sculpted angels over the altar by Louis Saint-Gaudens, and *The Ascension of Our Lord* (1888) by John La Farge, a large, dark mural in muted colors. Just across the street at 16 East 10th Street is the former home of the **Pen and Brush** (212-475-3669), an organization for women artists and writers, with juried shows and

Statue of Giuseppe Garibaldi
Washington Square Park

Washington Square Arch
Washington Square, north entrance

New York Studio School of Drawing, Painting & Sculpture
8 West Eighth Street
212-673-6466
www.nyss.org

Church of the Ascension
12 West 11th Street
www.ascensionnyc.org

Pen and Brush
29 East 22nd Street
212-475-3669
www.penandbrush.org

a public gallery. At press time, their new space at 29 East 22nd Street was due to open in winter of 2014. Contact them for details.

The **Salmagundi Club** is another artists' club. It is just around the corner at 47 Fifth Avenue. The first private artist's club in America, it has been in this brownstone since 1917. The first two floors are open so the public can explore the group exhibition galleries, and you can also walk around to see portraits and landscapes made by past member artists. There are many events for both amateur and professional artists; you will enjoy the old-fashioned clubby atmosphere here.

Across Fifth Avenue is **The New School**, 66 West 12th Street (212-741-5955). ❶ Open Monday–Saturday. (Closed Sunday.)

There is a surprising wealth of art within this building of the New School. The most important is, of course, the José Clemente Orozco murals from the 1930s. (Call for specific hours where they can be seen, as they are in a classroom.) Newly restored, these bold images depict themes of leftist politics, revolution, oppression and freedom, with portraits of Gandhi, Lenin, and Stalin among them. Mexican folk art, Italian Renaissance mural art, and political views are major influences. The New School, which was a haven for intellectuals fleeing the Nazis, was a perfect site for Orozco's work, some 300 square feet of art. (You can look at a schedule for the classroom to see when it is available to visitors on the bulletin board near the entrance.)

There is additional art in the hallways and outside classrooms, particularly on the fifth floor. On the third floor is more art, including a bronze sculpture by Isamu Noguchi, an abstraction of a Shaker rocking chair (it was used in Martha Graham's first production of *Appalachian Spring*) called *Jocasta's Throne* (1945). There are also three Sol LeWitt aquatints called *Untitled* (1987), and a wall piece by Carol Hepper, *Comet* (1988), which is made of wood, wire, and nails in a basketlike structure.

On the ground floor, you'll find the glass doors to the sculpture garden in the courtyard. Small but distinctive, this collection has a number of notable works. Among them are Chaim Gross's *Acrobats—Family of Five* (1951); *The Little Dinner* (1968), by William King (representing two couples seated at a dinner table);

MANHATTAN

Salmagundi Club
47 Fifth Avenue

The New School
66 West 12th Street
212-741-5955
www.newschool.edu

Noguchi's granite structure *Garden Elements*; and a stainless-steel abstraction, *Untitled* (1977), by Guy Miller. (Many other works are unidentified.)

Inside on the ground floor lobby is a bold work by Petah Coyne also called *Untitled* (1987–88); it is made of mud, rope, hay, cotton, cloth, wood, and barbed wire. Gonzalo Fonseca is represented by striking geometric murals made of mosaic; also called *Untitled* (1959). And don't miss Julian Schnabel's ocher and brown aquatint *Untitled* (2008).

Finally, as you leave the building, note the shrouded figure near the doors; *Clothed Figure* is a fiberglass piece by Muriel Castanis.

On leaving the New School, walk to the **Forbes Galleries** at 62 Fifth Avenue (212-206-5548). Free admission. Here you will see bits and pieces of Malcolm Forbes's collection of models, art jewelry, and so on.

At 80 Fifth Avenue, take the elevator to the 14th floor to see the gallery of the **National Association of Women Artists, Inc.**, which presents group shows.

Just south along Fifth Avenue is the well-known **Parsons The New School for Design** (212-229-8900), a division of the New School. It offers exhibitions of both faculty and students (and some alumni) in its elegant galleries. (Free admission.) One entrance is at 2 West 13th Street, and the other is at 66 Fifth Avenue. ❶ Monday–Saturday, 9 AM–9 PM. You'll find the work shown of high caliber and interest.

Our final stop on this outing is at 15 West 16th Street, just west of Fifth Avenue. This is the multi-arts **Center for Jewish History** (212-294-8301). ❶ Tuesday, Wednesday, and Sunday 11 AM–5 PM; Thursday 11 AM–8 PM. Free admission. Five institutions share this setting; they include Yeshiva University Museum and the Yivo Institute. There are a variety of evens and exhibitions, such as recent shows of modern quilts and early photographs.

Forbes Galleries
62 Fifth Avenue
212-206-5548
www.forbesgalleries.com

National Association of Women Artists, Inc.
80 Fifth Avenue,
14th floor

Parsons The New School for Design
2 West 13th Street and
66 Fifth Avenue
212-229-8900
www.newschool
.edu/parsons

Center for Jewish History
15 West 16th Street
212-294-8301
www.cjh.org

AND IN ADDITION . . .

The **New School of Social Research** (212-229-5600) offers lectures and special events.

Grey Art Gallery and Study Center (212-998-6780) also has lectures, symposia, seminars, and other special events in connection with each show.

The **Salmagundi Club** (212-225-7740) holds auctions, demonstrations, and lectures

The **New York Studio School** (212-673-6466) has art lectures, usually on Wednesday evenings.

A George Segal sculpture, *Gay Liberation* (1980), has been placed in Christopher Park at Seventh Avenue South and Christopher Street. It depicts, in Segal's ultrarealistic style, two couples—one male, one female.

Chaim Gross Studio, 526 La Guardia Place (212-529-4906) is where the noted American sculptor worked; it is open by appointment.

The **Center for Architecture**, 536 LaGuardia Place (212-358-6133), is a lovely spot featuring architecture from around the world (in pictures), as well as lectures, conversations, readings, and so on.

Union Square Park, between 14th and 17th Streets and Broadway, is home to several statues of distinguished historic figures, including George Washington, Abraham Lincoln, and Mohandas Gandhi. The park also has changing sculpture exhibits. A recent example was *Gran Elefandret* (2008), by Miquel Barceló.

19 The Inviting Morgan Library and Museum

DIRECTIONS» By subway, take the 6 line to 33rd Street (Lexington Avenue); the 4, 5, 6, or 7 line to Grand Central Station; or the B, D, F, or Q line to 42nd Street (Sixth Avenue).

The **Morgan Library & Museum** is located at 225 Madison Avenue at 36th Street (212-685-0008; www.themorgan.org). **H** Tuesday–Thursday 10:30 AM–5 PM, Friday 10:30 AM–9 PM, Saturday 10 AM–6 PM, Sunday 11 AM–6 PM. (Closed Monday.) Admission fee; free admission for children ages 12 and under.

The Morgan has been described as being "extra special, in a class of its own," and we could not agree more! This East Side gem, many blocks south from the city's busiest museums, has an impressive collection of art treasures in its own right: drawings and prints by great masters, historic and literary manuscripts, printed books and bindings, antique seals and tablets, and a collection of music manuscripts unequaled in the country. And in addition, these one-of-a-kind works are displayed in an elegant yet intimate setting, where you can walk around at your own pace without the usual crowds.

The Morgan's history begins with the man himself—the American financier Pierpont Morgan, who in addi-

Gay Liberation
51–53
Christopher
Street

Chaim Gross Studio
526
La Guardia
Place
212-529-4906

Center for Architecture
536 LaGuardia Place
212-358-6133

Union Square Park
between East 14th and East 17th Streets and Broadway to Forrth Avenue

Morgan Library & Museum
225 Madison Avenue at 36th Street
212-685-0008
www.themorgan.org

MANHATTAN

tion to everything else, was a patron of the arts. When he needed more space to accommodate his growing collection of art objects, Morgan hired the noted architect Charles McKim to design a library next to his brownstone on Madison Avenue. The result was a classic Renaissance-style marble building, completed in 1906. In 1924, the library was made into a public institution, and as the collection continued to expand (under the supervision of Pierpont Morgan Jr.), an annex was added to serve both as library and museum. The complex you see today includes these connected buildings, as well as a sleek, light-filled 2006 addition by distinguished world architect Renzo Piano. The original library has also undergone an important restoration and now sparkles more than ever before.

Despite their differences in architectural style, these buildings work well together as a harmonious whole—both outside and inside. The Morgan is filled with treasures; but because of its manageable size and contained spaces, a visit here is a pleasant—rather than an overwhelming—experience.

Among the highlights in the permanent collection are many Rembrandt etchings (we are told, the most complete collection in the country); and drawings by Degas, Dürer, Blake, Rubens, Watteau, and others; copies of the Gutenberg Bible; more than 1,300 manuscripts of Western illumination created over 10 centuries; literary manuscripts by Charles Dickens (including *A Christmas Carol*), and others by Charlotte Brontë, Mark Twain, Voltaire, Abraham Lincoln, and 20th-century authors; and original music manuscripts by Bach, Brahms, Mozart, Schubert, and Stravinsky.

You can visit the Morgan by guided tour or on your own. In either case, you can walk through the richly adorned rooms in the library. Note the Rotunda, with its marble columns, ornate floor, mosaic panels, and blue and white stucco apse containing much of Morgan's historic American manuscripts—including letters by George Washington and Abraham Lincoln; Morgan's dark red private study, with its extensive bookshelves and fine Italian and Flemish Renaissance paintings; the Librarian's Office, now used as a gallery of ancient Near Eastern tablets and seals dating as far back as 3500 B.C., as well as Egyptian, Greek, and Roman sculpture; and the intricately decorated East Room (the original library), with its incredible ceiling.

In addition, there are several galleries that offer changing exhibits—some of the most worthwhile around. The four we saw on a recent visit covered fascinating topics and were all beautifully presented: *Treasures of Islamic Manuscript Painting* (from the Morgan); *David, Delacroix, and Revolutionary France* (Drawings from the Louvre); *Charles Dickens at 200*; and *Ingres at the Morgan*.

Before leaving the museum, be sure to stop and take a look at the attractive gift shop (in our opinion, one of the most appealing of its kind). And stop for a bite at the new café and restaurant (in a glass-enclosed central court within the Piano addition), or dine in the original Morgan family dining room, where family portraits decorate the walls.

20 An Art Exploration of Tribeca, Soho, and the Bowery's New Museum

DIRECTIONS » By subway, take the A, C, or E line to Canal Street. We recommend visiting these sites Wednesday–Sunday.

Once the center of Manhattan's avant-garde, Soho (south of Houston) and Tribeca (triangle below Canal) may no longer be central to the city's art scene. The great loft spaces of these rows of cast iron-detailed manufacturing buildings of Soho were once populated by major galleries and artists' lofts. But rising rents, trendy boutiques, and restaurants drove the art world to other neighborhoods. Nevertheless, a number of iconic art sites remain in Soho, and several new venues have opened. And Tribeca and even the Bowery (east of Soho) have their share of galleries and even a glamorous museum.

We begin this unusual walk in Tribeca, several blocks south of Canal Street. There are a number of sites in this rather trendy neighborhood that will interest the art enthusiast.

Begin at where Church Street meets Franklin Street, to visit the **New York Academy of Art**, 111 Franklin Street (212-966-0300). Here in the of Tribeca is an unusual spot, given the area's past emphasis on modernism and abstract art.

At this academy you'll find artists and students who are working in figurative, representational styles. There is a lobby gallery displaying a few works and plaster

New York Academy of Art
111 Franklin Street
212-966-0300
www.nyaa.edu

**Synagogue
for the Arts**
49 White Street
212-966-7141

Art in General
79 Walker Street
at Church Street
212-219-0473
www.artingeneral.org

Apexart
291 Church Street
212-431-5270

James New York
27 Grand Street
at Thompson Street

casts from the 19th century representing ancient and Renaissance sculpture.

Return to Church Street and next visit 49 White Street to see the **Synagogue for the Arts** (212-966-7141). ❶ Monday, Wednesday, and Thursday 1 PM–7 PM. This is a contemporary synagogue that was designed in 1967 by William N. Breger. It has a basement exhibition space and a most unusual sanctuary. Also called the Civic Center Synagogue, it hosts a series of exhibitions.

At the corner of Church and Walker Streets is **Art in General**, 79 Walker Street (212-219-0473). ❶ Tuesday–Saturday noon–6 PM. (Closed Sunday and Monday.) Here some of the most thought-provoking exhibitions and events take place, ranging from dance performances to shows using analog technology for blueprints.

At 291 Church Street, look for **Apexart** (212-431-5270), which has interesting group shows.

When you cross Canal Street, you have come to Soho. Walk north to Grand Street.

Our next stops are two unusual hotels—both featuring artistic interiors.

At 27 Grand Street, at the corner of Thompson Street, you'll find the **James New York**, a sleek boutique hotel, one of the latest additions to this now chic and sophisticated neighborhood. Throughout its elegantly designed interior spaces—from the entrance hall to the glass elevator, luminous Sky Lobby, corridors, and guest rooms, you are surrounded with lots of art and light, and the bare minimum of decoration.

In selecting the pieces of art on display in the common and guest rooms, the hotel collaborated with Artists Space, a Soho collective (see page 85). The result is an eclectic and interesting mix. As of this writing the works of some 20 artists—both local and international, emerging and more established—are on display. (To learn more about the individual artists, you can check the hotel website.)

The hotel staff is most welcoming, and you are invited to look around—up to a point. (Obviously, as a visitor you have access to the common rooms, hallways, and lobbies only—and not the guest rooms.) As you walk in, you'll see on the wall of the foyer a striking installation, *QWERTY 5* (2010), by Sarah Frost, made up of thousands of recycled keyboard keys; it reminded us of a modern-day mosaic, with a nod to technology. (The fact that these are all recycled pieces speaks well of the hotel's environmental policies.) As you go up the glass elevator, a large-scale black image, *Untying Space* (2010), appears before you. Created by Korean artist Sun K. Kwak, it is dramatically set against the white wall of the elevator shaft and accompanies you in fluid motion on your brief journey. The elevator takes you to the all-glass Sky Lobby, which overlooks a pretty sculpture garden. Here you can enjoy the fine view, as well as the carefully selected one-of-a-kind furnishing and interiors.

Our next stop is the **Soho Grand Hotel**, 310 West Broadway at the corner of Grand Street. The first hotel built in Soho (during the 1990s), it—like the James—exudes elegance and sophistication. But here the ambience is quite different: Rather than light, airy, and contemporary in feel, the entrance hallways are dark, grand, and evocative of the past. Decorative elements are reminiscent of 19th-century warehouses or factories—the iron staircase leading from the entrance hall to the glamorous bar area, the iron railings (albeit sleek and modern), and the industrial-like tools and artsy objects you see hanging on the walls of placed around the common areas. On the wall going up the central staircase is a fascinating mural depicting Soho as it might have looked when it was an industrial center.

This focus on the historic roots of this neighborhood is a wonderful concept for a hotel, giving it mystery and allure and character—in fact, not surprisingly, this is a popular spot with honeymooners and romantics in general! You'll enjoy walking around the common rooms, imagining yourself in another time.

From Grand Street, head to Wooster Street to one of the area's favorite art sites. Start at the **Drawing Center** at 35 Wooster Street (212-219-2166). **H** Tuesday–Friday 10 AM–6 PM, Saturday 11 AM–6 PM. (Closed Sunday and Monday.) This attractive gallery, the nation's only museum devoted to drawing, recently has been renovated with 50 percent more exhibition space; it presents some of the finest works on paper shown in New York. Selected works on paper featuring both contemporary and earlier artists.

Next, walk east to Greene Street where you will find **Artists Space**, at 38 Greene Street, third floor (212-226-3970). **H** Tuesday–Saturday 11 AM–6 PM. (Closed Sunday and Monday.) This multiartist gallery space exhibits recent works, including such group

Soho Grand Hotel
310 West Broadway
at Grand Street

Drawing Center
35 Wooster Street
212-219-2166
www.drawingcenter.org

Artists Space
38 Greene Street
Third floor
212-226-3970

shows as *Painting as Paradox . . . From the Digital to the Figural.*

Continue east to Broadway, where galleries have given way to all kinds of trendy shops. Don't miss one with the most unusual—you might say arty—of décors: **Allsaints**, 512 Broadway near Spring Street. If walls of old-fashioned sewing machines and shoetrees and wooden bobbins can be described as "art" in an installation, why not here in a shop?

Walk out the back door to Crosby Street. Here, at no. 79, is one of our favorite sites: the **Crosby Street Hotel**. With a lobby filled with art (many unusual representations of dogs, as well as contemporary sculpture, an accessible sculpture garden, and a refreshingly aesthetic environment, you will enjoy a stop here. (You may like to know that there is a miniature farm—with chickens on the roof—which provides fresh eggs and vegetables for the hotel restaurant!)

On the nearby corner of Crosby and Spring Streets, you will come to the **MOMA Design Store**, 81 Spring Street (646-613-1367). 🕐 Monday–Saturday 11 AM–8 PM, Sunday 11 AM–7 PM. Like the flagship MOMA Design Store near the Museum of Modern Art on 53rd Street, this new branch features elegant and unique objects, furniture, and gifts representing 20th- and 21st-century designers of note. Here you'll see classical pieces, as well as the latest in design concepts and materials: coasters shaped like slices of toast, watermelon knives, spherical ice trays, colorful nesting tables, sleek cutlery, wooden models of the city's landmark buildings, sculptured flower scarves, unusual jewelry, books on art and architecture, prints, and much, much more. You could spend hours here, shopping or just browsing . . .

Walk north to Prince Street and turn right. If you walk several blocks east, you'll come to one of the city's newest, and most avant-garde museums. The Bowery is now dominated by a striking contemporary building, the latest home of the **New Museum of Contemporary Art**, 235 Bowery at Prince Street, between Stanton and Rivington Streets (212-219-1222; www.newmuseum.org). 🕐 Wednesday 11 AM–6 PM, Thursday 11 AM–9 PM, Friday–Sunday 11 AM–6 PM. (Closed Monday and Tuesday.) Admission fee; free admission to children under age 18.

The opening of this site in 2007 has marked an important change for the museum and its new commu-

Crosby Street Hotel
79 Crosby Street

MOMA Design Store
81 Spring Street
646-613-1367

New Museum of Contemporary Art
235 Bowery at Prince Street, between Stanton and Rivington Streets
212-219-1222
www.newmuseum.org

nity: The museum, which had been located in various downtown sites (the last being in Soho), has found its permanent home; and the Bowery has gained a dynamic art institution, which is attracting other art related sites—galleries, shops, restaurants. As in so many other New York stories, this once seedy neighborhood is reinventing itself, in this case largely thanks to the presence of the New Museum. What a transformation for both the museum—which began in a one-room office on Hudson Street—and the Bowery, whose reputation is changing!

This museum, the only one in the city dedicated exclusively to international contemporary art, sees its mission as breaking ground in finding what art and institutions can do to remain vibrant in the 21st century. This idea is reflected in its imaginative architectural concept. Designed by the noted Japanese architects Sejima + Nishizawa/SANAA, the building consists of a set of mismatched rectilinear boxes, stacked one on top of the other, appearing as though they might topple over at any moment (perhaps a metaphor for the state of art in our rapidly changing world!). The sculpturelike structure is made of shimmering aluminum mesh, an industrial material reminiscent of this gritty neighborhood's historic roots. The effect is bold, unconventional, and unpretentious, in contrast to the many new and often "glitzy" commercial buildings that are cropping up everywhere in the city.

The museum has seven floors, of which three are dedicated to gallery space; the others are for education, special events, and sometimes edgy theatrical presentations. The entrance welcomes visitors into a vast hall and elegant shop, all light and airy and transparent. Each floor is of a different height (the "boxes" being of various sizes), and some have skylights, adding even more light to the luminous interior. From the outside sidewalk you can watch what's going on inside the lobby, including works of art being moved in and out of the building (a loading dock sits right next to the lobby, a clever device to eliminate the separation between the art world and everyday life).

As to the art on exhibit, it's probably as innovative as you'll find in an institutional setting. Since the museum's opening in 2007, there has been an ongoing program called *Façade Sculpture*, in which a given artist presents a work just outside the entrance for a period of time. A recent one was Isa Genzken's *Rose II*

(2007), which appeared as a pink rose effectively set against the metal background of the building. Recent shows have included *Ostalgia* (the term refers to a nostalgia for the era before the collapse of the Soviet bloc and Berlin Wall), a combination of psychology, history, and art, in which 50 artists from Eastern Europe and the former Soviet republics focused on the power of art as a transformative agent.

AND IN ADDITION . . .

Ethan Cohen Fine Arts Gallery, 18 Jay Street, between Hudson Street and Greenwich Avenue, Tribeca (212-625-1250). Ⓗ Tuesday–Saturday noon–6 PM. (Closed Sunday and Monday.) This gallery focuses on Chinese contemporary art.

Masters and Pelavin Gallery, 13 Jay Street, Tribeca (646-926-2787). Ⓗ Tuesday–Saturday 11 AM–6 PM. (Closed Sunday and Monday.) The works shown here are by emerging and midcareer artists in a variety of media.

Clocktower Gallery, 108 Leonard Street, Tribeca (212-233-1096). In this historic building is a cutting-edge gallery featuring installations and other contemporary shows, such as *Arctic Hysteria*.

21 Two Not-to-Be-Missed Midtown Sites: The New York Public Library and the International Center of Photography

DIRECTIONS » By subway, take the B, D, F, or S line to 42nd Street (Sixth Avenue).

As we go to press, the famous landmark of midtown Manhattan, the **New York Public Library**, is debating a major renovation. Generations of scholars, art lovers, and readers of all kinds have loved this venerable building with its two iconic lions (designed by Edward C. Potter) in front. We do not yet know how much the interior will change; at the present time there are three floors filled with interesting and rewarding sights. This is a brief description, therefore, of how it has looked for decades—and we hope will continue to look!

To begin your visit, walk up the steps at the front of the building to the lobby and the small gallery where a nice series of exhibitions is held. Usually focusing on writers or art relating to literature, this small exhibition space is always worth a stop. Recent shows have included works by Raoul Dufy, Claes Oldenburg, and

Ethan Cohen Fine Arts Gallery
18 Jay Street, between Hudson Street and Greenwich Avenue, Tribeca
212-625-1250

Masters and Pelavin Gallery
13 Jay Street, Tribeca
646-926-2787

Clocktower Gallery
108 Leonard Street, Tribeca
212-233-1096

New York Public Library
Fifth Avenue and 42nd Street
212-262-7444
www.nypl.org

George Bellows. Also on the ground floor is the DeWitt Periodical Room, where a recent set of murals by Richard Haas, who specializes in trompe l'oeil paintings, can be enjoyed.

Take the elevator to the third floor. The halls are lined with prints and a variety of pictures. The Rare Book Room and special collection rooms are also on this floor. Don't miss the murals titled *The History of the Recorded Word*; they were produced for the WPA in 1940 by Edward Laning.

Of particular note is the great reading room, a giant and beautiful spot where generations of readers and writers have worked in a light-filled and vast, almost silent, space. Here, too, is work by Edward Laning; a painting of Prometheus can be seen on the ceiling.

As you leave the library, you'll find the charming Bryant Park just behind it. This well-kept, much-loved urban space has benches, a working fountain, a terrace, and a number of statues. Note in particular the bronze bust by Jo Davidson of his friend Gertrude Stein (on the terrace); a likeness of William Cullen Bryant (1911) by Herbert Adams and architect Thomas Hastings; a bust of Goethe (1832) by Karl Fischer; a statue of William Earl Dodge (1885) by John Quincy Adams; and *José Bonifacio de Andrade e Silva*, a 1955 life-size statue by the Brazilian artist José Otavio Correia Lima.

This is a lovely park for a rest before you set out to see the **International Center of Photography (ICP)**, 1133 Avenue of the Americas (Sixth Avenue) at 43rd Street (212-860-1777; www.icp.org). At thus museum you will see an extraordinary collection of

International Center of Photography (ICP)
1133 Avenue of the Americas (Sixth Avenue) at 43rd Street
212-860-1777
www.icp.org

89

photos, ranging from the avant-garde artwork to retrospectives by famous photographers, to historic images. This interesting site has a permanent collection of some 55,000 photographs from the earliest history of the camera to the present day and the high-tech innovations that are brand new. Anyone with an interest in the art of science or the history of photography will find this a rewarding visit.

You might also wish to visit several other photography sites:

Bonni Benrubi Gallery, 41 East 13th Street, Suite 1300 (212-888-6007); **Edwynn Houk Gallery**, 745 Fifth Avenue at 57th Street (212-750-7070); **Steven Kasher Gallery**, 521 West 23rd Street (212-966-3978); and **Robert Mann Gallery**, 210 11th Avenue (212-989-7600).

AND IN ADDITION . . .

The **Grolier Club**, 27 East 60th Street (212-838-6690; www.grolierclub.org), an elegant, private, East Side club, has a particularly charming gallery on its main floor, and another exhibition space upstairs. Here in intimate settings reminiscent of fine rare book rooms, is presented a series of shows relating to books and art and history that are open free of charge to the public. Recent shows have included *Torn in Two: The 150th Anniversary of the Civil War* (featuring maps and prints and photographs); *The Prints of Seong Moy*; and *Through a Papermaker's Eye: Artists' Books from the Collection of Susan Gosin*.

Look for the following sculptures along Sixth Avenue:

The Sun Triangle, by Athelstan Spilhaus, is on Sixth Avenue between 48th and 49th Streets. This geometric, stainless-steel work was made in 1973.

Cubed Curve (1972), a sculpture by William Crovello, is in front of the Time-Life Building at 1271 Avenue of the Americas (Sixth Avenue) and 50th Street.

Jim Dine's **Looking Toward the Avenue** (1989) at Sixth Avenue and 53rd Street. These three "classical" figures are well known in New York and a notable addition to midtown.

Grolier Club
27 East 60th Street
212-838-6690
www.grolierclub.org

The Sun Triangle
Sixth Avenue between 48th and 49th Streets

Cubed Curve
1271 Avenue of the Americas (Sixth Avenue) and 50th Street

Looking Toward the Avenue
Sixth Avenue and 53rd Street

22 The Sculpture and Architecture of the Tip of Manhattan: From the Financial District to the South Street Seaport

DIRECTIONS » By subway, take the 4 or 5 line to Fulton Street, or the 2 or 3 line to Park Place.

The very tip of Manhattan is a wonderful place to explore: narrow street with historic buildings, bustling areas of commerce, graveyards where important American are honored, several parks, contemporary headquarters in tall buildings with lobby art, and even a 14th-century Italian triptych. You will find all kinds of art and architecture on this outing, and you are never far from the water—making you very aware that you are walking through some of the earliest-settled areas on an island—Manhattan.

We suggest you begin your walk at 209 Broadway at Fulton Street, where you'll find **St. Paul's Chapel**, long a favorite downtown site. This is a charming and historic site—New York's only surviving prerevolutionary building, dating to 1766. It has a long and illustrious history, with its cornerstone laid in 1964. It has a light and spacious interior with fluted Corinthian columns and a barrel-vaulted ceiling. You'll see a bust of John Wells (1818) by early American sculptor John Frazee, as well as a pew where George Washington worshipped. Note the glory above the altar; it is by Pierre Charles l'Enfant (the French military engineer and architect who designed Washington, DC).

St. Paul's Chapel
209 Broadway
at Fulton Street

If you exit the church through the rear doors, you'll find yourself in St. Paul's historic graveyard. This is one of the oldest cemeteries in the city. It contains a number of 18th-century tombstones (some of Revolutionary War heroes), and a few still have original carved designs.

The northern boundary of the graveyard is Vesey Street. At 20 Vesey Street is the **Garrison Building** (1906), where the *New York Evening Post* was published from 1907 to 1930. There are four unusual statues in front of it; called the *Four Periods of Publicity* (1906), they were created by Gutzon Borglum (the same artist who made the Mt. Rushmore presidential heads sculpture). His wife, Estelle Rumbold Kohn, was his coartist. (You can see other Borglum works at the Cathedral of St. John the Divine, in Chapter 4.)

Garrison Building
20 Vesey Street

On leaving Vesey Street, walk south to the **Kalikow Building** at 195 Broadway. Once the AT&T Building, it

Kalikow Building
195 Broadway

91

has a lobby worth seeing. There is a prevailing Egyptian ambience with 40 huge columns, and a statue of winged Mercury with marble figures in relief by Chester Beach.

Returning to Broadway, walk 3 blocks south to Liberty Street. You'll come to Liberty Plaza, a bustling spot with people coming and going and resting on park benches. Note, however, that one person on a park bench is the creation of the artist J. Seward Johnson, whose lifelike figures can be seen in several spots in the city. This artwork, called **Double Check** (1982) is completely realistic, down to the open briefcase, calculator, pencils, tape recorder, and so on, and the typical dress of a downtown worker (probably in the financial district).

Nearby, also on Liberty Street at 120 Broadway, is the Marine Midland Building, which has its own plaza, graced with one of the city's favorite outdoor works of art. The huge orange and red cube is by Isamu Noguchi and is called **Red Cube** (1968). Balanced surprisingly on one corner, it has a hole through the center. Although it looks like a cube, it is actually a rhombohedron, or six-sided figure whose opposite sides are parallel at oblique angles, creating the illusion of dramatic force. Noguchi remarked that a cube on its point was like chance or a rolling of the dice.

The **Federal Hall National Memorial** is on the corner a couple of blocks south at the intersection of Pine and Nassau Streets. Although the building that saw Washington take the Oath of Office or the Bill of Rights enacted is gone, the present stately hall dates back to 1842. It is in the Greek Revival style (inspired by the Parthenon), and is now a museum filled with historic documents, prints, and Americana—including a diorama of Washington's inauguration. It is operated by the National Park Service and has a variety of visiting exhibitions of all kinds. Outside the building is a statue of Washington by John Quincy Adams Ward.

After so much historic art and architecture, you'll have a complete change of style and era at Louise Nevelson Plaza. Walk east to William Street, turn left; two blocks north at the intersection of William and Liberty Streets is a small, triangular plot devoted to Nevelson's work. Her seven black steel structures, **Shadows and Flags** (1978) form a cohesive decorative unit; in fact, the sculptures were conceived as parts of a whole, and the 40-foot-tall forms make a stunning art

Double Check
Liberty Plaza

Red Cube
140 Broadway and
Liberty Street

Federal Hall National Memorial
intersection of Pine
and Nassau Streets

Shadows and Flags
intersection of William
and Liberty Streets

environment. Nevelson commented that she wanted to place the sculptures on poles so they would seem to "float like flags"; she was always concerned with the interaction of light and dark, and the relationship of art to its environment; this example echoes many of the city's geometric shapes—jagged planes, cylinders, angled bars, and so on—all obliquely reflecting the city's shapes and forms.

Walk back on Liberty Street to the Chase Manhattan Building (between Nassau and Pine Streets). On the south face of the building is a well-known masterpiece, Jean Dubuffet's **Group of Four Trees** (1972), a 43-foot, 25-ton sculpture of aluminum and steel, fiberglass, and plastic resin—all covered with polyurethane paint. This bright, fanciful work was described by the artist as an "hourloupe" (meaning a wonderful or grotesque object). The placement of this odd and fascinating work by a notably antiestablishment artist in front of one of the world's most hallowed capitalist symbols, adds to the curious mix of art and life that characterizes New York.

Group of Four Trees and Isamu Noguchi's sunken garden
Chase Manhattan Bank Plaza, between Nassau and Pine Streets

Just below street level is **Isamu Noguchi's sunken garden**; it is an elegant, artistic statement of black basalt rocks, trickling water, a patterned floor suggesting waves, and many additional elements that bring to mind Japanese gardens. You can view the site from above, or walk down to see it up close; either way, don't miss Noguchi's effort to integrate art and nature in an urban setting. (The designer said that when the fountain was in operation, the adjacent rocks "seemed to levitate out of the ground." You don't want to miss the scenic beauty. (Inside the lobby is a tribute in sculpture to the rescue dogs of 9/11; the large art collection that used to grace this building has been dispersed.)

Back on Broadway is **Trinity Church** at 89 Broadway at Wall Street, one of New York's best-known churches. Built in 1839, this lovely Gothic Revival church was designed by Richard Upjohn. There are many art elements to notice within: bronze doors resembling Ghiberti's in the Florentine baptistery, doors on the west portal designed by Karl Bitter, a large stained-glass window above the altar (1846) designed by the architect, the baptistery triptych with its gold background. In the graveyard adjacent to the church are the graves of Alexander Hamilton, Francis Lewis, and Robert Fulton, among other notable Americans. The church has a small museum relating to its history;

Trinity Church
89 Broadway at Wall Street

Cunard Building
25 Broadway

Charging Bull
Bowling Green Park

Alexander Hamilton U.S. Custom House
1 Bowling Green

there is also an interpretive slide program about the parishioners and gravesites of interest.

At 25 Broadway you'll find the old **Cunard Building** (1921), now housing a post office. A modest entranceway leads to a Great Hall—which is indeed something to see. From its main dome (65 feet high), which rises over the vast octagonal hall, said to be inspired by Raphael's style, to the impressive frescoes, by the American painter Ezra Winter, to the emphasis on shipping scenes (as the might expect at a Cunard Building) this is a sight to see. Note the history of shipping and ships: from Vikings to Columbus's galleon, to Sir Francis Drake's crossing—these are scenes any student of maritime history will enjoy. This 1920s building captures that aura of excitement and possibility and exuberance.

Just across the street in the tiny Bowling Green Park is the financial district's favorite sculpture: Arturo Di Modica's huge bronze ***Charging Bull***—of course, a symbol of good times in the market.

In the park, you can rest on a park bench and get a good look at 1 Bowling Green, the **Alexander Hamilton U.S. Custom House**, a beautiful old Beaux-Arts–style building from 1907. It has 44 Corinthian columns, a fine arched entrance, a great flight steps, and an impressive set of sculptures in front of it. By Daniel Chester French, perhaps the nation's premier sculptor in his time, these four figures represent four continents. Each is a seated female. To our 21st-century eyes, the stereotypical symbols of the continents are indicative of a biased, 19th-century view of the world. But as works of art they are dramatic, allegorical sculptures with each figure gracefully posed. *America* and *Europe* are at the center. *America* is idealistic and fervent, holding the torch of prosperity, prepared to lead and inspire. *Europe* is symbolic of past eras, with a Grecian gown and images of ancient glories. She wears a crown, and seems to symbolize solid, classical virtues. *Africa*, leaning against a sphinx and a lion, slumbers, waiting to be awakened in the future. *Asia* holds Buddhist figure and a lotus flower; she is the mother of mysticism and appears in a meditative trance.

At the roof's edge, you'll find cornice sculptures, too; these 12 statues from 1907 symbolize nations in sea trade. Each wears a national costume. The statues were made by leading artists of the time: *Holland* and *Portugal* by Augustus Saint-Gaudens, *France* and *England* by Charles Grafly, *Greece* and *Rome* by Frank Edwin Elwell, *Phoenicia* by Frederick Wellington Ruckstull, *Genoa* by Augustus Lukeman, *Venice* and *Spain* by Mary Lawrence Tonetti, *Denmark* by Johannes Gelert, and *Belgium* by Albert Jaegers.

The Customs House is now the site of the **National Museum of the American Indian** (212-825-6700). ⓗ Friday–Wednesday 10 AM–5 PM, Thursday 10 AM–8 PM. Free admission. This fine museum, a small part of the vast Smithsonian Institution, was founded in 1916 by George C. Heye, and is devoted to the collection, preservation, and exhibition of all things having to do with the Native Americans in North, Central, and South America—from the Arctic to Tierra del Fuego. Although the collection is now smaller in this New York branch than it used to be, it is nonetheless a must-see for all the family. From Pomo feather baskets to Iroquois silverwork to Pueblo pottery and costumes, masks, weapons, and Apache playing cards—hundreds of items will fascinate you. Encompassing history (Crazy Horse's feathered headdress), ethnography (animal figurines from Central America) and fine art (beadwork embroidery), this is an intriguing and essential stop.

National Museum of the American Indian (former US Customs House)
1 Bowling Green
212-825-6700
http://nmai.si.edu

You are now near a New York historic site: **Fraunces Tavern**. Walk east on Bridge Street to the corner of Pearl Street (no. 54) and Broad Street (212-425-1778). ⓗ daily noon–5 PM. Admission fee. Originally built for a merchant named Stephen Delancey in 1719, it became Fraunces Tavern in 1762, and has functioned as an eatery ever since. But nowadays it also houses a museum, which documents such historic events as George Washington's visit there. Although it has undergone extensive reconstruction over the years, you'll still get a feel for a distant past in downtown New York as you visit to see the dioramas and old prints in the upstairs museum, or eat downstairs. You'll be particularly struck by the scale of this very small structure surrounded by high, glamorous recent buildings.

Fraunces Tavern
54 Pearl Street
at Broad Street
212-425-1778

The **New York Vietnam Veterans Memorial** is an entire plaza; it was created by several artists working together: John Ferrandino, William Fellows, and Timothy Marshall. Their tribute to the many who were lost in the Vietnam War is unusual. It consists of etched green glass boxes set into a design; each bears quotations from soldiers' letters home. It is hard to imagine a more touching memorial.

New York Vietnam Veterans Memorial
55 Water Street

95

77 Water Street at William Street

80 Pine Street at Water Street

One Seaport Plaza 199 Water Street

At **77 Water Street**, not far away (near William Street), is a lobby with sculptures of interest. Four works of the 1970s are displayed; they are by Victor Scalo, George Adamy, Rudolph de Harak, and William Tarr.

Continue up Water Street to the corner of Pine Street. At **88 Pine Street** is another plaza; there is a fountain (by James Ingo-Freed) as well as a striking sculpture. A large and deceptive geometric work, *Untitled* (1969), by Yu Yu Yang, has fascinated viewers since its arrival in the plaza.

Return to 199 Water Street, to **One Seaport Plaza**, where you won't want to miss three murals by Frank Stella in the lobby.

Now a word about the South Street Seaport, long a favorite venue both for New Yorkers and tourists. The huge Hurricane Sandy of 2012 decimated the coastal area here, and as of this writing, many sites along the river have yet to reopen. Hopefully, everything will be put back together soon.

The South Street Historic District encompasses a much-loved museum; many narrow, charming streets relating to the city's maritime history; two sailing ships; a recent museum of underground history of the area; and much, much more.

South Street Seaport Museum
12 Fulton Street
and 207 Front Street
212-748-8600
www.southstreetseaport
museum.org

Our final stop is the **South Street Seaport Museum**. It occupies two sites in close proximity: 12 Fulton Street and 207 Front Street (212-748-8600; www. southstreetseaportmuseum.org). ℍ daily 10 AM–6 PM. Admission fee; free admission for children under age 9 (all tickets are purchased at the museum between Beekman and Fulton Streets). Displays here concern all kinds of material relating to the maritime, from ocean liner posters to early prints of New York's busy harbor.

As of press time, the museum was in need of renovation due to Hurricane Sandy and was closed to the public. Call before you go.

8 Spruce Street by Frank Gehry
8 Spruce Street

AND IN ADDITION . . .
The 76-story, shimmering **8 Spruce Street** is New York's latest architectural wonder. Designed by Frank Gehry, its curving verticals give it a sense of movement; it's the tallest residential building in the Western Hemisphere.

BROOKLYN

23 New Art Venues: From Dumbo to Williamsburg

DIRECTIONS » **Dumbo:** By subway, take the A or C line to High Street, or the F line to York Street.

» Williamsburg: By subway, take the L line to Bedford Avenue.

If visiting the emerging-artists scene and the latest small galleries appeals to you, we recommend a visit to two neighborhoods in Brooklyn: Dumbo (Down Under the Brooklyn Bridge) and Williamsburg. The best time to visit the galleries in these regions is Wednesday–Sunday 11 AM–6 PM.

Nestled under the Brooklyn and Manhattan Bridges, Dumbo, a small neighborhood on the banks of the East River, is an unusually scenic and inviting place to walk. (Visit the spectacular 70-acre **Brooklyn Bridge Park**, at Pier 6 across from Furman Street, designed by Michael Van Valkenburgh, with its views of the Manhattan skyline and the great bridge.) This is a relatively new art district with many new sites; as of this writing, construction was still under way, but many galleries were open and busy.

Brooklyn Bridge Park
Pier 6 across from Furman Street

While visiting the riverside area, be sure to stop by the spectacular *Pavilion* (2011), designed by Jean Nouvel, the noted French architect. The $9-million transparent, jewel-like glass "box," reflecting the scenery around it, houses *Jane's Carousel* (1922), named after Jane Walentas and her husband, David, who bought and restored it. Each vintage horse is hand painted and different from the next.

Turn inland toward the small neighborhood of **Dumbo** and head for Plymouth, Washington, Jay, Pearl, and in particular, Front Streets. These are the major gallery sites; for example, visit 111 Front Street, where there are more than 20 galleries.

Proceed next to Williamsburg, where many artists live and work. It is a major site for galleries, including on Kent, Third, and Roebling Streets and on Bedford and Morgan Avenues. Your first gallery stop can provide you with a map and list of art sites.

Geido
Restaurant
331 Flatbush Avenue
at Seventh Avenue
718-638-8866

AND IN ADDITION . . .

One of the most recent and trendy Brooklyn gallery neighborhoods is in nearby Bushwick. Major galleries are on Morgan, Bogart, and Stanhope Streets and Wyckoff Avenue.

Geido Restaurant, 331 Flatbush Avenue at Seventh Avenue (718-638-8866), is a Japanese restaurant decorated with graffiti-like wall paintings reminiscent of Basquiat.

24 Green-Wood Cemetery: Artistic Monuments, Temples, and Obelisks amid the Greenery

DIRECTIONS» By subway, take the M, N, or R line to 25th Street (Brooklyn); the entrance to the cemetery is one avenue block away, up the hill on 25th Street to Fifth Avenue. For NYC Mass Transit directions from other locations, phone 718-768-7300.

» By car, from Lower Manhattan take Brooklyn Battery Tunnel and exit at Hamilton Avenue (after the toll plaza). Continue on Hamilton Avenue until it becomes Third Avenue, and go about eight blocks to 25th Street. Turn left on 25th Street and go two blocks. The cemetery entrance is straight ahead at Fifth Avenue and 25th Street.

Cemeteries can be fascinating art and architecture sites, and the historic **Green-Wood Cemetery** is particularly so. This remarkable 19th-century graveyard—now a National Historic Landmark—is a must-see Brooklyn destination. Founded in 1838 by Henry Evelyn Pierrepont, it was one of America's first rural cemeteries—and soon became a favorite spot for Sunday strollers and picnickers in mid-century, before public parks. (It's still popular for walking, exploring, bird-watching, or sightseeing.) The setting of this grand park is magical: 478 acres of lawns, flowering trees, ponds, winding pathways, and many, many extraordinary momuments. Indeed, Green-Wood is considered to have one of the most impressive outdoor collections of 19th- and 20th-century mausoleums and statuary in the nation. ⊕ daily 8 AM–5 PM (extended hours in summer).

Many notable Americans are buried on these vast grounds—from historic political figures and Civil War generals to sports legends, inventors, writers and artists. With the help of a cemetery map available at the

Green-Wood Cemetery
Fifth Avenue and
25th Street

office near the entrance gate, you'll be able to locate the graves of such luminaries as Leonard Bernstein, Elliott Carter, Jean-Michel Basquiat, Boss Tweed, Horace Greeley, and Louis Comfort Tiffany, to name just a few. Of course, there are also unmarked graves, as well as many of people whose names may not be familiar; and there are some "unusual" burial sites, such as the touching one showing an empty marble chair. The monuments are in varied architectural styles—from exotic Moorish Revival designs to classic Greek columned temples to Egyptian pyramids to Gothic Revival styles, and, of course, also much simpler designs—and whether intriguing, compelling, or curious, they will definitely be of interest to art and architecture lovers.

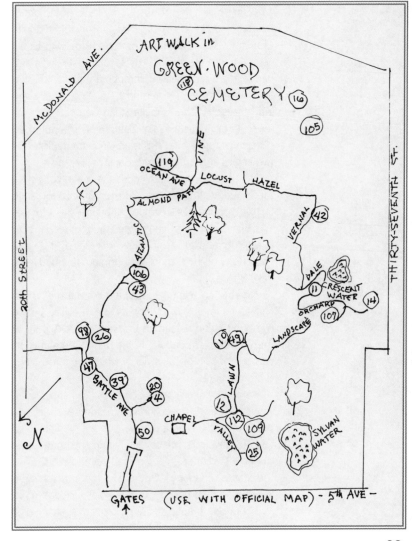

ART WALK in GREEN·WOOD CEMETERY

GATES (USE WITH OFFICIAL MAP) – 5th AVE –

Among the many people buried on these grounds (more than 500,000) at least 225 are identified on the cemetery map, but we will mention just a few that we find particularly worth pointing out. You can think of this outing as a sort of "treasure hunt," as it might take a bit of effort to find some of the monuments, but do persevere—it will be well worth it. (Of course you can also just wander about and enjoy whatever you chance upon!) Your route will be more or less circular, and you'll be on well-marked pathways, lanes, and avenues with such names as Syringa, Bayside, Border, Atlantic, Grove, Almond, Locust, Orchard, Landscape, Lawn, Valley, and many more. This is a vast cemetery!

It makes good sense to begin at the beautiful Gothic Revival gates near the entrance, which you can't miss. The 1860s work of the noted architect Richard Upjohn (whose designs included Trinity Church in Lower Manhattan), it is striking with its tall central tower, steep slate roofs, columns, reliefs, and bannerettes. After passing through the gates, turn left and look for the fine memorial (to David Stuart, the industrialist father of Isabella Stuart Gardner) by master sculptor Augustus Saint-Gaudens and reputed architect Stanford White. This is an eloquent depiction of two angles appearing as musicians.

Next (on Syringa Path) comes a grave carved by the noted sculptor Daniel Chester French, for "little Frankie"; opposite is a compelling bronze statue of De-Witt Clinton, of Erie Canal fame (though he was also a governor and senator of New York State). This work was designed by Richard Upjohn and cast by Henry Kirke Brown.

Nearby (on Battle Avenue) are several sites of architectural interest, including a Greek Revival temple with Ionic columns and an Egyptian pyramid. Both of these styles were popular in the mid-19th century, as was the Gothic Revival style, of which there are many examples here.

As you wander about, don't miss the spectacular views near the intersection with Borden Avenue; you will have to climb up a few steps to get the full effect. (By the way, there are several high points throughout the park that offer great views of such iconic sites as the Statue of Liberty.) One of the more picturesque spots is accessed from a tiny walkway called Almond Path, beyond Atlantic and Grove Avenues. Here you'll find a lovely shaded hillside with several impressive mausoleums nestled in. Several artists are buried here; look for the graves of John La Farge (master of stained-glass windows) and of contemporary artist Jean-Michel Basquiat.

If seeing particularly the resting places of artists and other creative people appeals to you, here are some additional ones to look for:

- John Kensett, Hudson River painter (Sassafras Avenue)
- Solon Borglum, noted American sculptor (near John Kensett)
- Samuel F. B. Morse, inventor of the telegraph and artist (Thorn Path)
- George Bellows, early 20th-century American painter (Landscape Avenue)
- William M. Chase, American painter (Crocus Path)
- Louis Comfort Tiffany, noted glass designer—buried next to his father, founder of Tiffany and Company (Lawn Avenue)
- Asher B. Durand, leader of the Hudson River painters (Landscape Avenue)
- George Catlin, American painter known for his depictions of Native Americans (Landscape Avenue)

As you make your way back toward the entrance gates, you'll come to Green-Wood's enchanting chapel and stained-glass windows, a sight not to be missed. The chapel was built in the early 20th century, and is based on a Christopher Wren design for his tower at Christ Church in Oxford.

We have given you just a sampling of Green-Wood's many offerings. Undoubtedly you will enjoy the process of discovering others on your own!

25 Colorful Stained Glass in the Churches of Brooklyn Heights

DIRECTIONS » By subway, take the 2 or 3 line to Clark Street.

It's best to visit Brooklyn Heights on Sundays between 10 AM and 2 PM, or weekdays during lunch hour. Most of the sites on this walk are closed at other times. Bear in mind that services may be going on, which should not prevent you from quietly viewing the church windows. To be sure of church and workshop hours, you

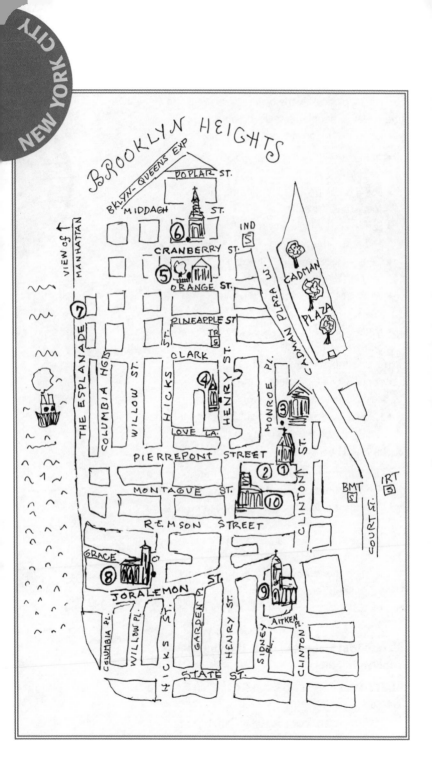

BROOKLYN HEIGHTS

BKLYN - QUEENS EXP

POPLAR ST.

MIDDAGH ST.

6.

CRANBERRY ST.

5 ORANGE ST.

IND S

VIEW of MANHATTAN

7

PINEAPPLE ST.

IRT S

THE ESPLANADE

COLUMBIA HGTS

WILLOW ST.

HICKS ST.

CLARK

4

HENRY ST.

LOVE LA.

MONROE PL.

CLINTON ST.

CADMAN PLAZA W.

CADMAN PLAZA

3

PIERREPONT STREET

2 1

MONTAGUE ST.

S

10

BMT S

IRT S

REMSON STREET

COURT ST.

GRACE

8

JORALEMON ST.

9

COLUMBIA PL.

WILLOW PL.

HICKS ST.

GARDEN PL.

HENRY ST.

SIDNEY PL.

AITKEN PL.

CLINTON PL.

STATE ST.

102

might wish to make a few phone calls before setting out.

Brooklyn Heights lends itself to a stroll—whether along the promenade that borders the East River, or through its charming street of brownstones and particularly lovely churches. This walk will take you to see one of its most unusual elements: its historic stained- and colored glass windows.

In the 50-block area known as Brooklyn Heights, you'll find some dozen churches built as early as the 1840s and reaching the height of stained-glass artistry with such designers as John La Farge, William J. Bolton, and Louis Comfort Tiffany. This is truly an interesting and historic way of exploring both a neighborhood and a form of art that in many ways defines an era of American life.

Before we start out on this walk, perhaps a few words about stained glass will introduce the walker to this particularly delicate and illustrative form of art. A taste for colored, illustrative glass came to the United States with European immigrants who were used to the colored, filtered light of Gothic churches. Here they found plain glass in colonial churches. They experimented in their own types of colored glass, including an iridescent milky and opalescent glass that did not transmit much light. The earliest American "stained" glass was actually painted onto this milky glass, and studios for painting glass were popular through the 1870s.

At about this time, however, American artists set about creating stained glass as it was made traditionally in Europe. The new names in this fully American endeavor were glass artists working in a 1,000-year-old tradition. When we visit the churches of Brooklyn Heights, you will see that they brought a thoroughly American sensibility to a European art form.

William J. Bolton and his brother John were among the first Americans to experiment with colored glass; as early as 1842 they were making bright, original stained-glass windows; we will see two churches with their windows on this walk (St. Ann's and Holy Trinity Episcopal Church).

Another artist to design colored windows was John La Farge, who had perfected the opalescent glass technique. Instead of practicing the European methods of making stained glass, he came up with his own technology merged with his personal artistic viewpoint in a

BROOKLYN

somewhat art nouveau style. He made some 300 colored windows, occasionally even inserting brightly colored glass jewels into his rather pale-toned windows.

Louis Comfort Tiffany, however, was the most notable of these American stained-glass artists. In 1878, he opened his first workshop, experimenting with brilliantly colored glass fragments in his own inimitable style (he made all kinds of items, such as his famous lamps out of glass, as well as windows—all bearing his distinctive colors, such as Mazarin Blue, Gold Lustre, and Aquamarine). Some were decoratively art nouveau in style; some he based on old master paintings (e.g., of Raphael, Ingres, Doré), and some had themes that we have all long associated with his work: clusters of wisteria, sailing ships, peacocks, as well as religious symbols, such as Biblical landscapes.

By the late 19th century, Tiffany windows and lamps were in great demand; one church after another commissioned him, and his workshop was the most famous one around. On this walk we'll see his windows at the First Unitarian Church. (Note that Tiffany windows can be seen in many other sites described in this book.)

While Holman Hunt and Otto Heinigke and Alexander Locke also produced stained glass of note, one outcome of the fashion for colored windows was a turn toward factory-produced stained glass, and many inferior products began flooding the market for windows in this era of church building. (Even some colonial churches, which depended for light on plain glass, were fitted with colored or opalescent glass, giving them dark interiors that were not appropriate to any earlier form of architecture.) By the early 1900s, leaded stained glass made in the European tradition finally arrived in the United States. On this walk, you'll see examples of all of these types of windows: opalescent, painted, and stained glass.

Among the earliest and more beloved Brooklyn Heights churches is **St. Ann's** at Pierrepont and Clinton Streets (718-875-6960). An English Gothic–style cathedral, St. Ann's merged with Holy Trinity. Its windows by William J. Bolton and his brother John date to 1844–47, making them among the oldest such windows in the nation. The bold, bright coloration was unusual for its time, and the well-known architect Minard Lafever thought they would complement his neo-Gothic design. Working in a small, cramped workshop

St. Ann's
Pierrepont and
Clinton Streets
718-875-6960

called the Priory Studio, the Boltons managed to cut, paint, and fire the glass for these windows—widely considered by art historians to be among the nation's best. Depicting the story of the Bible with Old Testament scenes on the clerestory windows, New Testament scenes on the gallery windows, and on the side aisles representations of the ancestors of Christ, including the Tree of Jesse, the colors are deep and bold—especially the reds and blues—you can walk up the stairs to the balcony for a closer look. While in the church, note the carved reredo behind the altar (by an unknown artist) and a sculpture by William Zorach near the vestibule.

Go left on Pierrepont Street and cross over to our next stop: the **Church of the Savior** (First Unitarian Church) on the corner at Monroe Place (718-624-5466). Built for a group of New England merchants, this dramatic sandstone building has a Gothic look with tall pinnacles and high gable. Unpopular for their liberal beliefs, they chose a site of an early British fort, and engaged the leading architect Minard Lafever. The church opened in 1844, and went on to become a notable scene of social activism.

Fifty years later, to celebrate its anniversary, the church engaged Louis Comfort Tiffany to design a new set of windows. The problem of combining stained-glass windows with the architectural design of side galleries can still be seen today.

The 10 opalescent Tiffany windows (eight of which are from the Tiffany studio) all suggest the quintes-

Church of the Savior (First Unitarian Church)
50 Monroe Place
718-624-5466

St. Ann's church window

sential Tiffany style: subdued colors, romantic nature scenes, heroic figures in flowing robes, naturalistic landscape (the Frothingham window), flowering magnolias (the Jessup Stevenson window), the angel Raphael (the Woodward window)—all in a notably art nouveau style. (Two non-Tiffany windows are by Alexander Locke, a student of John La Farge.) The fine rose window dates surprisingly to 1946; it pictures Christ proclaiming the Eight Beatitudes—in eight surrounding panels. It was designed by Charles J. Connick.

Continue to the right on Pierrepont Street, then right on Henry Street; halfway up the block at no. 124 is the **First Presbyterian Church** (718-624-3770). Dating to 1846, it is home to nine Tiffany windows in its imposing brownstone building. Its high steeple rises 90 feet above the street; its interior is elegant (though the balcony impedes sightlines for the windows). Note the geometric designs made of small squares of blue, green, and brown (reminiscent of Klee's *Magic Squares*). The Tiffany windows, such as the *River of Life* on the south wall, remind us of mid-19th-century American landscape paintings. Note also Maurice Cottier's 1893 *Children's Window*, and *Evening Time It Shall Be Light*. Don't miss Tiffany's *Alpha and Omega* window (a gift from Albert Bierstadt, the American landscapist), or his *St. John the Fisherman*, or the *Angel of Victory*, or the *Guardian Angel*.

For our next visit, turn left and left again to Orange Street, where you'll find the noted **Plymouth Church of the Pilgrims** at 75 Hicks Street (718-624-4743). This famous Congregational church has an illustrious history, from the time of its founding by Henry Ward Beecher. For more than 40 years he led the church in a controversial and nontraditional manner, involving it in the antislavery movement, woman's rights, and temperance battles. Abolitionists and social reformers spoke from his pulpit, and many of the most famous writers and activists of the time worshipped there (Mark Twain, Charles Dickens, Clara Barton, and Booker T. Washington—to name a few).

Much like a massive New England meeting house, this church was designed by the English architect J. C. Wells; it is austere and spacious, with cast-iron columns and seating for some 2,000 visitors. The somewhat stark interior is enlivened by its windows; by Frederick Stymetz Lamb, they depict more secular themes (*History of Puritanism*) and others devoted to religions and

First Presbyterian Church
124 Pierrepont Street
718-624-3770

Plymouth Church of the Pilgrims
75 Hicks Street
718-624-4743

St. Ann's
church window

political liberty. The Tiffany windows, however, adorn the adjacent Hillis Hall (open on Sunday afternoon, or by inquiring). Five of Tiffany's windows can be seen; note the center one, the *Life of Christ*. If you go out into the garden (with permission), you'll see a statue by Gutzon Borglum of Henry Ward Beecher.

On leaving, turn right onto Hicks Street to the **Church of the Assumption**, a Roman Catholic church (718-625-1161), which has an unusual mix of French royal–style design (fleur-de-lis motifs), a painted ceiling, and relatively modern windows, of which the most interesting are on the second tier.

Next, turn right, walk a couple of blocks toward the river, and take a few moments to enjoy one of Brooklyn Heights' most adored features: the 3,000-foot-long walkway called the **Brooklyn Heights Promenade**, where people-watching, Manhattan views, river traffic, and lovely architecture all combine to make this cantilevered walkway perched above the docks and highway below all the more magical.

Church of the Assumption
55 Cranberry Street
718-625-1161

Brooklyn Heights Promenade
base of Brooklyn Bridge
www.nyharborparks
.org/visit/brhe

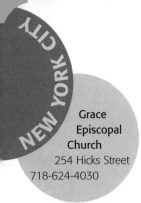

**Grace
Episcopal
Church**
254 Hicks Street
718-624-4030

**St. Charles Borromeo
Church**
31 Sidney Place between
Joralemon & State
Streets
718-625-1177

**Our Lady of Lebanon
Cathedral**
113 Remsen Street
718-624-7228

**Brooklyn Historical
Society**
128 Pierrepont Street
718-222-4111
ww.brooklynhistory.org

Walk to the end of the Promenade (to your left if you are facing the river) and make a left on Remsen Street. Go to Hicks Street, where you will turn right to find **Grace Episcopal Church** at 254 Hicks Street (entrance on Grace Court) (718-624-4030). Designed by Richard Upjohn in 1847, this unusually charming Gothic Revival, sandstone building has open wood vaulting and carved moldings. Three Tiffany windows and two by Holman Hunt add to the interest of the interior; with their subdued green and brown tones, they produce a subtle contrast with the brown wood vaulting. Don't miss the attractive rose window.

Next, turn right on Hicks, left on Joralemon Street, go several blocks, and turn right on Sidney Place to Aitken Place. Here you'll spot the deep red exterior of **St. Charles Borromeo Church** (718-625-1177). Built in 1869, it is a charming building with wood trim, and though its windows are not particularly noteworthy, behind the altar is a series of small colored glass panels that are quite attractive. The ceiling here is unusually interesting; divided by dark brown arches and moldings, it contains a series of lovely painted designs.

From Sidney Place and Joralemon Street, turn left to Henry Street. Here is a curious site: **Our Lady of Lebanon Cathedral** (718-624-7228). Although originally designed by Richard Upjohn, it was acquired in 1944 by Maronite Christians of the Lebanese community. The interior demonstrates this curious amalgam of styles: Upjohn's Romanesque Revival architecture with semicircular arches and slender columns is combined with Middle Eastern décor. Unusually bright colors would have surprised Upjohn, but here they fuse well with the graceful design of the interior, including the appealing mural of the Mediterranean over the altar and the calligraphic designs that suggest Arabic writing on the ceiling and the wall borders. Two porthole windows were rescued from the ocean liner *Normandie*, which burned in 1942. The windows themselves represent an attempt at an ancient style of stained glass, suggesting mosaics of the past.

AND IN ADDITION . . .
Brooklyn Historical Society, at 128 Pierrepont Street (718-222-4111), conducts Saturday and Sunday afternoon historic tours of the neighborhood, for which reservations are accepted. The society also

sponsors exhibitions and lectures. **H** Wednesday–Saturday noon–5 PM. Suggested admission fee.

Also in or near Brooklyn Heights are several notable sculptures: **Henry Ward Beecher** (1888–89), by John Quincy Adams Ward, can be seen at the south end of Cadman Plaza; the **Brooklyn War Memorial** with two classical figures (1922), by Charles Keck, is at Cadman Plaza's north section; and at the intersection of Court and Montague Streets you'll find Anneta Duveen's 1971 **bust of Robert F. Kennedy**.

In the large, ceremonial courtroom on the second floor (where new citizens are sworn in) of the **Federal Building**, 225 Cadman Plaza East, near the Brooklyn Bridge, you'll find some restored 1937 WPA murals by Edward Laning, who also painted the murals in the New York Public Library. Originally intended for the immigrants' dining hall at Ellis Island, these are appropriately entitled *The Role of the Immigrant in the Industrial Development of America*; and, in fact, they depict in dramatic scenes the newcomers of that era working hard in coal mines, on farms, and along railroad tracks.

At the **Urban Glass Workshop**, 647 Fulton Street at the corner of Rockwell Street (718-625-3685), the blazing kilns turning hot liquid glass into extraordinary art objects before your eyes, make this a not-to-be-missed stop. The workshop has a variety of programs and artists at work, as well as a small exhibition space. When we last visited, a number of artists and students were turning and twisting the molten glass or blowing it into unusual shapes. This form of sculpture dates back to ancient Egypt and reached high points in medieval Italy and 19th-century France. Today the techniques used produce three-dimensional works that vary from luminous neon glass tubes to sand-blasted objets d'art. The workshop offers a variety of seminars, classes, exhibitions, and events.

Chase Manhattan Bank, 4 Metrotech Center between Flatbush Avenue and Willoughby Street, has a distinctive high-tech lobby installation (1992) by Nam June Paik. There are 429 television sets displaying quickly changing video images. There is also a fluorescent installation, stretching 40 feet, by sculptor Dan Flavin (1993). Also at Metrotech is a sculpture called *Corrugated Rollers* (1994), by Ursula von Rydingsvard.

Contemporary Brooklyn artists are featured in the

Henry Ward Beecher
south end of Cadman Plaza

Brooklyn War Memorial
north section of Cadman Plaza

BROOKLYN

bust of Robert F. Kennedy
intersection of Court and Montague Streets

Federal Building
225 Cadman Plaza East

Urban Glass Workshop
126 13th St., Brooklyn
718-625-3685
urbanglass.org

Chase Manhattan Bank and Metrotech Center
between Flatbush Avenue and Willoughby Street

historic **BRIC Rotunda Gallery**, 33 Clinton Street (718-683-5604).

If, after seeing the Brooklyn Heights churches described here you would like to see more stained-glass windows, visit the following places in Manhattan (all contain windows by Tiffany): **Temple Emanu-El**, 1 East 65th Street at Fifth Avenue; **St. Michael's Episcopal Church**, 225 West 99th Street at Amsterdam Avenue; the **YWCA**, 610 Lexington Avenue at 53rd Street; **Collegiate Reformed Church**, 368 West End Avenue at 77th Street; **Congregation Shearith Israel**, 8 West 70th Street at Central Park West (for geometric, abstract Tiffany windows); and the **Church of the Holy Cross**, 329 West 42nd Street between Eighth and Ninth Avenues (note the Tiffany panels). Other windows of artistic interest are to be found at 714 Fifth Avenue near 56th Street. Here in the landmark **Coty Building** you'll find three René Lalique windows made in 1912.

26 Two Remarkable Treasures: The Brooklyn Botanic Garden and the Brooklyn Museum

DIRECTIONS » By subway, take the 2 or 3 line to Franklin Avenue/Eastern Parkway for the Botanic Garden, or Eastern Parkway–Brooklyn Museum for the museum. By car, take the Manhattan Bridge, whose continuation in Brooklyn is Flatbush Avenue; stay on Flatbush all the way to Grand Army Plaza at Prospect Park, and take the rotary three-fourths of the way around to Eastern Parkway, which borders the park. The Botanic Garden is immediately after the Central Library Building.

Combining a visit to the Brooklyn Museum and the Brooklyn Botanic Garden might seem like too much to undertake in one day—especially if you've never been to either of them before. Yes, there is indeed a great deal to see in both of these wonderful sites. But we put them together because they are so near to each other and also complement each other so well: after a visit to this world-class museum, a lovely walk through this remarkable garden—a work of art in itself—might be just the perfect thing. We leave it to you to decide what works best for you. You can always come back and do the other half of this outing on another day!

The **Brooklyn Museum**, 200 Eastern Parkway (718-638-5000; www.brooklynmuseum.org), is one

**BRIC
Rotunda
Gallery**
33 Clinton Street
718-683-5604
bricartsmedia.org

Brooklyn Museum
200 Eastern Parkway
718-638-5000
www.brooklyn
museum.org

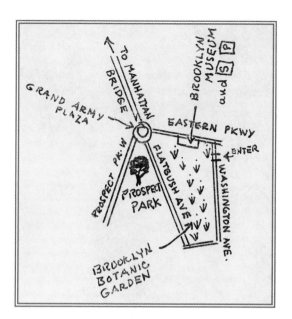

of the great museums of New York City. Filled with art treasures from around the world, it offers an enriching experience—and is rarely as crowded as its neighbors in Manhattan. Any art lover will enjoy a visit here. ❶ Wednesday, Friday–Sunday 11 AM–6 PM; Thursday 11 AM–10 PM. (Closed Monday and Tuesday.) Suggested admission fee.

As you walk up to the entrance (renovated several years ago) you'll see giant sculptures adorning the outside walls of the museum. These representations of ancient heroes and allegorical figures were created by noted sculptors, including Daniel Chester French, who made the two colossal figures on either side of the entrance; these represent Manhattan and Brooklyn and were to have been placed on either end of the Manhattan Bridge.

The museum has one the premier collections of ancient Egyptian, Greek, Coptic, and Nubian art, as well as first-rate collections of European art from the Renaissance to the 20th century. Its American collections are also impressive and include paintings from the 18th to 20th centuries and many examples in the decorative arts.

Contemporary art is also well represented at the museum. One of the more fascinating (and popular) permanent exhibits is Judy Chicago's installation *The Dinner Party* (1970) located in the Sackler wing. This one-of-a-kind piece of feminist art consists of a huge triangular banquet table laid with 39 place settings,

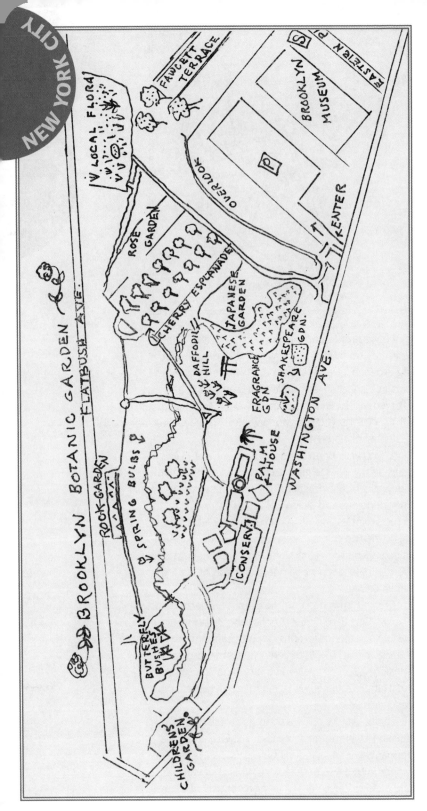

BROOKLYN BOTANIC GARDEN

NEW YORK CITY

FLATBUSH AVE.

LOCAL FLORA

FAWCETT TERRACE

BROOKLYN MUSEUM

EASTERN PKY

ENTER

OVERLOOK

ROSE GARDEN

CHERRY ESPLANADE

JAPANESE GARDEN

DAFFODIL HILL

FRAGRANCE GDN

SHAKESPEARE GDN.

WASHINGTON AVE.

ROCK GARDEN

SPRING BULBS

CONSERV.

PALM HOUSE

BUTTERFLY BUSHES

CHILDREN'S GARDEN

112

each celebrating an important historic or mythic female figure. Included in this original and symbolic work are gold chalices, utensils, painted porcelain, and embroidered runners. Beneath the table are white floor tiles with the names of another 999 women appearing in gold.

Recent exhibits have included *Gravity and Grace: Monumental Works by El Anatsui*, an artist from Ghana, now living in Nigeria. This work consists of 30 pieces in metal, wood, and combinations of sculpture and painting. Included in this large work are 12 monumental wall and floor sculptures made from bottle caps the artist found in a distillery in Nigeria. (This work reflects the artist's fascination with how things change and take on new shapes.) Another exhibit of interest was one called *Raw/Cooked*, which consisted of a series of exhibitions by lesser-known Brooklyn artists. One of them, Marela Zacarias, created *Williamsburg Murals*, which reflects her interest in urban renewal and the history of objects; large abstract forms seem to climb up the walls and interact with the museum's architecture.

Note the five WPA murals in the corridors (rescued from other sites): these works by American modernists Ilya Bolotowsky, Paul Kelpe, Albert Swinden, and Balcomb Greene were painted between 1936 and 1937 for a housing project. These abstract works may be the first such murals in the country.

The museum is active in many other areas, as well, sponsoring programs in dance and film, lectures, art classes, and craft demonstrations.

The **Brooklyn Botanic Garden**, 990 Washington Avenue (718-623-7200; www.bbg.org), is one of those delightful surprises you happen upon in New York. ❿ November–February, Tuesday–Friday 8 AM–4:30 PM, Saturday and Sunday 10 AM–4:30 PM; March–October, Tuesday–Friday 8 AM–6 PM, Saturday and Sunday 10 AM–6 PM. (Closed Monday.) Admission fee; free admission for children under age 12.

Brooklyn Botanic Garden
990 Washington Avenue
718-623-7200
www.bbg.org

Here you are, surrounded by urban sprawl, and in front of you, behind iron gates, is an inviting oasis. Once inside the gates, you find yourself in a world of complete enchantment, with artistic gardens, elegant walkways, weeping cherry trees, and the many sights and scents of the world's most appealing gardens. The garden includes about 50 acres (though it feels much larger), and you can walk through them as you wish,

or just enjoy the pleasure of being in such a magical landscape.

This is a garden for all seasons (though obviously at its best from late spring to early fall) and all tastes. All the plants are labeled (there are more than 12,000 of them) and come from almost every country in the world. If you are partial to literary references, you will especially enjoy the Shakespeare Garden, where plantings are related to passages from Bard's work; if you like horticulture, there is a Local Flora section waiting for you; if you wish to meditate, you might sit along the banks of the Japanese Garden's peaceful walkways; and, in our case, if you are interested in art and specifically the combination of art and nature, you'll find exhibits of interest here, too.

Following is a brief description of some of our favorite spots in this vast garden. Begin by picking up a useful map (at the main entrance), which will point you in the right direction.

A good place to start is the Herb Garden, right near the parking lot. Here you'll find hundreds of herbs (all labeled) that have been used for cooking and medicine since medieval times. Note the elegant Elizabethan knots that have been used to form a fascinating pattern amid the greenery.

From there it's a pleasant, leafy walk to the Cherry Esplanade, with crab apple trees, wisteria, and peonies en route. The best time to visit this garden is in late April and early May, when the Kwartzan cherry trees are in their full, delicious pink bloom. You might be reminded of similar scenes in Japanese paintings.

If you love roses, don't miss the Cranford Rose Garden, where you may be overwhelmed (as we were) by the sheer number (over 5,000 bushes) and variety (about 900) of plants. They are all labeled and spread out over a full acre—a spectacular display.

The Local Flora section will be of particular interest to those who study nature seriously. Here, different ecological zones have been re-created as dioramas or sorts, and you can learn about such habitats as the pine barren, wet meadow and stream, kettle pond, and bog, and see examples of the vegetation that grows in each.

The conservatory complex—known as the Steinhardt Conservatory—includes greenhouses with their various collections (cacti, flowers, palms, ferns, aquatic plants, etc.). On the lower floor are two exhibition galleries: one is devoted to bonsai and the many fascinating forms this Japanese art form takes; the other features horticultural displays and art exhibits relating to plants.

The exhibition gallery hosts several shows per year, featuring mostly small installations or two-dimensional pieces—photographs or paintings. Recent works have included *Terrarium* by Jennifer Williams, curator of interior displays. She has designed many different terrariums, or "gardens in a bottle" (an art form from the late 19th century), using antique glass containers from the Victorian era. In each is a tiny garden with such plants as orchids, mosses, or ferns, decorated with unusual rocks or petrified wood or figurines.

On the vast grounds you'll occasionally see outdoor changing art exhibits. Among our very favorites was an installation by Patrick Dougherty, *Natural History*, a monumental work that was constructed with a team of volunteers in the summer of 2010 to celebrate the garden's centennial. As with the artist's other works, this stunning sculpture was crafted from organic materials—in this case, pieces of vines and sticks woven into an architectural form (reminding us of an elephant's shape). If you entered this piece, you had the impression of being inside a nest.

Another exhibit we enjoyed was Nicole Dextras's whimsical *Wearable Art*: plant-based sculptures that were intriguing, if not long-lasting. Dextras uses a fabric base on which she sews layers of live moss, grasses, leaves, and flowers.

There are more gardens to discover, such as the enticing Fragrance Garden (where you might wish to linger, to take in all the delicious scents) and the aforementioned Shakespeare Garden. For us, the highlight of a visit to the Botanic Garden is probably the exquisite Japanese Hill and Pond Garden, designed by Takeo Shiota in 1914. Like Japanese gardens in general, this garden is filled with symbolism and invites quiet reflection. You walk past the imposing 17th-century komatsu stone lantern and find yourself in a welcoming circular viewing pavilion; in front of you is a idyllic panorama— a beautiful pond surrounded by cascades, grottoes, pathways along shrubberies, and pine groves. In the pond is a bright red torri (a wooden gateway), indicating a nearby temple; other splashes of color add their vibrancy during flowering season. You can walk around the pond, through winding paths, past grottoes, and up

Soldiers and Sailors Memorial Arch
Grand Army Plaza at Flatbush Avenue and Eastern Parkway

Prospect Park
bordered by Prospect Park West, Prospect Park Southwest, Parkside Avenue, and Flatbush Avenue/Ocean Avenue

the hill to the Shinto shrine—a quiet and mystical spot, where again you might wish to linger.

AND IN ADDITION . . .

BRIC Rotunda Gallery at 33 Clinton Street (718-683-5604, bricartsmedia.org) has changing exhibitions.

In the classical style is the **Soldiers and Sailors Memorial Arch** (1889–92) in Grand Army Plaza, not far from the Brooklyn Museum, at the intersection of Flatbush Avenue and Eastern Parkway. Here you'll find a great arch modeled after the Arc de Triomphe in Paris and decorated with exuberant sculptures by Frederick MacMonnies. Among its many heroic ornaments are bronze horses *Victory* and *The Army*; the entire construction was dedicated to the defenders of the Union in the Civil War. Of particular interest on the arch is the city's only sculpture by Thomas Eakins, better known as one of the country's leading realist painters and an early proponent of the art of photography. You'll find Eakins's work inside the arch: two bronze reliefs—one of Lincoln and one of Grant—each on horseback.

There are additional sculptures in and around Grand Army Plaza, including a recent bronze portrait head of John F. Kennedy by a Brooklyn sculptor, Neil Estern.

Adjacent to the Brooklyn Museum is one of New York's most beautiful open spaces, **Prospect Park**. Here you'll find a variety of sculptures at the various entrances and within the park itself. At the entrance to the Prospect Park Zoo is the bronze *Lioness and Cubs* (1899) by Victor Peter, a French sculptor. Another Daniel Chester French work, a Lafayette memorial, can be seen at the 9th Street entrance to the park. The 3rd Street entrance is flanked by a pair of heroic panthers by Alexander P. Proctor.

Frederick MacMonnies is well represented here by a statue, across from Grand Army Plaza, of James Stranahan (a founder of Prospect Park). Called *Horse Tamers* (1899), it stands on two pedestals designed by Stanford White, at the Park Circle entrance to the park; as well as the great arch mentioned earlier.

In the center of the park is a group of oddly chosen great composers' busts, including those of Edvard Grieg, Carl Maria Von Weber, Mozart, and Beethoven, by lesser-known sculptors. You'll find these sculptures in the Flower Garden, which also contains a bust of

Augustus Saint-Gaudens: Sherman Monument, Gand Army Plaza

Irish poet Thomas Moore (1879), by John G. Draddy (who also produced religious works for St. Patrick's Cathedral). Also near the Flower Garden is a World War I Memorial, including figures by Augustus Lukeman.

A major work is the *Bailey Fountain* (1932), north of the great arch. This elaborate creation includes a variety of nude bronze figures representing Triton, Neptune, Wisdom, and so on. It is by Eugene Savage, and its style has been described by some art historians as "grotesque."

The **subway station** at the Botanic Garden also has art to enjoy: *IL7/Square* (1999), by Millie Burns, which reflects the botanical theme at ground level.

Botanic Garden subway station
Franklin Avenue/Eastern Parkway (2 or 3 line)

QUEENS

27 A Neighborhood of Sculpture: Queens's "Left Bank" and Roosevelt Island

DIRECTIONS» **Noguchi Museum:** 9-01 33rd Road at the corner of Vernon Boulevard, Long Island City (718-204-7088; www.noguchi.org). Ⓗ Wednesday, Thursday, and Friday 10 AM–5 PM; Saturday and Sunday 11 AM–6 PM. (Closed Monday and Tuesday.) Admission fee. By subway, take the N or Q line to the Broadway stop in Queens. Walk 10 blocks west on Broadway to Bernon Boulevard; turn left and walk two blocks to 33rd Road. By car, take the Queensboro Bridge Upper Level. Exit at 21st Street. Turn right onto 21st Street and go north to Broadway. Turn left on Broadway. Broadway will dead-end at Vernon Boulevard. Turn left onto Vernon Boulevard. The museum will be two blocks farther on the left at 33rd Road. Note: There is a shuttle bus on Sundays from Manhattan, at the corner of Park Avenue and 70th Street (in front of the Asia Society).

» Socrates Park: 32-01 Vernon Boulevard at Broadway, Long Island City (718-956-1819; www.socratessculpturepark.org). Ⓗ Monday–Friday 10 AM–6 PM. (Same directions as above.) Free admission.

» Sculpture Center: 44-19 Purves Street, Long Island City (718-361-1750; www. sculpture-center.org). Ⓗ Thursday–Monday 11 AM–6 PM (Closed Tuesday and Wednesday). Suggested admission fee. By subway, take the E or M line to Court Square—23rd Street, or the 7 or G line to Court Square. By car, from Manhattan, take the Queensboro Bridge (Upper Level) and follow the signs for Jackson Avenue. At the light, turn right onto Thomson Avenue. Turn right on 44th Drive and right on Jackson Avenue. Take the first right onto Purves Street. The Sculpture Center is halfway down on the left side.

» FDR Four Freedoms Park: Roosevelt Island (www.fdrfourfreedomspark.org). Ⓗ Tuesday–Sunday, 9 AM–5 PM. Free admission.

» By subway, from Manhattan take the Queens-bound F line to the Roosevelt Island stop. Walk (about 15 minutes) south to the park. By tram, take the tramway car at 59th Street and Second Avenue. Exit at Roosevelt Island. Walk south to the park.

» By car, take the Queensboro Bridge (Upper Level) to 21st Street; take a right onto 21st Street and a left at 36th Avenue across Roosevelt Island Bridge. Turn left onto Main Street and left onto East Road. (Note: There is no parking at Four Freedoms Park and limited parking on Roosevelt Island. There is limited parking on East and West Roads.)

Anyone with an interest in sculpture should make an effort to visit this riverside area of Long Island City, Queens—very close to Manhattan—and filled with terrific sculpture. You might think this is an unlikely site for art, as it is a warehouse and industrial neighborhood, just off the 59th Street Bridge. But these large spaces and almost hidden treasures make this an unusually rewarding experience. There are four sculptural spots of interest in fairly close proximity to one another. Each brings a different aspect of sculpture and art history to us in unexpected ways.

Our first stop is the Isamu Noguchi Museum, dedicated to one of the 20th century's sculpture icons. Not far away is Socrates Sculpture Park, one of the city's major sites of today's art; it is a vast area just opposite Manhattan's skyline across the East River, featuring the latest works of contemporary sculpture. (Some of it is still being worked on as you visit.) Relocated to the area is the National Sculpture Center, which is also dedicated to today's art. And on nearby Roosevelt Island is the FDR Center for Four Freedoms, opened in 2012, an environmental and sculptural tribute to Franklin Delano Roosevelt.

We begin with the very elegant **Noguchi Museum**. Located in a nondescript cinderblock corner building at 9-01 33rd Road, it is a surprise from the moment you enter its luminous rooms. This is a setting of calm and contemplation that both celebrates Noguchi's life and work, and creates an ambience unlike that of any museum we have visited. Noguchi's stone sculptures are almost all abstract, and they sit in an appropriately abstract setting that adds to the tranquility and almost Zen-like atmosphere. (The surprisingly disguised museum seems to be one more warehouse in the neighborhood, but this just adds to the mysterious environment.) Noguchi believed that art should relate to its environment. "These are private

Noguchi Museum
9-01 33rd Road
at the corner of
Vernon Boulevard
Long Island City
718-204-7088
www.noguchi.org

sculptures," he said, "a dialogue between myself and the primary matter of the universe."

The museum owns some 350 works by Noguchi, as well as tools, his worktable, and maquettes. You can even see him at work on film. And there is the beautiful sculpture garden to walk through (or on a rainy day, view through the glass walls next to it). Here in a traditional Japanese garden you'll experience Noguchi's abstract sculptures, suggesting the most delicate of Asian gardens.

But Noguchi was indeed a 20th-century artist with a contemporary vision that melded the Eastern tradition with modernism. Searching for abstract realities, which he called "the brilliance of matter," he aimed to turn "stone into the music of the spheres." And in these light-filled, spacious white rooms, that's exactly what you sense as you walk among the sparsely arranged stone forms he created. They are characterized by subtle variations in tone (mostly grays and tans), in form (anthropomorphic and suggestive of nature), in size (some huge, others small), in texture (gradation of rough and polished), and in their great appreciation of the relationship between forms. It is these carefully conceived contrasts that make every work fascinating. The rough stone pillars, the round basalt mounds, the delicate carved marble, even the white paper lamps all show the artist's preoccupation with pure form and its relationship to its surroundings.

Several exhibits relate Noguchi to his fellow artists. Among them are Constantin Brancusi, with whom he worked in Paris as a young man; architect Louis Kahn, whose plans with Noguchi for a park in Manhattan can be seen in maquette form; and Martha Graham, for whom he designed dance sets. (Be sure to visit the second floor for a taste of these collaborations.)

A visit to this museum—even if you have little appreciation for abstract sculpture—is bound to change the way you look at stone. It will also show you how seemingly simple forms can create a sense of spirituality in Noguchi's hands.

Our next site could not be more different from the Noguchi Museum. Just a few blocks away—but a world apart—is the **Socrates Sculpture Park**. In this weedy, unmanicured 4.5-acre field at 32-01 Vernon Boulevard, you'll find the latest contemporary sculpture—much of it large, bold, exuberant, joyful, freewheeling, and original—some of it quite fascinating, some down-

Socrates Park
32-01 Vernon Boulevard
at Broadway
Long Island City
718-956-1819
www.socrates
sculpturepark.org

right unappealing. These odd combinations make a visit here all the more amusing. You are free to wander at will through these giant forms that are here on temporary display, amid rough-hewn constructions in the most imaginative of shapes. And all around you are spectacular river views.

This one-of-a-kind sculpture park was the creation of Mark di Suvero, who named it to honor the philosopher as well as the nearby Greek-American community of Astoria. Built in the 1980s on the site of an empty lot filled with rubble, it was dedicated to exhibiting large-scale outdoor woks chosen for their originality and vision, rather than the fame of the artist (in fact, most of the works here are by lesser-known artists). From the beginning, the surrounding community was invited to participate in the park's activities, and over the years it has helped run the park, offering the services of volunteers to aid in its upkeep and maintenance; on occasion local would-be artists have added their own works to the mix and neighbors have even assisted to set up shows. In short, the park has become an integral part of the community's daily life. Unlike most other outdoor sculpture parks, here you can touch any and all of the sculptures (much to the delight of kids!) and are free to roam about, perhaps watching artists busy at work nailing down giant constructions or handling huge steel parts. There is energy in the air here and a wonderful sense of possibility and freedom.

The exhibits at Socrates change once or twice a year, each lasting for several months. Since the 1986 inaugural show (in which di Suvero was among the contributing sculptors), such artists as Robert Stackhouse, Cristos Gianakos, Jody Pinto, and Alison Saar have shown their work here. Recent shows have included Malcolm Cochran's *Scrapyard Temple for Socrates*, whimsical granite pillars surrounded by colorful coffee tins with their labels; and *Folly*, by Jerome W. Haferd and K. Brandt Knapp, which consisted of fanciful structures with no particular use ("follies"), representing the intersection between architecture, design, and sculpture. If you like a lively party, be sure to attend one of the park's exhibition openings, where you may see performances by local actors, musicians, or dancers doing their thing in and around the sculptures.

And now, on to the **Sculpture Center**. Also located in Long Island City, at 44-19 Purves Street, this not-to-be-missed art site is situated in a fascinating in-

Sculpture Center
44-19 Purves Street
Long Island City
718-361-1750
www. sculpture
-center.org

dustrial space, once a trolley shop, renovated in 2002 by the renowned Maya Lin and David Hotson. Its vast space (some 6,000 square feet with 40-foot ceilings, and an enclosed sculpture yard) is ideal for exhibiting unusual and sometimes even cutting-edge works by emerging as well as established artists, both national and international. The center, founded in 1928 by artists, has presented many solo and group shows over the years, with such (now known) sculptors as Ursula von Rydingsvard, Monica Bonvicini, Ugo Rondinone, and Jeppe Hein. Recently show have included *A Disagreeable Object* (the title comes from Giacometti's surrealistic work), a group show that explored such contrasting themes as the familiar/unfamiliar and desire/repulsion; *Retainer* by Nairy Baghramian, in which most of the center's space was made to look like a giant corrective prosthesis (addressing art's dependency on its own context); and *Double Lift*, in which works of art were restaged, as an expression of a performance-based approach to sculpture.

FDR Four Freedoms Park
Roosevelt Island
www.fdrfourfreedoms park.org

Our last stop is nearby Roosevelt Island, a place not usually known for its art. But here, on the southern tip of the island, is a magnificent brand-new art site, inaugurated in the fall of 2012: Louis Kahn's **FDR Four Freedoms Park**. (The term *four freedoms* refers to a speech the president made in 1941, as he hoped for a better world.) This 4-acre memorial features a masterful design by the noted architect Kahn—his only work in New York City—and a 1933 bronze statue of Roosevelt by Jo Davidson, a highly regarded portraitist who sculpted other illustrious people, such as Albert Einstein, Helen Keller, Charlie Chaplin, Gertrude Stein, and Charles Lindbergh.

Designed by Kahn in 1971, this remarkable monument to a beloved president was never built (Kahn died very suddenly, soon after completing his drawing for the park, then the city experienced financial meltdown). While properly solemn and austere in its simple, uncluttered, and abstract geometric lines, this is an inspiring, uplifting work, beautifully situated overlooking the Statue of Liberty and the ocean beyond (appropriate in terms of Roosevelt's worldview). A giant (100-foot-wide) staircase leads to a small stretch of lawn and allée of linden trees (actually specified by Kahn himself) and tree-lined pathways. Beyond is a grand, open, granite enclosure, a roofless room with extended vistas and the impressive bust of FDR. This is a quiet spot that invites reflection, as you savor the site and its rare panoramic views. The nearby ruin of a 19th-century hospital lends an added tone of sobriety to this remarkable spot.

AND IN ADDITION . . .

MOMA PS 1 Contemporary Art Center, 22-25 Jackson Avenue at the intersection of 46th Avenue (718-784-2084; www.psl.org). ⊕ Thursday–Monday noon–6 PM. Suggested admission fee. This alternative space par excellence is housed in a large, brick, 19th-century building that was once a school. Since its renovation in 1976, it has included working studios, as well as galleries for innovative and unusual exhibits and some permanent installations. The 30 or so artists chosen to be in residence come from all over the world and usually stay for about a year. You can take a tour of the studios to see the artists at work and visit the first floor's eight galleries, where exhibitions change about every two months. The permanent displays include James Turrell's *Meeting* (1980–86), which can be seen daily (except in bad weather) immediately before, during, and after sunset; Alan Saret's *The Hole at P.S.1, Fifth Solar Chthonic Wall Temple* (1976); and Richard Serra's *Untitled* (1976).

Recent shows include *Kraftwerk*, an eight-channel video and sound installation, and *Now Dig This! Art and Black Los Angeles 1960–1980*. There are also many other events, such as studio visit, site-specific installations, and a schedule of musical and performance programming. If contemporary art is of special interest to you, don't miss this visit, which the institution describes as "a true artistic laboratory."

The **American Museum of the Moving Image**, 36-01 35th Avenue, Astoria (718-784-0077; www.movingimage.us). ⊕ Wednesday and Thursday 10:30 AM–5 PM, Friday 10:30 AM–8 PM, Saturday and Sunday 11:30 AM–7 PM. (Closed Monday and Tuesday.) Admission fee. Amid the movies, television, and video memorabilia and technology are works of non-electric art: a large, jolly pseudo-Egyptian Red Grooms installation called *Tut's Fever* (1986–88), and a delightful five-piece jazz band carved of wood and found objects that served as a prop for a 1977 movie. (This is a must-visit for kids of all ages.)

QUEENS

MOMA PS 1 Contemporary Art Center
22-25 Jackson Avenue at 46th Avenue
Long Island City
718-784-2084
www.ps1.org

American Museum of the Moving Image
36-01 35th Avenue
Astoria
718-784-0077
www.movingimage.us

**Fisher Landau
Center for Art**
38-27 30th Street
Long Island City
718-937-0727
www.flcart.org

The **Fisher Landau Center for Art**, 38-27 30th Street, Long Island City (718-937-0727; www.flcart.org). ⓗ Thursday–Monday noon–5 PM. Free admission. Not far from the Queensboro Bridge is a little known exhibition space that houses more than 1,000 paintings—only some on view at any given time. In this elegant yet stark, white and gray, three-floor gallery you can see an impressive collection of contemporary art from the 1960s to the present. Such masters as Andy Warhol, Willem de Kooning, Robert Rauschenberg, James Rosenquist, Ellsworth Kelly, Cy Twombly, Kiki Smith, and Jasper Johns are represented, as well as lesser-known artists. Exhibits change every six months, drawing from the center's vast collection kept in storage below. Once a parachute-harness factory (most new art spaces in Long Island City have been converted from industrial sites), the gallery has been in operation since 1991. It began as a repository for the private collection of Emily Fisher Landau (you can see her portrait by Warhol, in the lobby), a philanthropist in the New York art world. For many years, visitors were only allowed by appointment, but since 2003 the doors have opened to the general public. This once well-kept secret may not be so much longer!

BRONX

28 Art Finds in the Bronx: Wave Hill, the Bronx Museum of the Arts, and Lehman College

DIRECTIONS» Wave Hill: By bus, take the BX10 or BX7 bus to 252nd Street; walk for about 10 minutes.

» Bronx Museum of the Arts: By subway, take the B, D, or 4 line to 161st Street–Yankee Stadium.

» Lehman College: By subway, take the B, D, or 4 line to Bedford Park Boulevard, then walk (three minutes) to the campus. By car from Manhattan, take the Henry Hudson Parkway north to the Mosholu Parkway exit; at the second traffic light after the exit, turn right onto Paul Avenue; then turn right onto Bedford Park Boulevard, then left onto Goulden Avenue. The parking lots are on your right.

In this large and varied borough, we have selected our favorite art sites that are comparatively near one another, and can be visited on the same trip.

Wave Hill, 675 West 252 Street (718-549-3200; www.wavehill.org), is one of New York City's lesser-known gems. **H** March 15–October 31, Tuesday–Sunday 9 AM–5:30 PM; November 1–March 14, Tuesday–Sunday 9 AM–4:30 PM. (Closed Monday.) Admission fee.

Wave Hill
675 West 252 Street
718-549-3200
www.wavehill.org

There are not many Hudson River estates left in our city, but fortunately for art and nature lovers alike, Wave Hill is both beautifully kept and open to the public. This is that rare combination: a botanical garden and environmental center, as well as an active art center. So whether you simply want to visit a magnificent estate with manor houses and a conservatory high above the river in a landscape filled with great trees and elegant plantings, or are seeking an art site with gallery and environmental sculpture—this is the perfect spot for an outing. Its 28 acres form a parklike setting; you feel as if you are miles from the hustle of the city.

In fact, Wave Hill has long been just such a getaway for prominent New Yorkers. From the time the first of its two houses was built in 1848 by the jurist William Lewis Morris, it was occupied by illustrious people who often entertained members of New York society. As a boy, Teddy Roosevelt spent a summer here with his family, where it is said he learned to appreciate nature—birds in particular. William Makepeace Thackeray

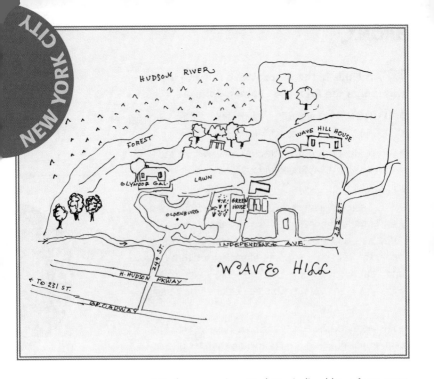

visited on occasion; Mark Twain lived here from 1901 to 1903 (and even built a tree house on the grounds); and Arturo Toscanini occupied the house from 1942 to 1945. In the 1950s it was home to the head of the British delegation to the United Nations, and visitors included the Queen Mother, Anthony Eden, Harold Macmillan, and Konrad Adenauer. Fortunately for all of use, Wave Hill was preserved through the years, even enhanced with formal and naturalistic landscaping. As recently as the 1980s, a financier named George Perkins (notable for his conservation efforts, and for organizing the Palisades State Park) expanded the estate. It was he who added greenhouses, pergolas (note the marvelous view of the Palisades from the pergola facing the Hudson), terraces, rare trees, and an English-style garden.

In 1960, the estate was deeded to the city, and now, known as the Wave Hill Center for Environmental Studies, provides all kinds of events, classes, exhibitions, lectures, crafts workshops, concerts, and so on. This is a very active place, but as you walk around it, you will feel peaceful and enjoy its artistic ambience.

Much of the art that you see as you wander through the grounds, is temporary. (Two sculptures are on long-term loan: Claes Oldenburg's *Standing Mitt with Ball* (1973), a steel and lead baseball mitt with a wooden ball), and Robert Irwin's *Wave Hill Wood* (1987), a group of ceremonial steel monkeys.) Other sculptures are dotted throughout the estate, across a field, along a wooded trail, and each piece has been carefully placed to harmonize with its natural surroundings.

There are two indoor galleries (one in each of the two manor houses). Wave Hill House, the 19th-century fieldstone building with white shutters and walls covered with ivy, has several rooms devoted to art. A recent exhibition featured bold black-and-white drawings of plant life by Mike Glier. While you are in Wave Hill House, pick up a map and all kinds of material relative to upcoming events.

The other indoor art site is called Glyndor Gallery. It is in the red brick Georgian Revival–style house (1920s). **🕐** Tuesday–Sunday, 10 AM–4:30 PM, year-round. (Closed Monday.) In these bright and airy white rooms, you'll find all kinds of shows; we recently saw contemporary sculpture by Jene Highstein.

We recommend visiting Wave Hill in growing season for a full experience of the gardens, and on a weekday, if possible, as it is often filled with visitors on weekends.

Bronx Museum of the Arts, 1040 Grand Concourse at 165th Street (718-681-6000; www.bronxmuseum.org). **🕐** Thursday, Saturday, and Sunday 11 AM–6 PM; Friday 11 AM–8 PM. Free admission. Changing exhibitions of modern painting, photography, and sculpture, as well as community art shows can be seen here and at satellite galleries throughout the Bronx.

This museum specializes in contemporary artists of Asian, Latin American, and African descent. Their shows, which tend to combine socio-political with aesthetic issues, have recently included *One Planet Under a Groove: Hip-Hop and Contemporary Art* and *Witness: Perspectives on Police Violence*, and works by pioneer video artist Juan Downey and street-level photography by Jamel Shabazz, a Harlem-based artist.

The 37-acre campus of **Lehman College**, 250 Bedford Park Boulevard (www.lehman.edu/gallery), is an unusually interesting place to visit, with both art and architecture of note. **🕐** Tuesday–Saturday 10 AM–4 PM year-round. (Closed Sunday and Monday.) We found the art gallery in the Fine Arts Building (designed by Marcel Breuer) in the center of the

Bronx Museum of the Arts
1040 Grand Concourse at 165th Street
718-681-6000
www.bronxmuseum.org

Lehman College
250 Bedford Park Boulevard
www.lehman.edu/gallery

campus to have a strikingly contemporary and interesting exhibit (*Sticks and Stones*, a show of various artists who work with nature). Be sure to notice this two-story clear glass building, with its unusual, undulating ceiling and wonderful light.

Next to it is a three-story, rectangular limestone building also by Marcel Breuer, called Shuster Hall. Note also the Apex Building (the gym) located on Bedford Boulevard. Designed by Rafael Viñoly, it features a spectacular roof—visible from within the campus—which resembles a giant wave.

In contrast, if you wander the campus, you'll see several Gothic Revival buildings dating to the mid-19th century.

AND IN ADDITION . . .

Bronx Central Post Office
558 Grand Concourse at 149th Street

On the walls inside the **Bronx Central Post Office**, 558 Grand Concourse at 149th Street, are a series of murals celebrating Americans at work, by Ben Shahn and his wife, Bernarda Bryson. Among the colorful scenes are those depicting farmers planting their fields and engineers surveying sites. One vignette depicts Walt Whitman speaking before a group of workers and their families, apparently discussing his poetry.

Romare Bearden,
City of Glass, 1993
Elevated subway station Westchester Square–East Tremont Avenue stop, 6 line

In the Westchester Square–East Tremont Avenue **elevated IRT station** for the 6 line, there is a stained-glass triptych by the noted artist Romare Bearden. This 9 by 6-foot work, *City of Glass* (1993, from the artist's 1982 proposal), depicts a luminous city.

29 Woodlawn Cemetery: Artists' Graves, Elegant Statuary, and Historic Monuments in an Idyllic Setting

DIRECTIONS » By subway, take the 4 line or Metro North Harlem line (from Grand Central Station) to Woodlawn. By car, take the Cross Bronx Expressway to Jerome Avenue; the entrance is on your right, opposite Van Cortlandt Park. Alternatively, take the Major Deegan Expressway and take exit 13 at East 233rd Street to Jerome Avenue.

Woodlawn Cemetery, Webster Avenue and East 233rd Street (718-920-0500; www.thewoodlawncemetery.org), is open daily year round, 8:30 AM–5 PM (the office is closed on Sunday). Maps are available at entrance; visitors are welcome to walk or drive around the grounds or take a shuttle bus. Guided tours are offered for a fee.

Woodlawn Cemetery is a peaceful oasis surrounded by a vast urban landscape. In its unusually lovely setting with magnificent trees, shrubs, and flowers is a remarkable collection of artistic and historic mausoleums. Some 300,000 souls are buried here—among them many noted figures in politics, sports, science, industry, and the arts. Their graves range from simple stone markings to grandiose monuments with sculptures, Gothic arches, stained-glass windows, and myriad decorations. To stroll on winding shaded pathways through these vast grounds—about 400 acres of gently rolling terrain—is a rare treat for anyone, especially those who love history, art, architecture, gardens, or even birds (nearly 120 species have been spotted here).

Woodlawn Cemetery
Webster Avenue and East 233rd Street
718-920-0500
www.thewoodlawn cemetery.org

Woodlawn was founded in 1863 as a "rural cemetery," in the tradition of Green-Wood in Brooklyn (see chapter 24). Like other garden cemeteries, it was an inviting spot for leisurely walkers, before urban public parks came into being. The site chosen was within the beautifully wooded Bronx River Valley, which was not yet part of the city at the time but was easily accessible. It soon gained the reputation for being the final resting place of many prominent people, not only from America but from all around the world.

Since the cemetery now has a greater number of interesting graves than one can possibly see at any given time, we have limited our suggested itinerary to some sites of artistic and architectural importance, as well as to those where noted artists are buried. Our list is by no means comprehensive, and we hope you will make your own discoveries as you zigzag through this labyrinth, searching for the sites.

We recommend that you pick up a map from security, just inside the entrance gates, before starting off, to help you locate sites. You'll find the staff unusually helpful. So don't hesitate to ask for directions, should you get lost.

Begin by walking to the cemetery's Central Avenue, the wide street directly in front of you. Your first stop is the Gates Mausoleum, a classical Greek temple on the left corner. Here you will note an impressive bronze door with grieving figure (1914). This is the work of Robert Aitken, a leading American sculptor in the

representational style, known for his busts of famous Americans (Thomas Jefferson, Edgar Allan Poe, and Henry Clay, among others).

The impressive French-style Ehret Mausoleum is next, guarded by stone lions (1913). These creatures protecting George Ehret (a prosperous beer magnate) are by John Massey Rhind, an architectural sculptor who also made commemorative portraits of notable Americans.

Nearby is the Egyptian Revival–style Woolworth Mausoleum, a stark white structure featuring two sphinxes (1920). This tomb (where F. W. Woolworth and his granddaughter Barbara Hutton are buried) was designed by John Russell Pope, the architect of the Jefferson Memorial in Washington, DC; the statues are by the sculptor J. C. Loester.

Continue on Central Avenue, past Park Avenue, to the "Walnut" plots. On your right is the H. A. C. Taylor Mausoleum, designed in 1902 by McKim, Mead & White. This is one of eight tombs at Woodlawn by this historically important architectural firm.

Next to it are the Leeds Mausoleum, designed by John Russell Pope in 1910; and the Bliss Memorial, created by Robert Aitken in 1917, with figures carved by the Piccirilli Brothers (one of whom, Attilio Piccirilli, was a sculptor of monuments in his own right).

Cross Central Avenue to Oak Hill. Here you'll find the St. John Memorial (1916), whose single figure is by noted sculptor William Ordway Partridge. An important creator of commemorative statuary and monuments, Partridge is known for his images of Thomas Jefferson, Alexander Hamilton, Horace Greeley, General Grant (on his horse), Beethoven, and Tennyson, among others.

Just down the road is the Goelet Mausoleum, again by McKim, Mead & White; it once was more elaborate, with a gilded front by Edward Sanford. Nearby is the Clark Memorial, a grand neoclassical temple decorated with Ionic columns and bas-reliefs (1897) by Paul W. Bartlett. This imposing tomb is the final resting place of William A. Clark, a spectacularly wealthy US senator from Montana who, among his many real estate holdings, owned a lavish 130-room mansion on Manhattan's Fifth Avenue.

Cross Prospect Avenue to the "Hawthorn" plots. Here is the Kinsley Memorial, by the legendary sculptor Daniel Chester French, one of the most influential artists of his time. French, especially noted for his seated Abraham Lincoln at the Lincoln Memorial in Washington, DC, is well represented across the country, with his many noted war memorials and images of national leaders and allegorical figures. (In New York you can see several of his works, including the famous *Alma Mater* (1903) in front of Low Library at Columbia University.)

Find your way back to Central Avenue, and make a left at Lawn Avenue. In this section ("Lake View") is the imposing Jay Gould Mausoleum, where the infamous 19th-century financier is buried. Designed in 1884 by H. Q. French, the Greek-style temple with Ionic columns sits majestically on top of a hill, surrounded by enormous weeping beech trees.

Walking left again, following small circular paths, you'll come to the Whitney Family Monument, a polished black granite structure designed by Stanford White. This group of gravesites hidden beneath individual shrubs (a custom from the Near East) includes that of the remarkable Gertrude Vanderbilt Whitney. A sculptor/philanthropist/founder of the Whitney Museum all in one, she created many works that can be seen in various parts of the country, in France, and even right here in Woodlawn (see the Untermyer Memorial).

Nearby, across Observatory Avenue, is our next site, the Warner Mausoleum, by noted architect Cass Gilbert.

Return to Central Avenue and walk to the "Evergreen" plots. On your left will be the Pulitzer Memorial. Here lie the illustrious newspaperman Joseph Pulitzer and his family, in front of a simple white stone bench. A black bronze figure (1913) by William Ordway Partridge (the same sculptor who made the solitary figure in the St. John Memorial, see page 130) sits in contemplative mode.

Continue on Central Avenue; on your right, in the "Catalpa" section, is the gravesite of the illustrator James Montgomery Flagg. He is perhaps best known for having created the "Uncle Sam Wants You" poster used to recruit soldiers during the two world wars.

Our next stop is farther down Central Avenue and to the left, within the "Magnolia" area. Here you'll come to one of the grandest mausoleums in Woodlawn, the Huntington Memorial, an imposing temple of granite and marble, majestically situated above a

grand staircase. The enormous bronze door (1932) features bas-reliefs by Herbert Adams, known for his architectural figures, war memorials, and allegorical pieces. Here lie the railroad magnate/robber baron turned philanthropist Collis P. Huntington, his son Archer, and his daughter-in-law, the prominent sculptor Anna Hyatt Huntington, noted especially for her powerful animal and equestrian works. (One of her most dramatic groups dominates the courtyard in front of the Hispanic Society Museum, in Upper Manhattan. See page 43.) She also sculpted the Arabella Huntington Memorial (commemorating Collis's second wife), which is just to the left of the mausoleum; surprisingly, it is Anna who is buried here, not Arabella.

To reach the next stop, you have to take a slight detour, up Ravine Avenue (right) to the intersection with Whitewood Avenue. On your right you'll find the Memorial to Henry E. Russell (1893), yet another work by McKim, Mead & White. On your left, off Whitewood, is the aforementioned Untermyer Memorial, situated on a beautifully landscaped quarter-acre hillside plot. This garden memorial includes waterfalls, terraces, and a walk leading to the bronze monument (1925) by Gertrude Vanderbilt Whitney. The unusual monument has a middle section open on three sides, like windows with bronze shutters. Fortunately, these are left open so that one can see the three evocative figures inside: a woman with arms stretched upward, a male figure kneeling beside her, and a young woman turning away.

Continue on Whitewood Avenue, turn right at Heather Avenue, and proceed (again) to Central Avenue. On your left, within the "Myosotis" area, are several graves to note. The first is the Cronin Memorial (2002), called *Memorial to a Marriage*, a work by the sculptor Patricia Cronin. Nearby is the elegant Garvan Mausoleum (1930), another classical design by John Russell Pope. This beautiful temple includes columns and a frieze of mourners by the sculptor Edward Sanford. Here lies Francis P. Garvan, a prominent chemist/entrepreneur who helped establish the modern American chemical industry.

The Piccirilli Memorial comes next. Designed by the most prominent of the six Piccirilli brothers, Attilio Piccirilli, this bronze image of a mother and child, called *Fortitude* (1913), is a tribute to the family matriarch buried here. Another of his sculptures on the same site is named *The Outcast* (1915). The Piccirilli brothers were noted stone carvers who operated their family sculpture studio right here in the Bronx. They carved stone decorations and sculptures on many public buildings, private mansions, and monuments in the city. Although some of the work was their own design, they also realized the designs of such prominent sculptors as Augustus Saint-Gaudens and Frederick MacMonnies.

Nearby, the Straus Family Mausoleum, designed by the architect James Gamble Rogers in 1928, includes a funeral barge, commemorating the deaths of Isador and Ida Straus. The couple perished together on the *Titanic*'s fateful journey.

Another longish detour takes you to our next site. Follow Myosotis Avenue and turn left at Alpine Avenue. Within this section is the modest stone grave of the artist Walt Kuhn, prettily set amid evergreens. Kuhn helped organize the explosive 1913 International Exhibition of Modern Art in New York, which featured works by the French modernists—and to which he personally escorted President Teddy Roosevelt.

Find Alpine Avenue again and turn right onto Park Avenue. Here, in the "Oakwood" section, you'll come to the Archipenko Memorial, where both the seminal cubist sculptor Alexander Archipenko and his wife, Angelica Bruno-Schmitz—a noted sculptor in her own right—are buried. The work of Archipenko, a leading figure in the history of early modern sculpture, is not represented at this site. Having outlived his wife, he decided to place a sculpture of hers, an abstract seated figure, at their common gravesite. (You can see a work by the great master himself later on this tour.)

You are now heading back to the main entrance, to see two not-to-be-missed mausoleums. The first, on the corner of Tulip and Whitewood Avenues, is the Bache Memorial, a very grand tomb, fit for a king—or, in this case, a pharaoh. In fact, Jules Bache, a prosperous stockbroker/art collector fascinated with world art, demanded that his architect, John Russell Pope, pattern his final resting place on ancient architecture. The result is a large rectangular temple with great columns carved in papyrus motifs and other symbolic decorations. (There are a few other Egyptian-style mausoleums at Woodlawn, though not on as grand a scale.)

The nearby Belmont Mausoleum, off West Borden Avenue, is perhaps the most magnificent of all at

Woodlawn. And, no wonder: it is an authentic replica of the Chapel of St. Hubert at the Château d'Amboise in the Loire Valley, originally designed by none other than Leonardo da Vinci! Oliver Hazard Perry Belmont (grandson of Commodore Perry and a banker who developed Belmont Raceway) and his wife, Alva Belmont (a socialite, once married to William Vanderbilt, and later a suffragette) are buried here. Built by the sons of the famous architect Richard Morris Hunt, this is an elegant structure with exquisite stone spires and carvings depicting the life of Saint Hubert, patron saint of hunting.

The nearby Borden Lot, off Fairview Avenue, is a nod to antiquity: This Roman sarcophagus on a pink marble plaza is an example of the work of architects Carrière & Hastings.

You are now near the entrance (and main office), having made quite a circle. If you're still feeling energetic, you can always check out further sites. Following are a few recommendations, among the many worth seeing.

In the "Park View" section (off Parkview Avenue) look for the grandiose Harbeck Mausoleum, an unexpected grave that includes its own pipe organ. The structure, designed in 1918 by Theodore Blake from the firm of Carrière & Hastings, is richly decorated with Biblical scenes.

The Hudnut Memorial, commemorating perfume manufacturer Richard Hudnut, is by sculptor Alexander Zeitlin.

The graceful Irene and Vernon Castle Memorial commemorates this famous early 20th-century dance team with an evocative sculpture by Sally Farnham, a protégé of Frederic Remington. Although mostly known for her images of western themes and horses, the artist here depicts a dancer, tired after a long day. *The End of the Day* also includes a graceful group of columns surrounding the seated figure.

Take Hickory Avenue to Filbert Avenue, to the Mori Memorial, in the "Clover" section. The figure in this 1927 memorial (designed by Raymond Hood) is the work of the illustrious sculptor Charles Keck. A student of both Philip Martiny and Augustus Saint-Gaudens (with whom he later collaborated), Keck is especially known for his commemorative portraits of Lincoln, among other notable Americans.

The Joseph Stella Mausoleum, off West Border

Avenue, commemorates the Italian-born artist who painted skyscrapers, bridges (his image of the Brooklyn Bridge has become an American icon), and other New York scenes.

From West Border Avenue, take Filbert Avenue, then Hickory Avenue, to the "Goldenrod" area. The two sites not to miss here are the Harkness Mausoleum and the Romney Memorial. The Harkness gravesite is one of our favorite spots in the cemetery. This unusually lovely setting includes a little stone chapel (designed by the architect James Gamble Rogers) and—of special interest to garden lovers—an intimate walled garden designed by the formidable landscape architect Beatrix Jones Ferrand. You will want to linger at this inviting place! Nearby is the Romney Memorial, which features a big bronze pot (1946) by Archipenko.

Walk along Filbert Avenue and turn right at North Border. In the "Rose Hill" section, on your right, you'll see the grave of Josef Stransky, a composer who conducted the New York Philharmonic from 1911 to 1923. What distinguishes this plot is that the gravestone is another work of Attilio Piccirilli's, from 1942. Continue on North Border and turn right on Birch Avenue; look for the marker on your right. The influential 19th-century illustrator and cartoonist Thomas Nast created popular Santa Claus images, the donkey and elephant symbols for our two political parties, and many other political cartoons. His tomb is one of the most modest to be found at Woodlawn, with only a simple (if rueful) inscription.

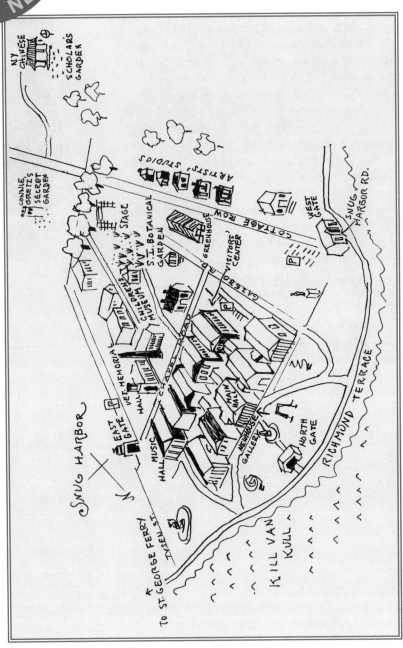

STATEN ISLAND

30 **Surprising Staten Island: Snug Harbor's Chinese Garden, Contemporary Art, and Nearby Art Sites**

DIRECTIONS» Staten Island is easily reached by public transportation, but you will need a car if you want to see in one day the many additional sites listed here. Snug Harbor is located on the north shore of the island, conveniently only 2 miles from the Staten Island Ferry terminal. The Snug Harbor trolley or the S40 bus will get you there. From Manhattan, the best route is by ferry (by subway, take the 1, N, or R line to South Ferry–Whitehall Street and follow the signs) and bus. From Brooklyn, Queens, or Long Island, you should drive via the Verrazano-Narrows Bridge (take Bay Street with the harbor on your right, until you find yourself on Richmond Terrace at the ferry terminal; Snug Harbor is on your left, after 2 miles). From New Jersey, take the Staten Island Expressway (I-278) to the Clove Road/Hyland Boulevard exit; at the traffic light, turn left at Clove Road, right at Richmond Terrace, and right at Snug Harbor. For specific auto routes, call 718-448-2500.

Whether art or gardens or architecture is your great interest, this spot will surely satisfy; **Snug Harbor** is a rare part of New York City. From its landmark buildings to its one-of-a-kind Chinese garden to its contemporary art, Snug Harbor is an unusual and harmonious place to visit. On the north shore of Staten Island, it was originally founded in 1801 as a hospital for retired sailors, and some of the old buildings date as far back as 1831. The elegant New York Chinese Scholar's Garden, on the other hand, was designed quite recently. Snug Harbor's grounds—some 80 acres—with additional gardens, a conservatory, and occasional outdoor exhibitions, are great for walking around. Inside the building complex you'll discover art shows and events. This is a particularly fine place to take visitors from out of town, as well as children (there's even a children's museum). One of the most surprising aspects of Snug Harbor is its sense of being totally removed from the bustle of Manhattan. Here, after a brief trip, you are in a pastoral, quite Victorian setting, an informal and inviting place to enjoy a day away. (Some city attractions,

Snug Harbor
1000 Richmond Terrace
718-448-2500
www.snug-harbor.org

such as the Metropolitan Opera, do occasionally come for a concert or play.)

You enter a main gate; begin your tour by picking up a map at the Visitor Center to decide what to see first.

As you leave the building, map in hand, note Chapel Street directly in front of you. Its small row of Victorian cottages once housed the farmer, gardener, baker, and so on. who helped keep the place running; some of the houses now have visiting artists living in them.

Opposite these little houses are the conservatory and some charming flower gardens. The Staten Island Botanical Garden, which opened in 1975, incorporates some delightful small gardens, including a butterfly garden, culinary paintings, a "white" garden, an herb garden, and a medicinal garden, among other specialties. Inside is the spectacular Neil Vanderbilt Orchid Collection. (Needless to say, the gardens are visited in the growing seasons.)

Not far away, see Charles Locke Eastlake's pagoda in the Chinese style—surrounded by flowers (a rather Victorian touch).

Staten Island Children's Museum
1000 Richmond Terrace
718-273-2060
www.statenislandkids.org

To your left is the **Staten Island Children's Museum**, 1000 Richmond Terrace (718-273-2060, www.statenislandkids.org), which has appealing displays, workshops, and events for the family.

If you continue along the same route (Cottage Row) you'll come to an outdoor setting for concerts and major events, and then to the Connie Gretz Secret Garden. To get there you actually cross a moat, go through a castlelike structure and find your way through a half-acre maze of hedges and pathways. The garden itself is a wonderful walled "secret garden" (perhaps reminiscent of a novel by that name). Don't miss that part of your tour.

New York Chinese Scholar's Garden
Snug Harbor

But our favorite garden spot is just off Cottage Row to your right. Worth a trip by itself, the **Chinese Scholar's Garden** is an exquisite evocation of an ancient aesthetic and philosophical tradition. **H** November 1–March 31 10:00 am–4:00 pm. April 1–October 31 10:00 am–5:00 pm. Closed Mondays. Admission fee. Modeled after a Ming Dynasty (1368–1644) scholar's garden, this 1-acre garden is the only one of its kind in the United States. It was designed by a noted Chinese landscape architect, and created by some 100 artisans working in China, and more than 40 here. They made pavilions, a teahouse, lotus ponds, waterfalls, rock foundations, and courtyards. The overall design (reminiscent of the famous Garden for Lingering in Suzhou, China) of this landscape invites strolling in enclosed spaces (as did scholar's gardens of the past.) Among the intricate carvings and designs are elegant calligraphy and sculpted stones, mosaics, pruned trees, bamboos and pines that reminded us of Chinese scroll paintings, and wonderful tracery windows. Completely separated from the outside world, you get a sense of the Taoist tradition as you contemplate earth and sky, light and dark—all visible in an exquisite setting. Among the gardens of note are Dwelling on Poetic Pleasure, the Hall for Listening to Pine, and the Chamber to Rest Head over Glowing Waters, or the Meandering Cloud Wall.

When you leave the garden, turn toward the building complex. Begin your tour by noting the architecture; some of these pale cream, charming buildings are in the Greek Revival style and were elegantly renovated.

The **Veterans' Memorial Hall** is the major venue for events; it also has a Music Lab, the Atelier Gallery, the Great Hall, and a profusion of sites, events, and lots of exhibitions. While there are Victorian-era (1884) murals with Italianate motifs in the Main Hall, most of the art is not permanent, so as you enter, discover for yourself what exhibitions and performances are scheduled.

Make a point of visiting the **Newhouse Center for Contemporary Art** in the Main Hall. This is the principal art site of Staten Island, and is an important center for contemporary shows. Recent exhibitions have included sculpture by Steven Foust and art by Gillian Jagger.

If you are interested in maritime and historical art, visit the **Noble Maritime Collection**, a permanent home for material about Snug Harbor and its history.

AND IN ADDITION . . .

Historic Richmond Town, 441 Clarke Avenue (718-351-1611; www.historicrichmondtown.org), is New York City's only historic village restoration. ⓗ Wednesday–Sunday 1 PM–5 PM. (Closed Monday and Tuesday.) Admission fee; free admission on Friday. It sits on the Greenbelt area of the island and can be reached by bus or car from Snug Harbor. It consists of 26 buildings that have been restored; 11 of them can be vis-

STATEN ISLAND

Newhouse Center for Contemporary Art
Enter through Visitor Center, Building C
Snug Harbor

Noble Maritime Collection
1000 Richmond Terrace, Building D
Snug Harbor

Historic Richmond Town
441 Clarke Avenue
718-351-1611
www.historicrichmond town.org

139

ited inside. They represent various historical periods of New York's past, ranging from the 17th through the 19th centuries. Among the attractions are the oldest standing schoolhouse in America, a general store, exhibitions of crafts and restoration techniques, and a historical museum. While there is little art visible as such, the atmosphere is pleasantly historic, and there are many interiors with genuine artifacts and decorations of the past. This is probably a place best enjoyed by families with children.

Overlooking the Port of New York in a particularly fine location is the **Alice Austen House**, Clear Comfort, 2 Hylan Boulevard, Rosebank (718-390-5100; www.aliceausten.org), a historic site that also houses an exhibition of works by the pioneer documentary photographer Alice Austen. **H** March–December, Tuesday–Sunday 11 AM–5 PM. (Closed Monday.) Suggested admission fee. This Victorian house, set in a nice green garden with a view of the Statue of Liberty, is the only museum in the country that commemorates a single photographer's life and pictures.

In the most unlikely setting imaginable—on a suburban Staten Island street—you'll find the **Jacques Marchais Museum of Tibetan Art**, 338 Lighthouse Avenue, Richmond (718-987-3500). **H** Wednesday–Sunday 1 PM–5 PM. (Closed Monday and Tuesday.) Admission fee. This is one of the largest private collections of Tibetan art in the country. The center includes a small garden in Tibetan style, artifacts, musical instruments, and many, many works of art—all housed in two stone buildings built to resemble a Tibetan monastery. Works from other Asian countries are also exhibited in the chock-full, rather small buildings.

Borough Hall, 10 Richmond Terrace, St. George (718-816-2000), has 13 murals by Frederick Stahr, depicting Staten Island's history; they were created under the WPA art projects in 1940.

The **College of Staten Island**, a branch of City University, has a campus at 2800 Victory Boulevard, which it is endowing with art both indoors and out. Visitors can enjoy a good-size collection of sculpture in the large grassy areas between buildings and in the Wooded Park, as well as a number of artworks in various media indoors in the Center of the Arts and other buildings. For a complete listing of this growing collection and information on how and when to see it, you

Alice Austen House
2 Hylan Boulevard
Rosebank
718-390-5100
www.aliceausten.org

Jacques Marchais Museum of Tibetan Art
338 Lighthouse Avenue
Richmond
718-987-3500
www.tibetanmuseum.org

Borough Hall
10 Richmond Terrace
St. George
718-816-2000

College of Staten Island
2800 Victory Boulevard
718-982-2364 or
718-982-2328
www.csi.cuny.edu

can telephone the Public Relations office of the college at 718-982-2364 or 718-982-2328.

Among these works are a wood and granite boulder, *Ark* (1995) by Daniel Wurtzel, on the Great Lawn, and a steel-wire cone called *Red Inside*, by Niki Ketchman, both in the Wooded Park. A fiberglass relief by Red Grooms is in the Sports Center. In the Center for the Arts are silkscreens and lithographs by George Segal, Jean Dubuffet, Robert Rauschenberg, Helen Frankenthaler, and Edouard Manet, among others. (Some artworks are hung in the Mezzanine Lounge, and others are in the Gallery itself.)

Visit the North Shore Esplanade at St. George's Ferry Terminal, where Siah Armajani's **Lighthouse and Bridge on Staten Island** is a not-to-be-missed art experience. With this 1996 work, Armajani—one of today's leading sculptors of public art—has added real panache to the area. Consisting of a 65-foot bridge and a 65-foot-tall tower topped with gold glass in a lighthouse vein, the structure is made of gray wood and steel, with splashes of yellow, orange, and green reminiscent of the sun's rays.

From this site you can enjoy spectacular vistas as you walk from the terminal to the plaza still undergoing development. Now somewhat solitary, the esplanade is expected to house art fairs and farmers' markets in the future.

Siah Armajani:
Lighthouse and Bridge on Staten Island, 1996
North Shore Esplanade at St. George's Ferry Terminal

STATEN ISLAND

SUBWAY ART

31 Art Underground: Discovering a Colorful World in the Subways

Everyone knows that New York City has a vast and impressive subway system with dozens of stations, and a network of different trains. What many people do not realize, however, is that a great many of these stations have first-rate art in them. Ranging from tile work to murals, mosaics to sculpture, steel constructions to glasswork—these works of art are both a surprise and a delight.

In 1985, the Arts for Transit program began. Its aim was to decorate gloomy, underground stations and passageways with fine art. They have succeeded beyond expectation; over 120 works have been commissioned, with many more to come.

Notable artists, including Faith Ringgold, Romare Bearden, Tom Otterness, Elizabeth Murray, Nancy Spero, Vito Acconci, Mary Miss, and Roy Lichtenstein, are among the leading artists whose work can be seen underground.

The questions of how to see these interesting pieces of art is perhaps to purchase a day pass to MTA system—available at any station—and to look at the groupings by borough and train line listed here to plot your route. You can also write for a free MTA booklet to Arts for Transit, 347 Madison Avenue, New York, NY 10017-3739; or call 212-878-7000.

MANHATTAN
Columbia University subway station at 116th Street (1 line): *Rail Riders' Throne*, a welded steel sculpture by Michelle Greene commissioned by the MTA in 1991.

Dyckman Street, 125th Street, 207th Street, 215th Street, Marble Hill–225th Street, and **231st Street** (1 line): three works by Wopo Holup, including reliefs, ceramic tiles, and murals.

Third Avenue/149th Street (2 line): José Ortega's *Una Raza, Un Mundo, Universo* (1996), a brilliant horizontal ceramic mosaic abstraction.

125th Street/Lenox Avenue (2 or 3 line): Faith Ringgold's *Flying Home: Harlem Heroes and Heroines* (1996), glass-mosaic murals with figures above familiar landmarks.

81st Street/American Museum of Natural History, at Central Park West (B or C line): *For Want of a Nail* (1999) is a mixed-media (ceramic tile, wall mosaic, granite, etc.) representation of many animals, extinct and otherwise, by a design team from the MTA. There are spirals, circles, time lines, and all sorts of natural history like that exhibited in the museum.

72nd Street/Broadway (1, 2, or 3 line): Nancy Spero's 22 brilliantly multicolored glass women in mosaic, called *Artemis, Acrobats, Divas, and Dancers* (2001), in keeping with the theme of performing arts.

Lexington Avenue/59th Street (4, 5, or 6; or N or R line): Elizabeth Murray's *Blooming* (1996; appropriately named, since Bloomingdale's department store is just above) is a 120-foot-wide mural of Italian mosaics depicting dramatic tree branches and swirling fantasies.

Fifth Avenue/59th Street (N or R line): *Urbane Oasis* (1997), by Ann Schaumberger, includes 17 glass-mosaic friezes and a granite-composite floor inspired by the flora and fauna of Central Park, with penguins!

57th Street/Seventh Avenue (N, Q, or R line): Josh Scharf's *Carnegie Hall Montage* (1994), in which the names of great performers (including Marian Anderson, Leonard Bernstein, and the Beatles) are inscribed on small, white porcelain tiles.

Fifth Avenue/53rd Street (E line): *53rd Street ArtStop* (2000) is a group of porcelain-enamel murals on the downtown-platform walls. These works were provided by several museums and cultural institutions in the area, including the Museum of Modern Art (MOMA), the Museum of Folk Art, the American Craft Museum, and the New York Public Library.

Times Square, mezzanine, between the S shuttle to Grand Central Terminal and the north entrance to the IRT 1, 2, 3, and 7 lines: Roy Lichtenstein's *Times Square Mural* (2002), a 6-foot-high, 53-foot-long panel depicting the history of New York transportation, in porcelain enamel on steel. Also, Jacob Lawrence's *New York in Transit* (2001), a richly colored mosaic mural that pictures subway riders and vignettes of city life, is located on the stairway wall between the N, Q, R, and S lines' mezzanine. At the Seventh Avenue and 41st Street entrance is Jack Beal's *The Return of Spring/The Onset of Winter* (2001/2005), a neo-Mannerist mosaic.

SUBWAY ART

Grand Central Station (4, 5, 6, 7, or S line): Terminal North: glass mosaic, patinated bronze, glass tiles, and glass reliefs by Ellen Driscoll, called *As Above, So Below* (1998). Cross passages: 45th Street (tracks 102, 107, 114–116), Native American and Australian works; 47th Street (tracks 12–15, 19, 32–37, 40–42), mythic images from Africa and Europe; northeast to 48th and Park Avenue, a series of Asian images from China, Tibet, India, and Nepal.

34th Street/Herald Square (B, D, F, N, Q, or R line): Works by many artists, including David Provan (kinetic aluminum sculpture), Nicholas Pearson (aluminum spheres), and Michele Oka Doner (bronze-colored tile art).

Penn Station (Long Island Railroad): Andrew Leicester's 1994 ceramic wall murals in terra cotta, *Ghosts*, in five separate locations, and his porcelain-enamel murals above the escalator; overhead at the Seventh Avenue end of the station is a Maya Lin clock, which uses sliding discs to evoke an eclipse.

33rd Street (6 line): James Garvey's *Lariat Seat Loops* (1997) are sinuous polished-bronze loops entwined around columns, forming seat rests for weary travelers.

23rd Street (N or R line): *Memories of Twenty-Third Street* (2002), delightful mosaics by Keith Godard, depict historical hats.

Union Square/14th Street (4, 5, or 6; or L, N, Q, or R line): Artist Mary Miss and architect Lee Harris Pomeroy have tackled three different subway stations that conjoin at this site, and they have managed to elucidate the various levels and eras with bright red enameled frames in 115 separate places; some have faceted mirrors showing the technical aspects of the subway's wiring and fixtures, while others show the concrete arches and architecture from these 1904, 1914, and 1930 stations.

14th Street/Eighth Avenue (A, C, E, or L line): Tom Otterness's *Life Underground* (2001) is easily recognized by his typically whimsical bronze animals.

Astor Place (6 line): Milton Glaser's *Untitled* (1986) is a porcelain-enamel mural, on station walls.

Broadway-Lafayette (6 [downtown only] or D or F line): Mel Chin's *Signal* (1997)is a stainless-steel and glass sculpture with electric light. Look at the mezzanine column bases and station walls.

Canal Street (A, C, or E line): Walter Martin and

Paloma Muñoz have created sculptured birds on railings and ledges and on a token booth, called *A Gathering* (2001).

City Hall/Brooklyn Bridge (4, 5, or 6 line): *Cable Crossing* (1996), by Mark Gibian, consists of spidery web of cables stretching across the ceiling of the station, reminiscent of the beautiful Brooklyn Bridge.

Fulton Center/Broadway/Fulton Street (2, 3, 4, 5, A, C, J, R, Z lines): *Sky Reflector-Net* by James Carpenter is a new installation. It is a curving, 79-foot-high net of reflective aluminum diamonds that rises above the station and sends sunlight down into it.

BROOKLYN

Prospect Park (B, Q, or S line): Susan Tunick's *Brighton Clay Re-Leaf No. 1* (1994), using leaves in a ceramic-mosaic mural.

Flatbush Avenue/Brooklyn College (2 or 5 line): Muriel Castanis's *Flatbush Floogies* (1996) are elegant, patinated-bronze relief murals showing female forms suspended from above, much like angels.

Franklin Avenue/Eastern Parkway (2, 3, 4, or 5, or S line): Millie Burns's *IL7/Square* (1999) reflects the nearby Botanic Garden's theme of nature and landscape.

36th Street/Sunset Park (D, M, N, or R line): *An Underground Movement: Designers, Builders, Riders* (1998) and *A Celebration of the Working People* are brightly colored mosaic murals (including dancing Rockettes) by Owen Smith.

Myrtle Avenue (J, M, or Z line): At this elevated station in the heart of Brooklyn, Verna Hart's *Jammin' Under the EL* (1999) suggests the neighborhood's lively cultural mix.

Beverly Road and **Cortelyou Road** (Q line): Patsy Norvell's *Garden Stops* (1994–96) is an outdoor installation (these stations are elevated) with garden trellises, columns featuring abstract flowers, and decorative squares from the original stations' fencing.

Broadway Junction/Eastern Parkway (J, L, or Z line) and **Broadway Junction/East New York** (A or C line): Al Loving's brilliant glass murals of geometric designs and curlicues decorate the entire complex, including the upper mezzanine.

Church Avenue (2 or 5 line): Louis Delsarte's *Transitions* (2001) are colorfully vibrant wall murals of people strolling in the Caribbean Day Parade.

Brighton Beach (B or Q line): Six sleek sculptures on this elevated platform are by Dan George; these abstract works present the Homeric myth of Dionysus and the Pirates.

Eastern Parkway–Brooklyn Museum (2 or 3 line): As of this writing, renovation of this station is taking place; it will include about 78 architectural fragments from demolished buildings around the city, including three-dimensional gargoyles and cherubs and other designs of terra-cotta stone.

BRONX

Intervale Avenue, mezzanine (2 or 5 line): Michael Kelly Williams is represented with two whimsically abstract glass-mosaic murals in shades of blue.

Tremont Avenue (B or D line): Frank Leslie Hampton's *Uptown New York* (2000) is a glass, stone, and marble mosaic mural depicting a typically urban scene of a tenement with a clothesline.

Westchester Square/East Tremont Avenue (6 line): Noted artist Romare Bearden's *Untitled* (1982) is a faceted-glass triptych to be found over the stairway.

161st Street–Yankee Stadium (4, or B or D line): Vito Acconci has made *Wall-Slide* (2002), a stone, tile, and fiberglass installation, which can be seen throughout the station.

QUEENS

111th Street, **104th Street**, **Woodhaven Boulevard**, **75th Street**, and **Cypress Hills** (J line): Kathleen McCarthy's *Five Points of Observation* (1990–93) are wire-mesh sculptures, including a striking human face, at five different stations (Note: Cypress Hills is in Brooklyn).

Woodside/61st Street (7 line): John Cavanagh's *Commuting/Community* (1986) are porcelain-enamel murals; and Dimitri Gerakaris's *Woodside Continuum* (1999) are handcrafted steel and stainless-steel railings.

23rd Street/Ely Avenue (7 line): Elizabeth Murray's *Stream* (2001), in the passageway, is a colorful mural.

33rd Street, **40th Street**, and **46th Street** (7 line): Yumi Heo's urban scenes, collectively entitled *Q Is for Queens* (1999), focus on one letter of the alphabet in three successive stations.

AND IN ADDITION . . .

For the adventuresome art lover, visit the "Underbelly Project," one of many abandoned stations in New York City's vast system. For example the 1904 Beaux-Arts station beneath City Hall can be visited via the **New York Transit Museum Tours** (718-694-5100; www .mta.info/museum).

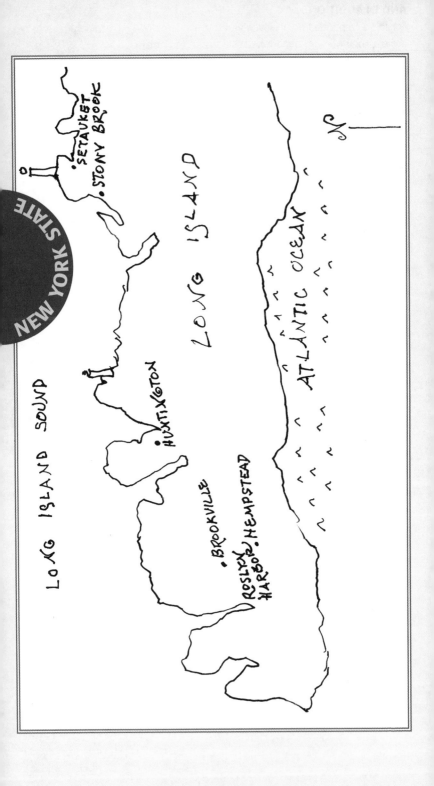

II. NEW YORK STATE
LONG ISLAND

32 **Sculpture in a Landscaped Garden: Nassau County Museum of Art, Roslyn Harbor**

DIRECTIONS» By car, take the Long Island Expressway (I-495) to exit 39N (Glen Cove Road North). Go approximately 2 miles to Northern Boulevard (Route 25A), and turn left. At the second light, turn right into the museum entrance.

The **Nassau County Museum of Art**, 1 Museum Drive at Northern Boulevard, Roslyn Harbor (516-484-9337; www.nassaumuseum.com/ncma). **H** Tuesday–Sunday 11 AM–4:45 PM. (Closed Monday.) Garden **H** Tuesday–Sunday 11 AM–5 PM, except holidays. (Closed Monday.) Admission fee to the museum; free admission to the garden. Tours are available by appointment. For full garden pleasure, we recommend visiting in spring or early summer. You can picnic on the grounds.

Nassau County
Museum of Art
1 Museum Drive
at Northern Boulevard
Roslyn Harbor
516-484-9337
www.nassaumuseum
.com/ncma

The elegant gardens on this site are like many formal gardens here and abroad; what makes them unique, however, is the juxtaposition a very traditional landscape with contemporary sculpture. While many classical statues adorn gardens here and around the world, this site mixes the boxwood hedges and gazebos, flower beds, and fine old trees with contemporary sculptural forms. This is an eye-opening experience, for it causes the viewer not only to look at abstract and semiabstract sculpture in formal terms, but also to relate it to nature as well.

There are fine paths and walkways here—including through a pinetum of hundreds of conifers from all over the world—and you will see sculpture set both on rolling fields and among the trees.

A distinguished collection of modern sculpture is displayed here. There is a special area devoted entirely to the works of Aristide Maillol. The walking tour will take you to see sculpture by Roy Lichtenstein (*Modern Head*, 1974), which is 31 feet tall and abstract in concept. More figurative works follow; among the artists represented are many of the 20th century's most prominent. You will see sculptures by José de Creeft, Anna Hyatt Huntington, Marino Marini, Fernando Botero, and Chaim Gross, among others. Among the

Nassau County
Museum gazebo

abstract works are sculptures by Mark di Suvero, Reuben Nakian, Barnett Newman, and Richard Serra.

If the arrangement of nature's beauty with art is particularly appealing to you, note the statues by Chaim Gross and José de Creeft set amid flower beds; a fountain surrounded by flowers that forms the backdrop for *King and Queen*, by Xavier Corer, a Spanish artist; and a 1979 work by Allen Bartholdi called *Homage to Noguchi* within the gardens. Don't miss Ellyn Zimmerman's *Triad* made in 1993, a 10-foot-high granite monument.

In addition to the sculpture garden, there is, of course, the museum, which occupies the former Henry Clay Frick estate. He purchased it from William Cullen Bryant; another Bryant site can be seen at Cedarmere, not far away at 225 Bryant Avenue.

The museum has more the 500 works by 19th and 20th-century artists, including paintings and drawings. Among notable European holdings are works by Rodin, Braque, Bonnard, and Vuillard, while Americans represented include Robert Rauschenberg, Frank Stella, Alex Katz, and Larry Rivers. There are frequent exhibitions, among them one focusing on relationships between different art forms (*Dance, Dance, Dance*), and one relating contemporary art to its surroundings—in this case, the Hamptons, also on Long Island.

33 Neoclassical Sculptures, Columns and Fountains: Old Westbury Gardens, Old Westbury

DIRECTIONS» By car from New York City, take the Midtown Tunnel to the Long Island Expressway to exit 39S (Glen Cove Road). Continue east on the service road of the expressway 1.2 miles to Old Westbury Road, the first road on the right. Continue 0.25 mile to the garden entrance on your left. The gardens are also reachable via the Long Island Railroad to Westbury from Pennsylvania Station in New York, then by taxi from the Westbury Station.

Old
Westbury
Gardens
710 Old Westbury Road
Old Westbury
516-333-0048
www.oldwestbury
gardens.org

Old Westbury Gardens are located at 710 Old Westbury Road, Westbury (516-333-0048; www.oldwesturygardens.org). **ⓗ** May–December, Wednesday–Monday 10 AM–5 PM. (Closed Tuesday.) Admission fee.

In this magnificent, European-style formal estate, you'll find the traditional combination of nature and sculpture that has made centuries of elegant landscapes so pleasing. Old Westbury Gardens are on a grand scale, bringing to mind Edwardian splendor and classical sculpture set among fine old trees and ele-

Old Westbury Gardens

gant garden beds. Used frequently for historic movie settings, this estate—with its great mansion—is a look at a glamorous on Long Island. Ornamental cherub fountains grace pools of lilies and lotuses, bronze peacocks have topiary tails, and there is even a shell mosaic in the style of a 17th-century Italian grotto decoration. Magnificent black iron gates and a grand allée lead the way to a landscape with groups of nymphs and satyrs (see the roof on the house),while a sculpture of the athlete Milo of Croton wrestles a stump from the earth. All along the walkways you'll make discoveries in this elegant, artistic nod to the past.

34 19th-Century American Paintings and Other Treasures: The Heckscher Museum of Art, Huntington

DIRECTIONS » By car, take the Long Island Expressway to exit 40. Go north on Route 110 (Old Walt Whitman Road) to Route 25A. Go east a short distance on Route 25A to Prime Avenue.

Heckscher Museum of Art
2 Prime Avenue
Huntington
631-351-3250
info@heckscher.org

The **Heckscher Museum of Art**, 2 Prime Avenue, Huntington (631-351-3250; info@heckscher.org), was founded in 1920 by the financier August Heckscher. Ⓗ Wednesday–Friday 10 AM–4 PM, Saturday and Sunday 11 AM–5 PM. (Closed Monday and Tuesday.) Admission fee; free admission first Friday evenings, 4 PM–8:30 PM and for children under age 10. While it is known particularly for its American paintings of the 19th and 20th centuries, this unusually fine collection is also a place where you can see first-rate works by Cranach, Murillo, and Courbet, among other European masters. The 19th-century American collection includes Eakins, Inness, Church, and Moran; among the 20th-century works is a notable George Grosz, *The Eclipse of the Sun* (1926). The Heckscher Museum hosts some half-dozen shows each year, in addition to its permanent holdings. These exhibitions are thematic: *Edward Weston: Life Work*, and recently *Artists of the Stieglitz Circle: Dove, Marin, O'Keeffe, and Others*. There are also various interactive art events, recently including installations of all environmental art projects.

35 William Sidney Mount: The Genre Painter of Long Island, Setauket

DIRECTIONS » The Long Island Museum of American Art, History, and Carriages: By car from New York City, take the Midtown Tunnel to the Long Island Expressway (Route 495) to exit 62. Proceed north on County Road 97 (Nicholls Road) to its end, then turn left onto Route 25A for 1.5 miles to the intersection of 25A and Main Street in Stony Brook. Stony Brook is also accessible by the Long Island Railroad.

» The Hawkins-Mount Homestead: After leaving the art museum, turn left at the bottom of the driveway and go about 0.5 mile to a fork. At the intersection of the fork, you'll see the house and barns immediately on your left.

» West Meadow Beach: Continue on Route 25A into the village of Setauket. Take Old Field Road (left) to West Meadow Road, and continue to the beach, from which you can view Crane's Neck as Mount did.

» Mill Dam: Continue on Stony Brook's Main Street from the museums; you will see the mill on your left.

The **Long Island Museum of American Art, History, and Carriages** (the art museum is the columned building on the hill), 1208 Route 25A, Stony Brook (631-751-0066, www.longislandmuseum.org). **🅗** Friday and Saturday 10 AM–5 PM, and Sunday noon–5 PM. Admission fee.

Long Island Museum of American Art, History, and Carriages
1208 Route 25A
Stony Brook
631-751-0066
www.longisland
museum.org

William Sidney Mount was a 19th-century genre painter and portraitist whose work focused on telling stories of real people living a rural life. With good humor and an unassuming manner, this pleasing artist chronicled everyday scenes on the farm, domestic events, and the comings and goings of plain folks of his native Long Island. A visit to his homestead and surroundings that he painted with good cheer and modesty will give you an idea of what life was like in those simpler times.

Genre painting—a popular art form by the middle of the nineteenth century—drew its subject matter from familiar, everyday scenes, often with a touch of whimsy. Gone were the rhetorical gestures of those historical panoramas so favored in the paintings of previous times: instead, genre painting captured people in such ordinary activities as farming, dancing, conversing, reading, playing, or fiddling. (In fact, Mount was also a talented musician who wrote music and played the violin, an interest reflected in much of his work.)

Mount's world focused on his neighbors, as they fished, danced, hunted, and fiddled. He rarely left his familiar territory—Stony Brook and Setauket—and was more interested in capturing its people while they were busily pursuing their lives, rather than the natural beauties of the region. Ordinary folks were his subject: "I must paint pictures as they speak at once to the spectator, scenes that are most popular, that will be understood on the instant," he wrote. He was, however, an independent thinker who did not paint just to please: "I must endeavor to follow the bent of my inclinations . . . and not be dictated by others." Like his fellow Democrat Walt Whitman, he was a champion of the common man, and believed in the dignity of all people. In fact, unlike other artists of his time, Mount depicted African Americans as individuals rather than as stereotypes—doing pretty much what other country boys did. One of his most famous works, *The Banjo Player*, shows a young African American busily engaged playing his instrument.

Mount was part of a large, cohesive, and apparently jolly family. The son of an innkeeper, he had a brother who painted signs (and encouraged William to seek formal training at the National Academy of Design, where he met Samuel F. B. Morse, who proclaimed him one of the pioneers of American art); one who painted portraits (the well-regarded Shepard Alonzo Mount); and a sister who painted flower pieces. Another brother was a traveling dancing master who sought William's advice on such matters as dancing tunes. Mount, who was also a prolific letter writer and diarist, corresponded with much of his family; many of these letters have been compiled and published in a large book on the artist.

Most of Mount's paintings—like the artist himself—have remained in his beloved region. A visit to the Long Island Museum of American Art, History, and Carriages will give you a fine sampling of his paintings, journals, letters, and inventions (yes, he was also an inventor!), and a feeling for what his life was like. You'll also find memorabilia relating to his talented and livery family.

The house in which Mount lived much of his life is still standing. Recently renovated, it is open to the public. Before visiting this homestead, be sure to see the painting Mount did of it. On the property are also the barns immortalized in so many of his paintings, including *Dancing on the Barn Floor* and *Dance of the Haymakers* (both are found in the Long Island Museum of American Art, History and Carriages) and *The Power of Music* (Cleveland Museum of Art).

If you have time, drive out to West Meadow Beach to see the view of Crane's Neck, another subject of a Mount painting housed at the museum. Another site reproduced by Mount is the Mill Dam in Stony Brook; you can view the mill and large waterwheel at the dam by taking a pleasant walk, though you might not recognize the mill—now much larger than it was when Mount painted it.

36 Melding East and West in Architecture and Design: The Charles B. Wang Center at SUNY—Stony Brook, Stony Brook

DIRECTIONS» By car, take the Long Island Expressway (I-495) to exit 62 north. Take Nicolls Road (Route 97) north for 9 miles. Turn left into the university's main entrance. There is public parking just across from the Wang Center.

Stony Brook, part of the State University of New York, has a contemporary campus that is spread out over acres and acres of forests and fields. Most of the buildings, which are in separated clusters across this vast campus, are typical midcentury, functional high-rise structures. But don't miss the **Charles B. Wang Center** (631-632-4400; wangcenter@stonybrook.edu)! This building, in the center of the main academic campus, is easily spotted by its bright red entrance pavilion. It should be of particular interest to architecture buffs.

Charles B. Wang Center
100 Nicolls Road
Stony Brook
631-632-4400
www.stonybrook
.edu/wang

While many public buildings have attempted to meld Eastern and Western design, none has been more successful than the Wang Center, designed by P. H. Tuan. Both contemporary in style and traditionally Asian in many details, this building is well worth a visit (the center is open to the public, so walk right in and look around).

Among the first design elements you'll notice are the use of water and the integrated gardens. Filled with natural light, the center is welcoming; at night, the pagoda (an octagonal 100-foot-tall edifice above the hall) is illuminated.

But it is the water—some placid, some rushing—that

SUNY at Stony Brook: The Charles B. Wang Center

NEW YORK STATE

particularly catches the eye. Much of the water design suggests the Asian influence; in front of the hall is a series of ornamental pools, while inside there are numerous fountains. (Note particularly the 12 Chinese Zodiac sculptures in the pool south of the lobby.)

In front of the center is a series of bright red geometric trellises and four 16-foot columns supporting clerestory window. All of these elements are reflected in the adjacent water.

Gardens are everywhere—inside and out. Designed in the Asian style, they provide settings for Chinese sculpture and many kinds of paintings. (For more information of the Wang Center, visit the office on the south side of the lobby.)

37 **Three University Campuses and Their Outdoor Art: Hofstra University Art Museum and Outdoor Sculpture, Hempstead; C. W. Post Campus of Long Island University: Sculpture Garden and Art Museum, Brookville; and Adelphi University, Garden City**

DIRECTIONS » **Hofstra University:** By car from New York City, take the Grand Central Parkway east to Meadowbrook Parkway (south) to exit M4 (westbound) onto the Hempstead Turnpike. The campus is 1 mile from exit M4.

» C. W. Post: By car, take the Long Island Expressway to exit 39N (Glen Cove Road). Turn right on Northern Boulevard (25A) until you reach the campus. Follow the signs for Hillwood Art Museum.

» Adelphi University: By car, take the Long Island Expressway (Route 495) to exit 34 south (New Hyde Park Road). Continue south on New Hyde Park Road for 3.2 miles; turn left onto Stewart Avenue; at the fourth light, turn right onto Nassau Boulevard, then turn left onto South Avenue. The Adelphi campus is on the right.

Hofstra University, Hempstead (516-463-5672, www.hofstra.edu/museum), has both an art museum with two galleries on South Campus—the Emily Lowe Galley, located in Emily Lowe Hall, and the David Filderman Gallery, located on the ninth floor of the Joan and Donald E. Axinn Library—and a fair amount of outdoor sculpture to enjoy. Emily Lowe Gallery 🅗 Tuesday–Friday 10 AM–5 PM, Saturday and Sunday 1 PM–5 PM. (Closed Monday.) David Filderman Gallery 🅗 daily 10 AM–5 PM. Free admission. The outdoor collection is on view daily. Among the museum's holdings are a variety of treasures (an African mask, a 17th-century Dutch painting, a head of Buddha, contemporary paintings) and changing exhibitions. The sculptures are spread throughout the campus, and children will enjoy the "Mystery Sculpture Map" that sends them to locate works by J. Seward Johnson Jr., Greg Wyatt, and Manolo Pascual, among others. (Pick up the map at the museum.)

Hofstra University
900 Fulton Avenue
Hempstead
516-463-5672
www.hofstra.edu/
museum

The **C. W. Post Campus of Long Island University**, Brookville (516-299-4073; www.liu.edu/museum) has both an art museum (Hillwood Art Museum) and a pretty hillside sculpture garden, with some notable (but unidentified) contemporary sculptures. Among them you might recognize a Nancy Graves steel and cast-iron work, giant spheres by Grace Knowlton, and a characteristic steel work by George Rickey. (The sculpture garden is far enough from the main campus to require driving; take Gold Coast Road to its end. At the museum you'll find changing shows; we happened upon a nice exhibition of contemporary sculpture. 🅗 Monday–Friday 9:30 AM–4:30 PM, Thursday 9:30 AM–8 PM, Saturday 11 AM–3 PM. (Closed Sunday.)

C. W. Post Campus of Long Island University
720 Northern Boulevard
Brookville
516-299-4073
www.liu.edu/museum

Dan Christoffel: *Requiem 9/11*, 2006, terra cotta and steel, Adelphi University

Adelphi University
1 South Avenue
Garden City
800-233-5744
www.adelphi.edu

Adelphi University, Garden City (800-233-5744; www.adelphi.edu), is a large, sprawling campus dotted with sculpture (More than 17 were visible when we visited). The majority can be found between the student center and the library. They are primarily shown on a biennial rotation (lasting from fall to spring, for example). There are also three centers of art that are open to the public: the Adele and Herbert J. Klapper Center for Fine Arts Gallery, the University Center Gallery, and a series of displays at Swirbul Library. ⓗ Monday–Friday 9:30 AM–4:30 PM, Thursday until 8 PM, Saturday 11 AM–3 PM. (Closed Sunday.)

WEST OF THE HUDSON

38 **Edward Hopper's Boyhood Home, Nyack**

DIRECTIONS» By car, from the George Washington Bridge take the Palisades Parkway north to exit 4. Go north on Route 9W to blinking light after 5.5 miles. Bear right at light to Broadway. Take Broadway past Main Street in Nyack, to Hopper House on your left.

The **Edward Hopper House**, 82 North Broadway, Nyack (845-358-0774; www.yearofedwardhopper. com). **H** Thursday–Sunday 1 PM–5 PM, or by appointment, with many special events at the art gallery there. Admission fee; free admission for children and students.

Edward Hopper House
82 North Broadway
Nyack
845-358-0774
www.yearofedward
hopper.com

Edward Hopper (1882–1967) can be said to have captured the isolation and loneliness of American life in the first half of the 20th century. His scenes—built of carefully constructed diagonal and horizontal planes—suggest the transience of his time: empty rooms, deserted streets, isolated figures. The Edward Hopper House is his boyhood home. Built in 1858, it is now an intimate gallery that shows some small works by Hopper and Rockland County artists. The house provides short walking tour maps of some of the local places Hopper knew and painted.

39 **A Picturesque Site for Indoor and Outdoor Exhibitions: Rockland Center for the Arts (RoCA), West Nyack**

DIRECTIONS» By car, from the George Washington Bridge take the Palisades Interstate Parkway to exit 5N, to Route 303 north for about 3 miles. Turn right at

Grace Knowlton: Installaton, Rockland Center for the Arts

Route 59 east exit, which puts you on a service road; make your first right from the service road onto South Greenbush Road. The center is about 0.2 mile away on the left.

Rockland Center for the Arts (RoCA), 27 South Greenbush Road, West Nyack (845-358-0877; www.rocklandartcenter.org), is an intimate site nestled within 10 acres of woods and meadows, dedicated to visual, literary, and performing arts. Here you'll find something of interest for all ages: There are indoor exhibits by both established artists and students, as well as outdoor shows in the bucolic sculpture park; art classes (for children and adults), workshops, concerts, even "interactive exhibit tours" to foster young people's creativity. We enjoyed wandering about the sculpture park, where the works on display (especially those of the well-known artist Grace Knowlton) seemed to us well integrated into the very green landscape. Sculpture shows change about every two years, so there is plenty of time to go back and revisit one you particularly liked. Gallery **Ⓗ** Monday–Friday 10 AM–4 PM, Saturday 1 PM–4 PM. Suggested donation for admission. Sculpture park **Ⓗ** dawn to dusk daily, year round; free admission.

The center—originally located in the nearby river village of Nyack—was founded in 1947 by an impressive list of creative people: Aaron Copland, Kurt Weill, Paulette Goddard, Lotte Lenya, Maxwell Anderson, and Helen Hayes. The Hudson River Valley has a long tradition of attracting artists, and local talent continues to flourish in the area; so it is not surprising that the center remains active and busy.

40 A Touch of "Easter Island" in Rockland County, Haverstraw

Ted Ludwiczak, "Easter Island"
14 Riverside Avenue
Haverstraw

DIRECTIONS » By car from New York City, take the Palisades Parkway to exit 5N (Route 303). Stay on Route 303, which leads to Route 9W north. Continue until you reach Haverstraw. Route 9W intersects with Riverside Avenue.

14 Riverside Avenue, Haverstraw, is an outdoor exhibit only; the house is private.

This is an unusual collection of carved stone heads (created with a bent lawnmower blade that the artist discovered in this garden). It will remind you of more exotic locations!

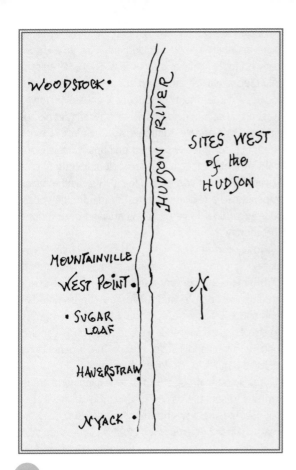

41 Arts and Crafts in the Catskills: A Village Visit, Sugar Loaf

DIRECTIONS » By car, take the New York State Thruway to exit 16; Route 17 west for 8 miles to exit 127. Turn left and follow the signs.

Sugar Loaf, in Orange County (845-469-9181; www. sugarloafnewyork.com), is open year-round. Most businesses are open Wednesday–Sunday 11 AM–5 PM (with extended hours in summer; closed Tuesday). A visitor's guide is available at the Chamber of Commerce.

Sugar Loaf, a quiet village amid rolling hills, apple orchards, and wineries, is known as "the village of craftsmen." This vibrant community of creative people has been for years a popular destination for visitors interested in seeing artisans and artists at work. Here you can see their studios, visit the galleries that show and sell their work, or even participate in craft workshops (a wide variety are offered during the summer months).

Sugar Loaf's history as a craft center dates to the

Sugar Loaf
Orange County
845-469-9181
www.sugarloaf
newyork.com

161

1700s. First a sacred burial ground for the Minisink Indians and then a colonial settlement, it became known early on for its crafts and provisions. By 1830, artisans included a blacksmiths, two cooperages, a cabinetmaker, a carpet maker, a tannery, a cheese factory, a wagon maker, and a sawmill owner, among numerous others. Craftspeople continued to work in this small mountain community (named perhaps for its curious bald mountain that reminded colonial settlers of a sugar loaf), but it was only in the 1960s, as the nation experienced a revival of interest in handmade goods, that Sugar Loaf began to draw artisans from around the country.

Today this tiny hamlet includes more than 50 independent artists and artisans, many of whom work in original 18th-century barns. Most of the working studios are open to the public. You can visit studios and shops that create everything from leather goods to stained glass, wood designs to handmade candles, pottery to hats and jewelry, musical instruments to rag dolls, and quilts to handmade furniture.

You'll find that Sugar Loaf is an inspiring and amusing way to spend a day away. Bring the children! They will love seeing how the many things used daily are made by hand. After your visit to this picturesque Warwick Valley site, you can take the family apple picking at several nearby orchards.

AND IN ADDITION . . .

Off Route 17 (at exit 129) is the **Museum Village of Orange County** (845-782-8247; www.museumvillage.org), which comprises more than 30 buildings housing demonstrations of crafts and early American life.

Museum Village of Orange County
1010 Route 17M
Monroe
845-782-8247
www.museum
village.org

42 America's Best Known and Largest Sculpture Park: Storm King, Mountainville

DIRECTIONS » By car from New York City, take the George Washington Bridge to the Palisades Parkway north, to the New York State Thruway. Take exit 16 (Harriman) to Route 32 north. Go about 10 miles and follow the signs to Storm King Art Center.

If you have never been to **Storm King Art Center**, Old Pleasant Hill Road, Mountainville (845-534-3190; www.stormking.org), you can look forward to an ex-

Storm King Art Center
Old Pleasant Hill Road
Mountainville
845-534-3190
www.stormking.org

traordinary experience; this is a great museum that can be enjoyed again and again, with new discoveries to be made on each visit. ❶ April 1–November 30, Wednesday–Monday 10 AM–5 PM. (Closed Tuesday.) Admission fee. Because of its vastness, Storm King never seems crowded, so you should not fear coming on weekends. Free walking tours are offered daily at 2 PM: no reservations are required. We recommend bringing a picnic lunch on your visit—there are few restaurants in the vicinity and a charming picnic spot with tables (in a grassy area near the lower parking lot) awaits you. Pick up a map at the gate.

Can you imagine 400 rolling acres with world-class contemporary sculpture dotted throughout? This is Storm King, the country's most expansive sculpture park, featuring more than 200 grand works of art. Ranging from dramatic abstractions by many of the world's most noted artists to more delicate works (both on the grounds and inside the museum/manor house). If you have foreign visitors, no place we have visited so dramatically embodies the vastness and free spirit of America, so bring them here.

Tal Streeter: *Endless Column*, **Storm King Art Center**

There is varied terrain—grassy walkways, fields, and wooded paths with eye-catching art stunning at every turn. You can walk up to each piece of art, or admire it from a distance, or even climb on two of them (bring the children to experience this).

Here are Siah Armajani's *Gazebo for Two Anarchists: Gabrielle Antolini and Alberto Antolini* (1998), a recent acquisition, and Isamu Noguchi's *Momo Taro*, an impressive 40-ton granite sculpture that was created with the idea that people would sit in it. You will often see family groups crowded inside its inviting hollows, posing for a photo—a scene that would undoubtedly please the artist. Considered to be one of Noguchi's major works, *Momo Taro* sits on a small hill that was especially created the accommodate the sculpture.

A lawyer named Vermont Hatch owned this estate and built the stone mansion (now the museum featuring changing exhibits of art from their permanent collection). It was his neighbor, Ted Ogden, who had the foresight to transform the property into a center for sculptures. (He was influenced by the sight of Henry Moore sculptures displayed on a sheep ranch in Scotland.) Ogden bought 14 David Smith sculptures. They

became the centerpiece of the collection. A pioneer in 20th-century metal sculpture, Smith used steel wire and rods to weld together his abstract designs, which set the stone of modernism at Storm King.

Your walk (assuming you go without a tour) can be as long as wish, but you won't want to miss seminal works by such notable artists as Henry Moore, Louise Nevelson, Mark di Suvero, Alexander Calder, Isamu Noguchi, and Alexander Liberman. Consult your map.

Surrounding the house are some of the smaller works, as well as semiformal gardens. Don't miss Louise Nevelson's *City of the Mountain*, Calder's stabile *Sandy's Butterfly*, and his *The Arch*, a dramatic black steel construction that suggests a prehistoric being. Several more representational works are also near the house by such artists as Henri Étienne-Martin and Emilio Greco, set within view of a group of Ionic columns.

The view from here is of the best at Storm King; from this spot you overlook much of the vast valley before you, dotted with Mark di Suvero's monumental *Mother Peace* and *Mon Père, Mon Père*, and Alice Aycock's *Three Fold Manifestation II*. Also near the columns is an area dedicated to temporary exhibits.

Farther from the house you'll find larger spheres by Grace Knowlton, Kenneth Snelson's *Free Ride Home*, Maneshe Kadishman's *Suspended* (a construction of steel that seems to defy the laws of gravity), and Tal Streeter's *Endless Column*, a zigzag in orange metal.

Alexander Liberman:
***Adonai*, Storm King**
Art Center

New works appear periodically and the museum often shows "emerging" artists. Storm King effectively combines vast space with striking images, and this melding of nature with contemporary art forms the essence of this site.

43 Military History and Art at West Point's Museum, West Point

DIRECTIONS» By car, take the George Washington Bridge to the Palisades Parkway, to Bear Mountain Circle. Take Route 9W north; follow the signs to Highland Falls and West Point.

The **West Point Museum**, 2110 New South Post Road, West Point (845-938-2638; www.usma.edu). ♿ Almost all buildings are open to the public April–November 8:30 AM–4:30 PM. (For schedule of special events, contact them first.) The West Point Museum ♿ daily 10:30 AM–4:15 PM. Free admission.

A visit to West Point United States Military Academy is unlike any other such experience to look at art. Here you'll find a spectacular campus with lots to see (historically, scenically, architecturally, etc.) as well as a museum devoted primarily to warfare. The large collection has exhibits and displays depicting every aspect of military history: there are paintings, dioramas, and models, ranging from ancient Greek battles to logistics of the Revolutionary War, from Gettysburg to the everyday life of the soldier, from honors and medals to early paintings of West Point itself.

West Point Museum
2110 New South Post Road
West Point
845-938-2638
www.usma.edu

44 Environmental Art: The *Opus 40* Quarry, Saugerties

DIRECTIONS» By car from New York City, take the New York State Thruway north to the Saugerties exit. Take Route 212 west through Woodstock and follow the signs along the road.

If you have ever visited an abandoned stone quarry, you know what a dramatic and beautiful sight it can be. Perhaps you have made a comment about nature imitating art, for the picturesque quality of the light and shadow on stone and water has long been a favorite subject for artists. A visit and walk to *Opus 40*, 50 Fite Road, Saugerties (845-246-3400; www.opus40.org). ♿ Thursday–Sunday and Holiday Mondays

Opus 40
50 Fite Road
Saugerties
845-246-3400
www.opus40.org

11:00 AM–5:30 PM There is a small admission fee; free admission for children under age 12. Group tours are available. Rubber-soled shoes are recommended.

Long a favorite subject for artists, quarries are inherently beautiful, as the light and shadow play upon the rock faces and occasional water below. The combination of art and nature has been irresistible to painters, and now, to environmental artists, as well.

A visit to Opus 40, the abandoned quarry that has been the lifetime enterprise of Harvey Fite, will make you wonder where art and nature divide—or whether such environmental art is the ultimate merging of them. For as you walk in and around Opus 40 you will be fascinated by the variety of shapes, pathways, circular foundations, springs, trees, and so much more.

In 1938, Harvey Fite bought the 6-acre abandoned bluestone quarry, and over about four decades transformed it into the monumental sculptural environment you see today. He originally thought of it as a setting for his own sculpture, but the magnificent natural surrounding overpowered any individual works; he moved his pieces to the grassy knoll nearby, and began turning the quarry into Opus 40.

Thousands of tons of stone have been arranged; there are pathways, abstract monuments, walls and shapes—and all of it can be walked through, or climbed on. Views—including one of nearby Overlook Mountain—are great in every direction. In the center is a monolith, by the artist—a 9-ton stone column, which occasionally serves as backdrop for concerts and events and as a place for meditation for many visitors.

There is a museum on the property; the Quarryman Museum houses artifacts and tools of stone work, and offers a slideshow of the construction of Opus 40.

This is definitely one of the most interesting art sites we have visited. You may wonder whether an abandoned quarry is more beautiful or interesting in its natural state or as a carefully designed work of environmental art—but it is just such questions that make this a rare and inspiring place to visit.

EAST OF THE HUDSON

45 **The Hudson Valley: Landscape Painters and Vistas of the 19th Century: the Hudson River Museum, Yonkers; the Jasper Cropsey House and Studio, Hastings-on-Hudson**

DIRECTIONS » Hudson River Museum: By car, take Henry Hudson Parkway north to Saw Mill River Parkway. Immediately after junction with Cross County Parkway, you will find Yonkers Avenue. Ramp leads to Ashburton Avenue. Turn right; go 2 to 3 miles to Warburton Avenue and go to Trevor Park.

» Jasper Cropsey House: From Yonkers, return by car to the Saw Mill Parkway, again go north, and exit at the Hastings-on-Hudson sign and continue on Main Street to the village of Hastings-on-Hudson. At the intersection of Main Street and Warburton Avenue, turn left and go one block to Washington Avenue, where you make another left. The Cropsey house and studio will be on your left.

The Hudson River painters, the great romantics who glorified America's natural wonders on canvas, were inevitably drawn to the Hudson Valley Highlands. In their quest for what they called the "sublime landscape," they sought vistas that embodied their aesthetic and philosophical ideals. These artists, who flourished between 1820 and 1880, were dazzled by the scenic grandeur of the West Point region, where dramatic mountain ranges meet the majestic Hudson. Here they captured the spectacular scenery in its many variations, following the lead of the painter Thomas Cole, who advised artists to go out into nature, not only for the beauty of the scenery, but for its "heroic associations." The second generation of Hudson River painters was led by Asher B. Durand, John Kensett, and Frederick E. Church. Referring to Thoreau's comment that "the universe is not rough-hewn, but perfect in its details," they believed in the careful observance of the natural world. The next generation (in the 1870s) favored a more French approach and its move toward all increasingly impressionistic style. All of them found in the Hudson Valley scenery that inspired great works.

In this chapter we take you to a museum devoted to Hudson scenery and art, and to the nearby home and studio of one of its most notable artists

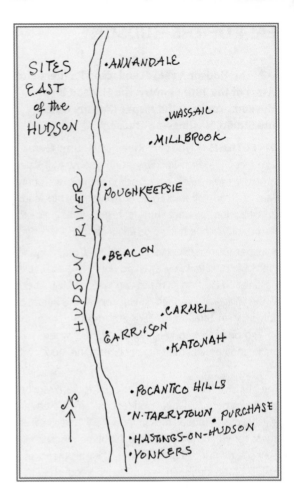

SITES EAST of the HUDSON

- ANNANDALE
- WASSAIC
- MILLBROOK
- POUGHKEEPSIE
- BEACON
- CARMEL
- GARRISON
- KATONAH
- POCANTICO HILLS
- N. TARRYTOWN
- PURCHASE
- HASTINGS-ON-HUDSON
- YONKERS

HUDSON RIVER

N

NEW YORK STATE

Hudson River Museum
511 Warburton Avenue
Yonkers
914-963-4550
www.hrm.org

The **Hudson River Museum**, 511 Warburton Avenue, Yonkers (914-963-4550; info@hrm.org), is located in a restored Victorian house. ♿ Wednesday–Sunday noon–5 PM. (Closed Monday and Tuesday.) Admission fee. It showcases American painting, particularly of the 19th century, with an emphasis on the Hudson Valley and its landscapists, so it is a good place to begin your outing. In addition to art, there are also a planetarium, collections of decorative arts and furniture, and many programs relating to astronomy and the history of the Hudson valley.

There is also a trail offering terrific views of the Palisades along the Hudson (pick up a trail guide at the museum).

Jasper Cropsey House
49 Washington Avenue
Hastings-on-Hudson
914-478-1372

Jasper Cropsey House, 49 Washington Avenue, Hastings-on-Hudson (914-478-1372) can be visited by appointment only, Monday–Friday 10 AM–1 PM. Free admission.

168

While most artists' homes of the 19th century have vanished or been changed beyond recognition, here is a wonderful exception. Due to the vigilance and care of his granddaughter, the pretty yellow house where Jasper Cropsey lived is still intact. You can visit the grand studio where he painted his Hudson River views and see the attractive Victorian setting in which he lived from 1885 until his death in 1900. It was made into a museum by his descendants (who had continued to live there) in 1970. You'll find many examples of his oils, prints, and fine line drawings—including numerous images of the Hudson and nearby communities. In addition there are portraits, clothing (his wife's elegant dresses), and all kinds of items that show how the artist's household functioned (we were particularly intrigued by the elaborate system of pulleys he designed to bring in fresh air!). Like many artists of his time, Cropsey was apparently one of those ingenious 19th-century Americans who did many things well—designing buildings (among them, two churches), inventing gadgets, and interior details for his home and studio—as well as painting his notable landscapes.

EAST OF THE HUDSON

46 Icons of the 20th Century at Kykuit: The Rockefeller Estate, North Tarrytown

DIRECTIONS » By car, take the New York State Thruway to exit 9 (Tarrytown); follow Route 119 to Route 9. Tours leave from Philipsburg Manor on Route 9. To visit Kykuit, leave your car at Philipsburg Manor and take a bus to the site.

Kykuit means "lookout" in Dutch. **Kykuit**, 381 North Broadway, Sleepy Hollow (914-631-8200; www.hudsonvalley.org/historic-sites/kykuit). This is an imposing Hudson Valley villa, dating from the early 20th century, with magnificent views of the river. Inside the grand mansion and in the lovely gardens is an impressive art collection—a must-see for any art lover.

Kykuit
381 North Broadway
Sleepy Hollow
914-631-8200
www.hudsonvalley.org
/historic-sites/kykuit

To visit the site, you take a two-hour tour, which turns out to be quite informative. The estate, relatively modest in its earliest version, evolved with succeeding generation of Rockefellers; and artworks and objects were added accordingly. Fee; hours vary. Admission by timed tours only.

William Welles Bosworth, a personal friend of John D. Rockefeller Jr., designed the original gardens, which were later enhanced by Abby Rockefeller, an avid gardener herself. But what you especially want to focus on while visiting here is the first-rate collection of modern sculptures in the gardens and other outdoor spaces.

Nelson Rockefeller, a very knowledgeable art collector, placed some 70 significant sculptures on the lush grounds (these had remained in his possession after he had donated most of his art to major museums). You will enjoy walking around the elegant terraces and gardens while viewing these significant 20th-century works. Almost all of them have been left at the very spot Rockefeller had chosen for them; most are within the formal gardens, gracing the lovely plantings, though you may be surprised to find a few in such unlikely spots as the golf course.

Among the most notable sculptures here are Brancusi's *Grand Oiseau* (near the entrance to the mansions), Maillol's *Bather Putting Up Her Hair* (in the garden), Henry Moore's *Nuclear Energy* (near the pool), Louise Nevelson's *Atmosphere and Environment* (on the "putting green"), and Shinkichi Tajiri's *Granny Knot* (under a giant tree). Dozens of other great works are placed around grounds (unfortunately, the tour barely allows time to see them all).

Indoors you will find—in addition to notable tea services and memorabilia—a fine collection of tapestries (Picasso), rugs (Leger), portraits (Warhol), and more, much more.

Fountains on the grounds of Kykuit

Calder, Arp, Giacometti, Noguchi, Lipchitz—practically every name associated with the history of twentieth-century art is represented—either outdoors or in—at Kykuit. Despite the strict requirements of reservations and tours, this is a must-see outing for any art lover.

A visit here may easily be combined with an outing to Union Church in nearby Pocantico Hills.

47 A Special Treat: Stained-Glass Windows by Chagall and Matisse: Union Church of Pocantico Hills, Pocantico Hills

DIRECTIONS » By car from New York City, take the New York State Thruway (I-87) north to exit 9; go north Route 9 to Route 448 (Bedford Road) and turn right. Go up the hill to Union Church on your right.

Union Church of Pocantico Hills is located at 555 Bedford Road, Pocantico Hills (914-332-6659; www .hudsonvalley.org). ⓗ April–December, Monday and Wednesday–Friday 11 AM–5 PM, Saturday 10 AM–5 PM, Sunday 2 PM–5 PM. (Closed Tuesday.) Guided or self-guided tours are available. Admission fee.

Union Church of Pocantico Hills
555 Bedford Road
Pocantico Hills
914-332-6659
www.hudsonvalley.org

This delightful spot is such a surprise in its rural setting that you will be astonished when you walk in. It is a small stone church that features exquisite stained-glass windows—not just ordinary windows but jewel-toned designs by Marc Chagall and Henri Matisse. Dedicated in 1956, they were commissioned by the Rockefeller family (whose art-filled Kykuit is nearby). They are the only cycle of stained-glass church windows that Chagall completed, and are Matisse's last completed work. The combination is a not-to-be-missed treat.

The near wall features a large, colorful window by Chagall: a Biblical passage from St. Luke's Gospel, the parable of the Good Samaritan. Chosen by the Rockefeller family, it emphasizes "Love Thy Neighbor," a clear reference to John D. Rockefeller and his philanthropy.

In 1966, eight side windows were completed by Chagall. Verses from six prophets are illustrated, and of particular interest is the *Crucifixion*, a memorial to Michael Rockefeller, who died while on an anthropological expedition in New Guinea.

Using an unusual technique in creating stained glass, Chagall etched colored glass with acid, then assembled the pieces and painted upon them, as if on a canvas, using "grisaille" (a special type of paint). He worked in a studio in Reims, France.

171

NEW YORK STATE

Marc Chagall:
stained-glass window,
The Crucifixion,
Union Church of
Pocantico Hills

Note the rose window, Matisse's contribution to this lovely interior. Using paper cutouts to design its free-form abstraction, he used both opaque and translucent glass. It, too, was created in France.

Pick up a flier in the lobby for additional information on these windows.

48 Decorative Arts, Unique Design: A Visit to Manitoga, the Russel Wright Design Center, Garrison

DIRECTIONS» By car from New York City, take the George Washington Bridge to the Palisades Parkway, and the parkway to its end. Cross the Bear Mountain Bridge and turn left (north) onto Route 9D. The entrance to Manitoga is 2.5 miles from the bridge, on the right.

Manitoga/The Russel Wright Design Center,
584 Route 9D, Garrison (845-424-3812; www.russel wrightcenter.org), is a unique site unto itself. **Ⓗ** house staffed Monday–Friday, 9 AM–5 PM; house and landscape tours May–October, selected weekdays 11 AM, Saturday and Sunday 11 AM and 1:30 PM. Suggested donation. Reserve tour in advance; fee for tour. You

Manitoga/The Russel
Wright Design Center
584 Route 9D
Garrison
845-424-3812
www.russelwright
center.org

can take self-guided walks in the grounds daily year-round, during daylight hours.

Situated on the edge of an abandoned quarry on a wooded hillside with giant rocks and rushing water, the barely visible house and studio of the great industrial designer Russel Wright are perfectly integrated into the surrounding forest. The seamless union between the constructed and the natural make this rustic woodland retreat appear almost timeless, as if it has always been here. But, in fact, Manitoga (or "place of the great spirit" in Algonquin) was carefully designed down to the last detail (including the landscape) and conceived and fashioned over a period of many years. The site is a fascinating combination of architecture, interior design, and landscape architecture, all in one.

One of the most important American designers of decorative arts from the 1930s through the '50s, Wright created this unusual place. He first discovered the property in 1942; it had been ravaged by years of quarrying and lumbering. Over the next three decades he slowly and deliberately transformed it into his domain. He built Dragon Rock, the house and studio, atop a dramatic rocky cliff overlooking the quarry; reconfigured the surrounding 75 acres with trees, mosses, ferns, mountain laurel, and wildflowers; moved giant boulders to create dramatic effects; redirected the waterfall so its bubbly sounds could be heard near the house; and designed more than 4 miles of paths winding through the woods. The result is as beautiful a setting as any artist could ask for—a most inviting place to visit.

It is not surprising that this one-of-a-kind masterpiece is listed on the National Register of Historic Places. (Wright considered it his best work of all.) It represents, however, the exception to Wright's creative output: he was known as a designer of objects for the home, rather than as an architect or landscapist. (In fact, he has even been called the Martha Stewart of his generation!) His sophisticated yet inexpensive designs—including furniture, dishes, glassware, table linens, and pottery—were so popular at the time that they were mass produced in the millions and had a profound impact on the American home. Many of his designs are still collector's items.

Dragon Rock, the only 20th-century modern home open to the public in New York State, is a fascinating place to visit, combining architecture, landscape, products, archives, and even philosophy. To see it you must take a guided tour, which begins at Mary's Meadow (named after Wright's wife). It meanders along, past the former quarry, with amusing diversions along the way (we leave you to discover these yourself!); and finally culminates with a visit to the house itself. Be sure to wear sturdy shoes, as you'll be walking on uneven terrain, across a log bridge, and up massive stone steps to the house.

Although the blue-gray house may seem small on the outside, it is actually on 11 levels and is filled with original and unexpected touches that make it a delight to walk through. A committed naturalist, Wright literally brought the outside into the house; you will find boulders, trees (including an uncut floor-to-ceiling cedar trunk supporting the main part of the roof), flagstone flooring extending onto the terrace, and laminated leaves and grasses used for decoration. In the studio—Wright's favorite retreat—pocket windows actually slip down into the walls, so that you are practically outside, enjoying the sounds and fragrance of nature.

Throughout you will see examples of industrial and domestic design that Wright pioneered. Furniture and housewares are carefully crafted in organic shapes and materials; for example, a ceiling light fixture is made from—of all unexpected things—burlap.

A champion of democracy, Wright claimed, "Good design is for everyone." His legacy lives on in his many clever and original creations, epitomized in the rustic and down-to-earth sophistication that is Manitoga.

Manitoga/The Russel Wright Design Center

49 Contemporary Art in a Converted Warehouse: Dia Art Foundation, Beacon

DIRECTIONS » By car, take the Palisades Parkway north to end. At the rotary, take Route 6 east/202 across Bear Mountain Bridge. Take the first left onto Route 9D north. Continue 16.5 miles north on 9D into the city of Beacon. At the fourth traffic light in Beacon (just past Beacon City Hall), make a left turn onto Beekman Street. Continue 0.5 miles on Beekman Street. Dia:Beacon's entrance is on the right, marked by a gray sign.

EAST OF THE HUDSON

Beacon, once a quiet mill town along the Hudson, has since the early 2000s reinvented itself as a bustling arts community. Now a popular destination with trendy galleries and related sites and events, it features primarily a major contemporary arts museum that attracts visitors from everywhere. The museum, **Dia:Beacon**, 3 Beekman Street, Beacon (845-440-0100; www.diabeacon.org), housed in a converted Nabisco box printing factory with about 24,000 square feet of exhibition space, contains expansive galleries designed to show selected works of noted artists from the 1960s to the present—Donald Judd, Sol LeWitt, Agnes Martin, Louise Bourgeois, Andy Warhol, Blinky Palermo—are just a few of the names in a distinguished list. Each of the elegant and spacious galleries is devoted to a single artist and designed specifically for his or her featured work. ⓗ January–March, Friday–Monday 11 AM–4 PM; April–October, Thursday–Monday 11 AM–6 PM; November and December, Thursday–Monday 11 AM–4 PM. Admission fee.

Dia:Beacon
3 Beekman Street
Beacon
845-440-0100
www.diabeacon.org

The museum's unusually vast spaces and reflected natural light (there are many skylights) make it ideal for viewing installations, paintings, and sculpture in a setting that can accommodate many visitors without ever seeming crowded. You and any children you may have with you will enjoy the freedom of roaming throughout these wide open galleries, experiencing everything from Richard Serra's monumental steel sculptures and Dan Flavin's fluorescent wonders, to Andy Warhol's room of extensive iconic images.

Dia:Beacon also offers temporary exhibitions, monthly gallery talks, community free days for neighboring counties, and an educational program. Be sure to walk around the grounds surrounding the building (which, by the way, appears boxy from the outside, as befits a former factory, and is not particularly beautiful). Designed by Robert Irwin, the landscape includes an entrance court, a grove of flowering fruit trees, and a small formal garden. And take a moment to enjoy the spectacular river view before driving to the center of town to check out the galleries and artsy boutiques.

50 Locust Grove: the Home and Studio of "America's Leonardo," Samuel F. B. Morse, Poughkeepsie

DIRECTIONS» By car from New York City, take the Henry Hudson Parkway north to the Saw Mill Parkway to the Taconic State Parkway. Take the exit for Poughkeepsie (Route 55) and go west for several miles, almost to the Mid Hudson Bridge, then take US Highway 9 south for about 2 miles. The entrance to Locust Grove is on your right.

Locust Grove
2683 South Road (US 9)
Poughkeepsie
845-454-4500
www.morsehistoric
site.org

For an outing focusing on the extraordinary career of a true 19th-century phenomenon, Samuel F. B. Morse, we take you to **Locust Grove**, 2683 South Road (US 9), Poughkeepsie (845-454-4500; www.morsehistoricsite.org). ℍ The gardens and grounds are open dawn to dusk year-round; house tours are offered daily May–November from 10 AM–3 PM. Tour fee.

Samuel F. B. Morse was the quintessential 19th-century "Renaissance man." He had consummate skill as a painter of both landscape and portraits, was a founder of the National Academy of Design, and was the inventor of Morse Code and the machine for telegraphing it. A visit to his home is awe-inspiring, as well as beautiful and educational. For here we see the vast reach of Morse's interests and abilities all kept just as he kept them.

Known as the "American Leonardo" for his inventions, he revolutionized communications of his day; his telegraphing machine became known as "the invention of the century." (You can see a replica of the machine here at the visitors center.)

As an artist, Morse excelled in painting (and sculpture as well) and a visit to Locust Grove will introduce you to his skilled work. His finely drawn paintings established him as a preeminent painter of the Romantic School. (When his invention became famous, however, he abandoned art and lived a life of ease—as can be imagined at this idyllic spot.)

The house itself, which he redesigned after a memorable trip to Italy, is in Italianate style; it became his summer home in 1847. There is a fine collection of furniture (Chippendale, Empire, and Federal styles), in addition to paintings by other artists.

All around this beautiful house are 150 acres of trees and a spectacular view of the Hudson River. Pick up a self-guided tour brochure at the visitors center. (The house is seen by a guided tour.)

51 Notable Art and Architecture on the Vassar College Campus, Poughkeepsie

DIRECTIONS» By car, take Routes 44/55 from either the New York State Thruway (I-87) or the Taconic State Parkway. Follow the signs to Raymond Avenue. Park at the South Parking Lot on Raymond Avenue.

Vassar College, 124 Raymond Avenue, Poughkeepsie (845-896-9560; www.fllac.vassar.edu), is an unusually interesting campus to discover from both an artistic and architectural viewpoint. Its museum houses an exceptional collection. To see the museum or other public buildings, visit Tuesday–Saturday 10 AM–5 PM, or Sunday 1 PM–5 PM. As you enter the campus, pick up a map from the guard on duty.

Vassar College
124 Raymond Avenue
Poughkeepsie
845-896-9560
www.fllac.vassar.edu

The visitor with an interest in architecture will want to walk through this campus, map in hand, for here are notable buildings—styles ranging from Beaux-Art to Brutalist, Arts and Crafts to postmodern. But our first stop is to see the art collection.

The fine museum is called the Frances Lehman Loeb Art Center. It has a contemporary glass pavilion entranceway into a traditional museum gallery. The 1994 addition was designed by César Pelli and Associates, and it has a bright, modern look.

Among the excellent holdings in the collection are American and European paintings and sculpture from medieval to modern eras, a fine collection of Greek and Roman antiquities, the Magoon Collection of Hudson River School paintings, early photographs, and many old master prints. At any time, about 350 works (out of a collection of some 12,000 items) are on view. Recent shows suggest the wide range of the museum's collection: Japanese prints, contemporary photos and film, and American mural drawings of the 1930s.

Just behind the museum (on the Raymond Avenue side) is a pretty sculpture garden designed by Diana Balmori.

177

The next building to see is Vassar Chapel. A Norman Revival structure (designed by Shepley Rutan and Coolidge, 1904) it was built of granite with sandstone trim. It is a huge and imposing building with an asymmetrically positioned tower, and a series of arched doorways reminiscent of medieval churches. There are notable stained-glass windows: one group on the west nave is by John La Farge, while the other series is by Louis Comfort Tiffany (on the east side), and the nave window is also by Tiffany. On both sides of the organ you'll find windows by Robert Leftwich Dodge.

Several architecturally interesting buildings are next on your tour.

To your left is the New England Building (named for its alumnae donors). Notable for its Beaux-Arts style, it was designed by York and Sawyer Architects in 1901. (If you look carefully, you'll see a piece of Plymouth Rock ensconced above the door.

Next is Olmsted Hall (1972), a fortresslike, functionalist brick building. Its rather forbidding exterior is unbroken by windows or any decorative elements, suggesting the Brutalist style of architecture.

The Seeley C. Mudd Chemistry Building of 1984 is next. It is a glass-oriented postmodern structure from 1954.

It is followed on our tour by the Vogelstein Center for Drama and Film. Designed by César Pelli and Associates (2003), this horizontally striped building is attached to 19th-century Avery Hall. Both buildings are worth looking at from an architectural standpoint.

Ferry House, designed by Marcel Breuer in 1951, is an example of the famous architect's international style; it was the first modernist building on campus. Walk in to see the attractive interior.

Kautz Admission House of 1908 (renovated in 1995) is an Arts and Crafts–style building with notable details of design, such as the dark woodwork associated with the period.

There are many other interesting architectural sites; on your map you'll see Noyes House, designed in 1958 by the Finnish architect Eero Saarinen. This building, in a circular shape, uses expressionistic, sculptural forms.

Your map will also guide you to the well-known Main Building, designed by James Renwick Jr. in 1865; the Students' Building, designed by McKim, Mead and

White in 1913; and the Frederick Ferris Thompson Memorial Library (1905, 1977, 2007.)

52 Spectacular Campus Additions in Architecture and Art: Bard College, Annandale-on-Hudson

DIRECTIONS » By car from New York City, take the Henry Hudson Parkway north to the Saw Mill River Parkway, and then the Taconic State Parkway. Exit at Red Hook/Route 199 and go west 10 miles on Route 199 through Red Hook. Turn right onto Route 9G, continue for 1.6 miles, and follow the signs to Bard. Alternatively, take the New York State Thruway (I-87) north to Kingston (exit 19) and take Route 209 over the Kingston-Rhinecliff Bridge. Turn left onto Route 9G and go north for 3.5 miles to Bard.

Bard College, 30 Campus Road, Annandale-on-Hudson (845-758-7472) is open year-round. Guided tours of the campus are offered regularly, Monday–Friday 9:30 AM–3:30 PM; call in advance. Or you can walk around on your own to view the buildings from the outside (inside access is limited, except for special events). Pick up a map of the campus, available at the Admission Office.

Bard College
30 Campus Road
Annandale-on-Hudson
845-758-7472
www.bard.edu

Nowadays, some of the most interesting architecture and art seems to be on college campuses. And a good example is Bard College, a dynamic institution with many creative people. Here you'll find several relatively new buildings that stand out for their prominence as well as their artistic merit, being the works of internationally acclaimed architects.

Two of Bard's newest buildings—also the most dramatic—are in themselves worth a trip here: the Richard B. Fisher Center for the Performing Arts and the Gabrielle H. Reem and Herbert J. Kayden Center for Science and Computation.

Bard, a small liberal arts college beautifully situated high above the Hudson, was founded in 1860 on the site of two historic riverfront estates. The scenic grounds include some 550 acres of meadows, woodlands, wetlands, gardens, an arboretum, and many fine views. The buildings on campus are of different styles and eras, but somehow work well together. Because of the vastness of the campus, you are best off driving around (with a few stops now and again) to see the campus and its varied structures—from old stone houses to contemporary examples.

The striking Center for the Performing Arts stands alone, apart from the other buildings. It is one of the best-known works by Frank Gehry, a superstar in the world of architecture. (Gehry has built on other American campuses, including Princeton University.) The structure, like others he has designed, seems to come from another world: bold, defiant, with twisted shapes and billowing forms. The giant (110,000 square feet!) sculpturelike center is made of steel and glass, topped by a massive roof (some say that is appears to move like a wave reaching the sky). You will want to spend time walking around this most original work of art and architecture, and if possible go inside to see the state-of-the-art studios, rehearsal halls, and theater.

The other recent building of note on campus is the Center for Science and Computation, designed by Rafael Viñoly, an Uruguayan-born architect who also enjoys an international reputation. Whereas Gehry's building on campus is bold and massive, this structure is sleek and elegant, with elongated lines. It fits well with its surroundings (in the middle of the campus). Less than half the size of the other (49,000 square feet), it is located within a plaza with walkways. The materials used are gently curving glass and concrete, with an aluminum structure cantilevered over a walkway. The interior is designed to encourage flexibility and easy interaction, with an open floor plan.

You can continue to wander about and discover additional buildings of architectural and artistic interest on this inviting campus—the library, for one, has a relatively new addition by Robert Venturi; and the Center for Curatorial Studies and Art in Contemporary Culture (another recent addition) has nice space for exhibitions.

53 A Chinese Landscape in Dutchess County: Innisfree Garden, Millbrook

DIRECTIONS » By car from New York City, take the Henry Hudson Parkway (it becomes the Saw Mill River Parkway shortly) and follow the signs for the Taconic State Parkway. Take the Taconic exit at Poughkeepsie/ Millbrook (Route 44), and go east on Route 44. Look for Tyrrell Road on your right. The entrance to Innisfree is from Tyrel Road.

The artistic gardens of **Innisfree Garden**, Tyrrel Road, Millbrook (845-677-8000; innisfreegarden.com), are well worth a foray into the countryside. **H** May–October, Wednesday–Friday 10 AM–4 PM; Saturday and Sunday 11 AM–5 PM. (Closed Monday and Tuesday.) Admission fee.

Innisfree Garden
Tyrrel Road
Millbrook
845-677-8000
innisfreegarden.com

Traditional Chinese gardens, known for their rare beauty, delicacy, and symbolism, have long inspired artists, scholars, nature lovers, and others. The exquisite gardens of Innisfree, near Millbrook, offer a fine example of this ancient Chinese art form. A stroll through them is like walking through an outdoor art gallery: you experience the essence of Chinese landscape paintings, and bring them to life, as you go from one to the next.

This remarkable site, created in the 1920s, was the culmination of 25 years' dedication on the part of Walter Beck, a painter, and his wife, Marion. Inspired mostly by the Chinese scrolls of the eighth-century poet/painter Wang Wei, they based their design for Innisfree on the "cup garden," an ancient tradition in which an object is "framed" and set apart from its surroundings. Lester Collins, the landscape architect at Innisfree for years, explained the concept as follows: "You build a picture out of nature; you control the floor and the walls, and you bring the sky down."

At Innisfree you walk from one "picture" to the next, each time focusing on one element: it could be a lotus flower, a meadow, a moss-covered rock. Although the setting is made to appear naturally wild, it has been carefully planned and put together. Nothing has been left to chance. The two quintessential elements in Chinese gardens—water (yin) and mountains/rocks (yang) are well represented here, with rocks of all shapes and sizes, as well as cooling fountains, streams, and pools. Complemented by shrubs, trees, and occasional groupings of iris or primrose (Chinese gardens do not focus on flowers per se), this harmonious arrangement is said to occasion spiritual well-being, tranquility, and reflection.

Before beginning your walk, be sure to pick up a map and self-guided tour (near the parking area). You will follow pathways around a pretty lake with its own little island and wind your way through hemlock woods, and discover a waterfall, an intriguing cave, stone statues, incredible rock formations (some are shaped like exotic animals), and other pleasures. You may well feel like a traveler exploring a wondrous land filled with surprises that come unfolded as you make your way, reminiscent of a Chinese handscroll painting.

54 An Artists' Collaborative: The Wassaic Project, Wassaic

Wassaic Project
37 Furnace Bank Road,
the Maxon Mills
Wassaic
347-815-0783
www.wassaic
project.com

NEW YORK STATE

DIRECTIONS » By car from New York City, take the Sprain Brook Parkway/State Highway 987F and continue onto Taconic State Parkway (north). Take the Saw Mill Parkway exit toward Brewster (north). Take the exit toward I-684 north, keeping left at the fork. Follow the signs and merge onto I-684 north. Continue onto Route 22 north, which becomes Route 22 north/Route 55 east. Turn right onto Furnace Bank Road.

Located in a refurbished grain elevator and mill is a multiarts, artist-run community: the **Wassaic Project**, 37 Furnace Bank Road, the Maxon Mills, Wassaic (347-815-0783; www.wassaicproject.com), which provides year-round activities by resident artists, such as workshops, exhibitions, and studio visits. There is an annual free summer festival of multidisciplinary events, including over 100 artists, bands, poetry readings, films, and more.

55 Buddhist Symbols and Influences in Rural Putnam County: Chuang Yen Monastery, Carmel

DIRECTIONS » The Chuang Yen Monastery is located 10 miles east of Cold Spring, on Route 301. By car from New York City, take the Henry Hudson Parkway north to the Saw Mill River Parkway to the Taconic State Parkway to Route 301 east toward Carmel; go 1.7 miles to the entrance on the left, at 2020 Route 301.

Chuang Yen Monastery
2020 Route 301
Carmel
845-225-1819
www.baus.org

A visit to the **Chuang Yen Monastery**, 2020 Route 301, Carmel (845-225-1819; www.baus.org) makes one think of a movie set. **H** April–December, daily 9 AM–5 PM. (Closed January–March.)

As you arrive at the extraordinary walkway to the Great Buddha Hall, flanked by sculpted elephants and 19 statues of disciples, you will see a giant, eye-catching edifice, the main building of the Chuang Yen Monastery. This brightly colored, glamorously set building is overwhelmingly huge and grand, and more or less Asian in design. It looks more like an imaginary Chinese palace than a religious building, but as such is still one the most startling art sites around.

Epitomizing the idea of postmodern mélange in architecture, it is vaguely Tang Dynasty (a.d. 618–907) with stepped roof lines and huge, unsupported empty hall space. It is purported to be the largest such building in the Western Hemisphere (24,000 square feet within) and can accommodate 2,000 people. Apparently such grand edifices were designed to hold thousands of monks.

The architectural design, with its many levels of roofs and shadowing eaves, is traditionally associated with historic Chinese architecture, but its overall look is a blend of the traditional and a grandiose American version of an ancient culture.

Inside you'll find 10,000 small Buddhas in the vast space, a mural, a lotus terrace, and a predominant color: orange.

There are a number of additional buildings in the enclave, as well as the pretty Seven Jewel Lake, which is adorned by a 10-foot-high statue of Buddha.

As you walk around, you'll see a library, dining hall, living quarters for the monks etc., but your eye will be drawn back to the Great Hall. While it may not be the place for those truly interested in Chinese art of the past, it is a fascinating amalgam of a traditional Asian idiom and a "Disney-esque" sensibility. Visitors are welcome, but check hours and events in advance.

EAST OF THE HUDSON

Chuang Yen Monastery

56 Focusing on Changing Points of View: The Katonah Museum of Art, Katonah

Katonah Museum of Art
134 Jay Street/Route 22
Katonah
914-232-9555
www.katonah
   museum.org

DIRECTIONS» By car, take I-684 to exit 6, onto Route 35 east. At the first traffic light, turn right onto Route 22 south. Drive 0.25 mile to the museum.

An unusually interesting exurban museum, the **Katonah Museum of Art**, 134 Jay Street/Route 22, Katonah (914-232-9555; www.katonahmuseum.org), presents 10 to 12 exhibitions a year, covering a wide range of topics. For example, recent shows included *The Surreal Worlds of Kay Sage and Yves Tanguy*; and *The Human Comedy: Portraits by Red Grooms*. In a building designed by Edward Larrabee Barnes, the Katonah Museum shows curated exhibits (this is a non-collecting museum) with "focused and original points of view." There are numerous events and educational workshops. 🕐 Tuesday–Saturday 10 AM–5 PM, Sunday noon–5 PM. (Closed Monday.) Admission fee; admission free for children under age 12.

57 A One-of-a-Kind Sculpture Park on Corporate Grounds: The Donald M. Kendall Sculpture Park at PepsiCo, Purchase

DIRECTIONS» By car from New York, take the Hutchinson River Parkway north to exit 28 (Lincoln Avenue). Note the sign indicating SUNY/Purchase. After the exit, go left on Lincoln Avenue to its end. Turn right onto Anderson Hill Road; the entrance is on the right.

This walk is one of our favorites, with or without children, with friends or family visiting from afar, or by ourselves. If this is your first visit to the **Donald M. Kendall Sculpture Gardens at PepsiCo**, you are in for a wonderful surprise. Yes, this is an inviting site with impressive art beautifully displayed throughout a vast landscape; but what makes it unusual is that this corporate collection is open to the public.

These 112 acres to the public daily, free of charge, year-round, without restriction—a rarity these days, in the case of corporate art!, once the site of a polo field, are dotted with more than 40 sculptures by noted contemporary artists. The former CEO of PepsiCo, Donald M. Kendall, had the idea of collecting and displaying sculpture to inspire creativity in the corporate world. The imposing headquarter building (a somewhat austere 1970 structure of square blocks by Edward Durrell Stone) is surrounded by courtyards, fountains, and intimate flower gardens.

The landscape, planned by internationally known designer Russell Page, includes some formal gardens with smaller works carefully set amid clipped hedges and other groomed plantings. A pleasing lake with fountain and winding pathway is set near the main building. Beyond are vast fields where massive works stand dramatically for all to view from a distance, and in back are well-tended woodlands.

Begin your walk, once you have parked your car in one of the discreet parking areas, hidden by plantings. (Everything here at PepsiCo is tastefully designed and maintained.) At the Visitor Center you'll find a map indicating each and every artwork and suggested routes. You can follow the Golden Path, which winds around the entire area, or set forth on your own, consulting the map now and again.

Among the many works you'll see is Alexander Calder's *Hats Off* (1973), a giant work easily identified as Calder's by its orange-red metal. Set against a backdrop of white fir and blue spruce, it is a striking abstraction. Jean Dubuffet's *Kiosque L'évidé*, a 1985 black-and-white painted abstraction, does look like some fantastic kind of kiosk with its whimsical shapes and painted designs. Dubuffet described his works in this style not as sculptures but as "unleashed graphisms, drawings which extend and expand in space." Arnaldo Pomodoro's *Grand Disco* (1968) is a variation on the form of the globe—eaten away by mysterious forces; his *Triad*, one of the most memorable and dramatic works in the park, consists of a group of three modern, but ancient-looking, columns set starkly against the landscape. David Smith's *Cube Totem Seven and Six*, is typical of his style in this delightful shiny metal work. Marino Marini's charming *Horse and Rider* (1950) is now somewhat of a "classic"; although Marini's signature horse and rider images are familiar, they always a pleasure to see anew. In Alberto Giacometti's *Large Standing Woman II* and *Large Standing Woman III* (1960), their tall, thin figures are sharply defined against the main building's wall. Max Ernst's *Capricorn* (1948) is one of the most interesting works. Kenneth Snelson's *Mozart II* (1985) is a giant aluminum construction of geometric shapes and wires, a most contemporary tribute to Mozart. Auguste

EAST OF THE HUDSON

Donald M. Kendall Sculpture Gardens at PepsiCo
Anderson Hill Road
Purchase

Rodin's *Eve* is perhaps the most traditional work on this artwalk, but it is interesting to see the origins of contemporary sculpture in this lovely 1881 work. It is charmingly set among holly trees and shrubbery. George Segal's *Three People on Four Benches* (1979), a characteristically superrealistic work, may remind you of PepsiCo's workers relaxing during their lunch break. Claes Oldenburg's *Giant Trowel II* (1971–76) is one of the most memorable sights at PepsiCo. It is so starling against its background of pine and dogwood trees that you blink to see whether the giant spade is really there, digging into the green earth. George Rickey's *Double L Eccentric Gyratory* II is a typical Rickey work made up of stainless-steel windmill-like blades that shift gently in the breeze. Judith Brown's 1982 sculpture *Caryatids* is an interesting postmodern work that is reminiscent of ancient art—using old car parts in a highly contemporary manner. Don't miss this impression of crumbling ruins made of steel bits. David Wynne, with five sculptures displayed on the grounds—*Dancer with a Bird*, *Girl on a Horse*, *Grizzly Bear*, *Girl with a Dolphin*, and *The Dancers*)—is the best represented of all. Louise Nevelson's *Celebration II* (1979) is a dark collection of geometric metal forms set in soft ground

Henry Moore:
Reclining Woman,
Donald M. Kendall
Sculpture Gardens

cover amid a stand of copper beech trees that reflect the color of the sculpture. Robert Davidson's *Totems* (1984) consists of three giant totems that will remind you of northwest-coast Native American carvings. This work stands out for its audacity, bright colors and dramatic design. Henry Moore's *Double Oval* (1968–70), on the edge of the lake, is a splendid monument to modern art. These are just some of the highlights of works gracing these magnificent grounds.

If you enjoy nature as well as sculpture, notice rare plantings, including some from Japan and China. A list of these trees is available at the Visitors Center; but we will also mention a stand of birch trees, an oak grove, a stand of witch hazels, lacebark pine from China, European hornbeam, black locusts, sweet gum, walnut, hemlock, cypress, and dawn redwood. Among the wonderful flowering plantings are azaleas, rhododendrons and crab apples, so you might want to take this walk in April or May—at the height of the flowering shrub season. In any case, we think you'll find this combination of natural and artistic pleasures a rare treat.

Just across the street (Anderson Hill Road) you can see more modern art at the **Neuberger Museum of Art, SUNY**. (914-251-6100, www.neuberger.org) ❿ Tuesday–Sunday noon–5 PM. (Closed Monday.) Entrance fee.

Neuberger Museum of Art, SUNY
735 Anderson Hill Road
Purchase
914-251-6100
www.neuberger.org

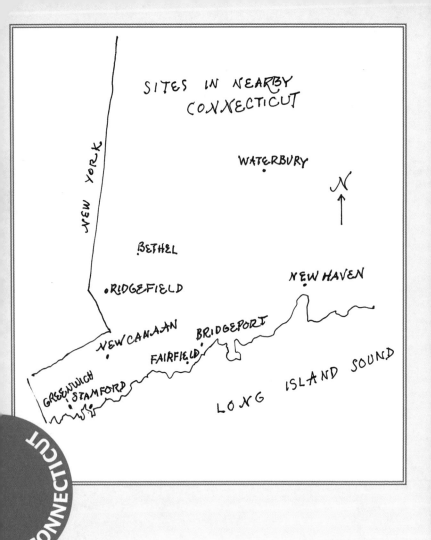

SITES IN NEARBY CONNECTICUT

NEW YORK

WATERBURY

N

BETHEL

•RIDGEFIELD

NEW HAVEN

NEW CANAAN

BRIDGEPORT

FAIRFIELD

GREENWICH

STAMFORD

LONG ISLAND SOUND

CONNECTICUT

III. CONNECTICUT
SOUTH

58 A Gathering Place for American Impressionists: Bush-Holley House, Cos Cob

DIRECTIONS» By car from New York City, I-95 north to exit 4 (Indian Field Road) to Cos Cob (Greenwich) and continue for less than 1 mile. Take a left at Indian Fields Road, then right onto Strickland Road/Station Drive. You will soon see the Bush-Holley site on your right.

Around the turn of the 20th century, a colony of American impressionists gathered at a very old and charming boardinghouse. The 1794 **Bush-Holley House** historic site, 39 Strickland Road, Greenwich (203-869-6899; www.hstg.org)—and its barn, shed, and wash house—are interesting as a historic Connecticut site (the house was once used as a post office), but it has a much more artistic history as well. ♿ The house and grounds are open Tuesday–Sunday noon–4 PM. (Closed Monday.) House tours are given at 12:15, 1:15, 2:15, and 3:15 PM. Admission fee.

Bush-Holley House
39 Strickland Road,
Greenwich
203-869-6899
www.hstg.org

Originally housing David Bush, who ran a mill there from 1764 on, the house had numerous additions (including Victorian windows) over the years. It was purchased by Edward P. Holley in 1884.

In the 1890s, the painter John Henry Twachtman asked Holley if he could open his house to Twachtman's art students, and from that time on, the Bush-Holley House became a meeting place and inspiration to several generations of American impressionists and every early abstractionist. Twachtman was joined by J. Alden Weir (see chapter 65), Childe Hassam, Theodore Robinson, and many other painters. Among them were several organizers of the 1913 Armory Show. In addition to the many artists who gathered there, literary folks came to visit, too, among them Willa Cather and Lincoln Steffens.

You can visit the house (now a museum) and even take a walking tour on Sundays to see some of the favorite sites painted by the many landscapists who gathered in Cos Cob. Childe Hassam, in fact, described the colony as "the Cos Cob Clapboard School of Art."

59 Bruce Museum, Greenwich

DIRECTIONS » By car, take I-95 to exit 3 to Arch Street, which becomes Museum Drive. Follow the signs to the museum.

The **Bruce Museum**, 1 Museum Drive, Greenwich (203-869-0376; www.brucemuseum.org). **🕐** Tuesday–Saturday 10 AM–4:30 PM, Sunday 1 PM–4 PM. (Closed Monday.) Admission fee; free admission for children under age 5. This imposing building just off the thruway is a century old; it is both an art museum and a science center. There are a number of large sculptural works set in the grassy expanses surrounding the museum. They include works by Luis Arata, Lynn Chadwick, David Boxley, and Elizabeth Strong-Cuevas. Changing exhibitions include photography, textiles, fossils, drawings, and Native American art and artifacts—and there are many events for children.

60 A Modernist Design in Architecture and Stained Glass: Stamford's Fish-Shaped Church, Stamford

DIRECTIONS » By car, take the Merritt Parkway to exit 34. Take Long Ridge Road to downtown Stamford. Make a right on Summer Street, a left on Bedford Street, and then another left on Bedford Street.

Certainly one of the most unusual and eye-catching of churches, the **First Presbyterian Church**, 1101 Bedford Street, Stamford (203-324-9522; www.fishchurch.org), is worth a visit. In early Christian symbolism, the fish was representative of the Church: Because they were forbidden to practice their religion, early Christians drew a fish in the sand to direct worshippers to their services. Here we have a modern version of an ancient tradition: the First Presbyterian Church is shaped like a fish and is certainly one of the most unusual religious structures we have ever seen.

In melding symbolism with modernism, the architect, Wallace K. Harrison (who also designed Lincoln Center, Rockefeller Center, and the United Nations Building) created an eye-catching design that is flanked by the tallest carillon tower (260 feet) in New England. Some of its 50 bells can be seen through its surprisingly transparent construction.

The "fish church" itself is in two sections (suggesting the body and tail of the fish). Its scales are represented by small pieces of Vermont slate.

There is a soaring interior space with a dramatic sanctuary (open to visitors), and of particular note, a vast use of stained glass. More than 20,000 jewel-like pieces of stained glass make up these extraordinary windows that seem to combine a magnificent Gothic tradition with a modern sensibility. The windows were made in Chartres, France, by a noted stained-glass artist, Gabriel Loire. He used 86 different colors and tones—particularly the blues, greens, and reds, which reflect the light and seem to change as the sky darkens. Although most of the windows appear abstract in design, you can occasionally discern crosses of white glass, or a Crucifixion scene, among others. (Be sure to note the windows behind the altar.)

The vast, soaring space, and the exquisite stained glass seem to be both modern and Gothic at the same time—a rare accomplishment.

Pick up a flier at the desk; it will detail the origins of various elements, including the 32-foot-high wooden cross, which came from Canterbury Cathedral after the bombing of World War II.

61 Stamford Museum and Nature Center: A Surprising Sculpture Trail amid the Greenery, Stamford

DIRECTIONS» By car, take Hutchinson River Parkway to the Merritt Parkway to exit 35. Go left at the bottom of the ramp. Continue 0.75 mile and go left at the traffic light. The museum is on your right.

Stamford Museum and Nature Center, 39 Scofield Town Road, Stamford (203-322-1646; www.stamford-museum.org). Ⓗ Monday–Saturday 9 AM–5 PM, Sunday 11 AM–5 PM. Admission fee.

Stamford Museum and Nature Center
39 Scofield Town Road, Stamford
203-322-1646
www.stamford museum.org

While the nature center here is well known for its many classes and events; and the museum, for its Native American artifacts (among other treasures), not many out-of-towners are familiar with its surprising sculpture trail. On its 120-acre preserve—amid animals, maple sugaring, an 18th-century farm, and other picturesque natural sights, you'll find this sculpture trail (which begins at the lower parking lot) nestled among towering trees. One of the delights of the setting is the changing light seen and reflecting through the tree branches onto the contemporary sculpture.

191

In addition to those along this evocative trail, there are sculptures on the museum's patio, a terrace, and a large lawn near a lake. Most of the artwork is modern and abstract, so if you enjoy 20- and 21st-century sculpture, such as the X-shaped metal work by Peter Forakis or the COR-TEN steel sculpture by Lila Katzen or the abstract forms of Reuben Nakian or Grace Knowlton, this will be a visit you won't want to miss. (There are also earlier works here as well—even a Gutzon Borglum.)

The museum and nature center date originally to 1936, when surgeon G. R. R. Hertzberg founded it as an educational and scientific center for children. This property was added in 1957. But the outdoor sculpture collection began only in 1987, with a grant from the National Endowment for the Arts.

The combination of art and nature is always a fascinating exploration of forms, light, and space—and this sculpture trail is no exception. Here you can even enjoy old-fashioned fountains and stone lions among the large symbolic forms of modernism and the natural forms of trees, geese, ducks, and plantings.

62 John Rogers Studio, New Canaan

DIRECTIONS » By car, take Merritt Parkway to exit 37. Go north on Route 124 to New Canaan.

As one of several structures in this historical New Canaan Historical Society complex, the **John Rogers Studio**, 13 Oenoke Ridge, New Canaan (203-966-1776; www.nchistory.org), is a small wooden building that was the studio of a 19th-century sculptor. Between 1878 and 1904, Rogers produced numerous works here; some 30 of his *Rogers Groups* remain here. ❶ Tuesday–Friday 9:30 AM–4:30 PM, Saturday 9:30 AM–12:30 PM. (Closed Sunday and Monday.) John Rogers Studio tour by appointment only.

63 Housatonic Museum of Art, Bridgeport

DIRECTIONS » By car, take the Connecticut Turnpike (I-95) to exit 27 (Lafayette). Take the exit ramp straight to Lafayette Boulevard and turn left. The museum entrance is 1 1/2 blocks farther.

An unusually strong collection of modern and contemporary art can be seen at the **Housatonic Museum of Art**, 900 Lafayette Boulevard, Bridgeport (203-

CONNECTICUT

John Rogers Studio
13 Oenoke Ridge
New Canaan
203-966-1776
www.nchistory.org

Housatonic Museum of Art
900 Lafayette Boulevard
Bridgeport
203-332-5000
www.hcc.commnet.edu

332-5000; www.hcc.commnet.edu). ⏰ Monday, Wednesday, and Friday 8:30 AM–5:30 PM; Thursday 8:30 AM–7 PM; Saturday 9 AM–3 PM. (Closed Sunday and Tuesday.) Free admission. Among the noted artists represented by drawings, paintings, and sculpture are Picasso, Matisse, De Chirico, Warhol, Lichtenstein, and Dine.

64 Yale University: From Notable Buildings to Memorable Art, New Haven

DIRECTIONS » By car, from I-95 (Connecticut Turnpike) take exit 48 and take Route 34 into New Haven to Church Street. Turn right on Church Street to Chapel Street. Park in the vicinity of the New Haven Green (there are both metered street parking and a parking garage on College Street).

Yale University, 246 Church Street, New Haven (203-432-2700; www.yaleuniversity.edu). Visit Yale University Information Center at 149 Elm Street (which borders the New Haven Green). We recommend a campus map available at the center.

Yale University
246 Church Street
New Haven
203-432-2700
www.yaleuniversity.edu

A tour of this venerable university in downtown New Haven will take you to a number of notable and historic buildings—among them several important art sites.

We recommend that you begin your walk (map in hand) at New Haven Green, which has three notable 19th-century churches to see. Continue to Phelps Gate (1895), a Tudor-style entry to the campus, and continue on to Dwight Hall, designed in the 1840s in the Gothic Revival style by the notable Henry Austin.

Turning to your right, you'll find the Old Arts Building with its Romanesque arches and castlelike towers. In it you'll find some original Tiffany windows.

Continue along Chapel Street to the Yale University Art Gallery, our first visit to the university's unusually fine art collection and programs. Yale's Art Gallery complex, just recently renovated, now includes three contiguous buildings: the 1953 Louis Kahn modernist building, the 1928 old Yale Art Gallery, and the 1886 neo-Gothic Street Hall. The extraordinarily rich collection now includes 65,000 square feet of exhibition space. Here you'll find an outstanding collection, ranging from Italian Renaissance paintings to African sculpture; great paintings, such as Van Gogh's *Night Café* and Joseph Stella's *Brooklyn Bridge*; pre-Columbian

César Pelli's Malone
Center at Yale
University

art, Henry Moore sculptures, and excavations from Dura-Europos.

Directly across the street, at 100 Chapel Street, is the more recent Louis Kahn building, the Yale Center for British Art (also known as the Mellon Center). The Kahn building, the first "modern" structure on the campus, was the subject of some controversy with its blank, four-story brick façade and interior open concrete work. It represented a departure from the historical styling of traditional college buildings; today it is one of the many modernist structures at the university. Kahn was a consultant to Yale's architecture program for many years; his buildings made an indelible impression on the campus. Built in 1977, this distinguished museum houses a fine collection of British art within an architectural work of art. Considered the "best" building at Yale by many critics, Kahn's structure (which was built several years after his death) is a rectangular, four-story building with a flat roof and many skylights. Its outer cladding is subtly graded in color, allowing reflections of sky and light, and the interior is airy, bright, and spacious. Its façade is divided into numerous rectangles of brushed metal. Kahn's building integrated shops with its street façade—an unusual gesture to the urban streetscape. Although the building may be described as "functional" architecture for

its unadorned geometric form, it uses its modernity to reference the other art buildings on the Yale campus. Kahn described his efforts as combining "silence and light," an attempt to explore the expressive powers of simple forms with reference to historical styles.

The museum houses a truly remarkable collection—considered the best of its kind outside of England. Ranging from drawings to prints, sculpture, and rare books to great paintings including works by Stubbs, Gainsborough, and Turner.

Continue on Chapel Street to the corner of York Street. The Art and Architecture Building (180 York Street) is your next stop. Designed by the architect Paul Rudolph, it was built in 1963 and is another example of modernism on the urban campus. Rudolph was the first chairman of Yale's Architectural Department. The A&A Building, as it is known, has been the subject of controversy since its dedication (it was described critically as "architecture as art"); even a major fire in the building in 1969 was viewed with suspicion. In fact, it seemed a typically grand modernist gesture in rough concrete, composed of a wide variety of rectangles. Plagued with many technical problems, it has now been renovated by Gwathmey Siegel & Associates, which has also constructed a new adjacent building.

Your tour will take you to York Street and Broadway to see a 1961 complex, Morse and Stiles Colleges by Eero Saarinen, one of the best-known 20th-century architects. At Elm Street you'll also see Sterling Library designed by James Gamble Rogers in 1930, and the Gilmore Music Library.

If medieval manuscripts and letters by famous people are of interest, don't miss one of Yale's most important collections. You'll find the Beinecke Rare Book and Manuscript Library on Grove Street. This very elegant building of bronze, glass, and thick translucent marble walls (which capture the changing light outdoors) was designed by James Gamble Rogers in 1931. Among the notable manuscripts and prints are original works of Audubon, letters of Mark Twain, Gertrude Stein, and Ernest Hemingway. You can also see an original Gutenberg Bible.

There are many other notable buildings to see, representing different eras and styles of architecture; in fact the Yale campus can be seen as a panoply of American architecture. This is an outing for art and architecture enthusiasts of all kinds.

FARTHER NORTH

65 J. Alden Weir, Impressionism and the "Group of Ten" at Weir Farm, Wilton

DIRECTIONS» Weir Farm is located in southwestern Connecticut in the towns of Ridgefield and Wilton. By car from New York City, take the Merritt Parkway to Route 7 north, through Wilton and Branchville. Go left on Route 102; take the second road on your left, Old Branchville Road; turn left on Nod Hill Road to Weir Farm. The Weir Preserve is entered at either Pelham Lane or Nod Hill Road; signs are posted.

Weir Farm National Historic Site, 735 Nod Hill Road, Wilton (203-762-0237). ♿ The Visitor Center is open April–November, Thursday–Sunday 10 AM–4 PM; December–March, Saturday and Sunday 10 AM–4 PM. The grounds are open year-round from dawn until dusk. Free admission to grounds and Visitor Center.

Western Connecticut is an area of gentle hills, stone walls, fine old oak trees, and red barns. Its rolling landscape is tranquil and picturesque, rather than dramatic. It is the kind of place that is inviting for walkers, particularly at its greenest, in late spring or summer, when the light and the colors seem wonderfully fresh.

Sometime after dozens of painters had begun flocking to Giverny in France to learn about impressionism from the master, Claude Monet, a small but significant group of Americans started painting outdoors in Connecticut, taking the first steps toward American impressionism.

These outdoor artists were brought to the area by the artist J. Alden Weir, who purchased an old farm in Branchville (now part of Ridgefield) in 1882 for $10 and a still-life painting, six months after Monet moved to Giverny. With his colleague John Henry Twachtman, and many friends including John Singer Sargent, Childe Hassam, and Albert Pinkham Ryder, Weir explored the Connecticut landscape. Weir and Twachtman began painting outdoors and examining the light's effect on color—taking the first gentle steps toward the European style of impressionism. Weir Farm was the scene of great artistic activity from the 1880s until Weir's death in 1919. Its studios and the surrounding landscape (a delightful stroll covering 62 acres) were saved from development at the last minute. Although the farm has shrunk from its original 238 acres, it is still large enough to include many a picturesque landscape, and even a lily pond that Weir built, perhaps with Giverny in mind.

Weir, the son of a drawing professor at West Point, Robert Weir (who taught both Generals Grant and Lee, by the way), and younger brother of landscapist John Ferguson Weir, was for many years a conservative, academic painter. When he went off as a young man to study art in Paris, he wrote back in 1877, "I went across the river the other day to see an exhibition of the work of a new school, which call themselves 'Impressionists.' I never in my life saw more horrible things. They do not observe drawing nor form but give you an impression of what they call nature."

Weir had come from an American academic artistic background, painting realistic topographical scenes and giving major importance to drawing and form in his compositions. The hazy impressionistic painting that he saw abroad opposed the principles with which he had come to Europe. He shared American's anti-European feeling about "foreign" styles of art, though he—like all young artists—went there for traditional art study.

On his return to the United States, Weir settled in New York, where he was a successful painter of delicate, naturalistic still-lifes, flower pieces, portraits, and domestic scenes. But Weir was a great nature lover, having been raised on Emerson and "back to nature" themes.

In 1882, he moved his family to the farm in Connecticut to escape urban life; soon the beauty of his surroundings beckoned him to begin outdoor painting. Before long, Weir—a gregarious and magnetic figure in the art world—had brought other painters to his home in Branchville. He was to paint there every summer for 37 years. By 1890, he and Twachtman were experimenting with impressionistic canvases of scenes on the farm, using pure colors from the prism to create the sense of flickering light and changes in the atmosphere. They became so excited by outdoor painting that they even devised a portable winter studio. (You will see the sites of these forays on the farm when you visit.)

Weir went on to guide and organize the Ten, a loosely knit but nonetheless influential group of American impressionists. Their collective withdrawal from the established exhibitions in New York to show their works together was a revolutionary moment in

American painting. But Weir and his colleagues did not consider themselves rebels. They never abandoned entirely their American artistic roots; American impressionism retained subject matter and interest in the factual (though Weir didn't mind adding or transposing a tree or flower—he called it "hollyhocking").

Their paintings and explorations of light were an outgrowth of a tradition of luminism in American art, and they saw their experiments in painting light through the use of prismatic color as a natural step forward. They never issued a manifest of impressionism, nor sought to make dramatic political statements. Both Weir and Twachtman, as well as their colleagues in the Ten, were somewhat surprised by their designation as American impressionists.

Weir Farm became a center for artists, and Weir himself held open-air classes. Nearby Cos Cob soon became an art colony where Weir's friends took summer homes. Weir was a busy man, painting, teaching, encouraging and supporting his colleagues; and serving on the board of the Metropolitan Museum of Art and as president of the National Academy of Design. His personal charm and dynamism (he was known as "the diplomat") enabled him to move the static world of academic art forward, without dramatic means or revolutionary art.

Weir lived at the farm until his death. His daughter married the sculptor Mahonri Young, who built the beautiful second studio and continued to work there. Your tour of the farm will include studios used by both artists, and a variety of memorabilia from both of their careers.

Weir Farm has recently been dedicated as a National Historic Site, the first National Park in Connecticut. To visit its buildings, you must telephone for an appointment. When you arrive, you will receive a map and walking guide that identifies the sites of some of the Branchville paintings by Weir.

The grounds are always open for walking. We particularly liked the studios, with their clutter and confusion, including friezes, potbellied stoves, plaster casts, old photos, souvenirs, shelves of still life, and quite a bit of nice carved wainscoting.

Other views of Weir Farm painted by Weir and his colleagues include the barns, the pond, laundry on a line, and trees in the snow.

You will also find a nature preserve adjacent to Weir

Farm. The Weir Preserve consists of 110 additional acres of unspoiled Connecticut landscape given by the artist's daughter and several other residents of the area. A map with listings of wildflowers and trees is available at Weir Farm.

66 A Connecticut Sculpture Outing: Kouros Sculpture Center, the Garden of Ideas, the Aldrich Contemporary Art Museum, Ridgefield

DIRECTIONS » Kouros Sculpture Center: By car, from I-684 (in New York State) take exit 7 to Route 116 east (North Salem Road), which also becomes Route 121. Stay on 116; after the road divides, take a sharp right and look for a small, unpaved road on your left, Wallace Road. Follow for about a mile; when it becomes paved look for first driveway on the left.

» Garden of Ideas: From the Kouros Center, retrace your route to 116. After a few miles, you'll find the Garden of Ideas on your left. Look for a small green sign and a rustic fence.

FARTHER NORTH

Kouros
Sculpture Center
150 Mopus Bridge Road
Ridgefield
203-438-7636

David Hayes:
Screen Sculpture
(1995), Kouros
Sculpture Center

Juan Bordes:
La Construcción
(ca. 1990), Kouros
Sculpture Center

» **Aldrich Museum:** Return to the center of Ridgefield (following Route 116) and look for the museum at 258 Main Street (after the center of town) on your left.

Kouros Sculpture Center, 150 Mopus Bridge Road, Ridgefield (203-438-7636; for an appointment, phone the Kouros Gallery in New York City at 212-288-5888 or e-mail camillos@kourosgallery.com). ⓗ Open spring, summer, and fall, noon–6 PM. Appointments suggested. Admission fee.

Kouros is a truly remarkable place to see today's sculpture. On 6 acres of a rolling countryside in rural Connecticut, dozens of sculptures from all over the world are displayed in a beautiful, spacious landscape. These large works are part of the Kouros Gallery's collection (all are for sale), and they represent many styles and media. We have seldom seen a more interesting sculpture display, and we recommend a visit. Among the artists are the Greek sculptor Alexandra Athanassiades, who works with driftwood and metal, Bill Barrett, who produces abstract works; Spanish sculptor Juan Bordes, who is represented by a number of large thermoplastic bodies and bronze constructions; Curt Brill, whose *Diana* will catch your eye; David Hayes, whose painted steel works decorate the landscape; and John von Bergen, who works in patinated bronze in abstract mode. Other interesting sculptures are by Emanuele

De Reggi, Marianne Weil, Nicolas Vlavianos, Ron Mehlman, Lin Emery, and Bruno Romeda. Ms. Camillos, who will greet you at her home on the property, is a helpful and knowledgeable guide to the artworks.

The **Garden of Ideas**, 647 North Salem Road, Ridgefield (203-431-9914; www.gardenofideas.com). Ⓗ Mid-March to the end of November, Monday–Sunday 8 AM–6 PM (open until 7 PM during summer months). You could call the Garden of Ideas a boutique farm, an imaginative garden, or an intimate outdoor sculpture gallery: it's all of the above, described in its brochure as "the destination of choice for plant enthusiasts, nature lovers, art collectors, tomato growers, slow foodies, and bird freaks." We found it to be one of the most creatively designed green spaces we have discovered in our explorations.

Set on acres of marshes, woodlands, and meadows, this bucolic site combines native plants artfully set amid the greenery. Here herbs and peppers live alongside unusual woody plants and herbaceous perennials in a natural looking—yet well-tended—arbore-

FARTHER NORTH

Garden of Ideas
647 North Salem Road
Ridgefield
203-431-9914
www.gardenof
ideas.com

Stephen Cote: *Tin Man*, Garden of Ideas

tum-like setting. It's fun to explore the grounds, as you make your way along winding paths through little gardens and farm plots, noting the trees and decorative sculpture (which, by the way, is for sale and changes regularly). There is a great deal of whimsy in the way everything has been put together, something that will amuse children, too (so be sure to bring them along).

In the early 20th century, the property was part of a large family farm and gristmill. When farming stopped by the 1950s, a few houses were built, including the owners' present house. The 6-acre garden was created in 1995 by Joseph Keller and Ilsa Svendsen, who run it. (The remaining portion of the 12-acre property, including the lovely old barn, which was part of the original farm, is still privately owned.)

The sculpture at the Garden of Ideas is primarily in a folk art style, with figures and objects made of mixed media, painted tin, and so on. Unlike the more grandiose and impressive sculptures at the other sites in this chapter, these are small, intimate, and homemade-looking, and they fit well into their unusual surroundings of shrubbery and pathways.

The attractive **Aldrich Contemporary Art Museum**, 258 Main Street, Ridgefield (203-438-4519; www.aldrichart.org/visit), is particularly noted for its modern sculpture garden and very trendy changing exhibitions. ⓗ Tuesday–Sunday noon–5 PM. (Closed Monday.) Without visiting the galleries in New York, you can get a taste of the latest in avant-garde paintings, sculpture, constructions, and conceptual art.

The Aldrich is one of the few American museums devoted to showing contemporary artists (but not to collecting art). Therefore, whenever you visit, you'll see different exhibitions that feature emerging or mid-career artists.

The sculpture area—in a large grassy field behind the museum buildings—is a particularly intriguing part of the museum. Using a map given out at the desk, you can walk around on your own to spot the large sculptures. Among them in the past have been works by Tony Rosenthal, Arnaldo Pomodoro, Robert Morris, Lila Katzen, David Von Schlegel, Sol LeWitt, Alexander Liberman, and many other contemporary sculptors and construction artists. Admission fee for the museum; free admission on Tuesday. The sculpture garden can be seen separately without going indoors.

Aldrich Contemporary
Art Museum
258 Main Street
Ridgefield
203-438-4519
www.aldrichart.org/visit

ACROSS THE REGION

67 **The Stained-Glass Tradition in Connecticut Churches: Greenwich, Old Greenwich, Stamford, Fairfield, Bethel, and Waterbury**

DIRECTIONS » St. Paul's Roman Catholic Church, Greenwich: By car, take I-95 south to exit 2 or 3.

» Christ Episcopal Church, Greenwich: By car, take I-95 to exit 4.

» Old First Congregational Church of Greenwich, Greenwich: By car, take I-95 to exit 7.

» First Presbyterian Church, Stamford: By car, take the Merritt Parkway to exit 34. Take Long Ridge Road to downtown Stamford. Make a right on Summer Street, a left on Bedford Street, and then another left on Bedford Street.

» First Church Congregational, Fairfield: By car, take I-95 to exit 23.

» St. Thomas Episcopal Church, Bethel: By car, take Route 37 from Danbury.

» Holy Trinity Greek Orthodox Church, Waterbury: By car, take I-684 to I-84 east. Take exit 21. Take South Main Street to Tourist Information (between Grand and Center Streets.) Pick up a map of the city there.

» First Congregational Church, Waterbury: By car, take I-84 to exit 21 (Meadow Street).

The art of stained glass has been an integral part of church design since the Middle Ages; it only became common in America in the mid-19th century. The full use of stained glass—whether in abstract patterns, or as illustrations of religious stories and characters—became a major facet of Connecticut churches from the era of Louis Comfort Tiffany to today. As we tour a number of nearby Connecticut churches, we will see how the filtering of light and color into large interior spaces enhanced the architecture and the ambience of each building. Following are a few of our favorite stained-glass sites—some by notable designers, and others anonymous.

GREENWICH

St. Paul's Roman Catholic Church, 84 Sherwood Avenue (203-531-8466). The Willet Stained Glass Studios of Philadelphia made the attractive windows at

St. Paul's Roman
Catholic Church
84 Sherwood Avenue
Greenwich
203-531-8466

Christ Episcopal Church
254 East Putnam Avenue
Greenwich
203-869-6600
www.christchurch
greenwich.org

this church. Divided into semiabstract patterns of bright tones, they were created in 1962 and enhance the circular design of the building.

Christ Episcopal Church, 254 East Putnam Avenue (203-869-6600; www.christchurchgreenwich.org). Three fine Tiffany windows—including a particularly graceful angel in a field of lilies—grace this church. Made in the late 19th century, they were supplemented in the first two decades of the 20th century by windows designed by the Gorham Company (ca. 1910), Heaton, Butler & Bayne (1910 and 1915), and the Mayer Company (1910). The church has available a booklet about its outstanding windows.

OLD GREENWICH

Old First Congregational Church of Greenwich, 108 Sound Beach Avenue (203-637-1791). Not far away in Old Greenwich is a fine stone church with unusually nice windows dating to the late 19th and 20th centuries. Perhaps the most spectacular is the chancel window, created by Willet Studios in 1960s; its brilliant tones of red and blue are used to depict (on the middle panel) Christ on a donkey entering Jerusalem on Palm Sunday. Another window on the north transept dates to the 1890s. It is said to include the work of the artist John Singer Sargent. The glass is opalescent, and was made by Lamb Studios in Tenafly, New Jersey. Other windows in this church portray historical events of local interest.

Old First Congregational Church of Greenwich
108 Sound Beach Avenue
Old Greenwich
203-637-1791
www.fccog.org

CONNECTICUT

First Presbyterian Church
1101 Bedford Street
Stamford
203-324-9522
www.fishchurch.org

STAMFORD

You won't want to miss the strikingly modern, jewel-like designs of the stained-glass windows designed by French glass artist Gabriel Loire at the **First Presbyterian Church** in Stamford.

FAIRFIELD

First Church Congregational, 148 Beach Road (203-259-8396; www.firstchurchfairfield.org), which dates to 1892, is the sixth to occupy the site. Here you'll see Tiffany windows made not by his studio, but by Tiffany himself, though others are by the studio. (Note the booklet available at the church that describes his work.)

First Church Congregational
148 Beach Road
Fairfield
203-259-8396
www.firstchurch
fairfield.org

BETHEL

In **St. Thomas Episcopal Church**, 95 Greenwood Avenue (203-743-1494), which dates to the early 1900s, are several Tiffany windows, including one with a particularly striking image of Jesus with open arms, and two smaller angel windows on either side of the altar.

The more recent (1970s) windows were mostly the work of an artist named L. Ysbrend Leopold.

St. Thomas Episcopal Church
95 Greenwood Avenue
Bethel
203-743-1494

WATERBURY

Holy Trinity Greek Orthodox Church, 937 Chase Parkway (203-754-5189). Typical of the Eastern Orthodox tradition, the stained-glass windows in this church are filled with dramatic, rich color and an emphasis on iconography. They are made by Willet Hauser. The church's symbolism extends to its architecture (for example, there are 12 columns, representing Christ's 12 disciples). You can get more information on the windows, at 800-533-3960.

Holy Trinity Greek Orthodox Church
937 Chase Parkway
Waterbury
203-754-5189

First Congregational Church, 222 West Main Street (203-757-0331). Like so many of the windows in this area, the stained glass here was made by Willet Glass Studios in around 1965. They are definitely representative of that era, with modern, fragmented patterns.

First Congregational Church
222 West Main Street
Waterbury
203-757-0331

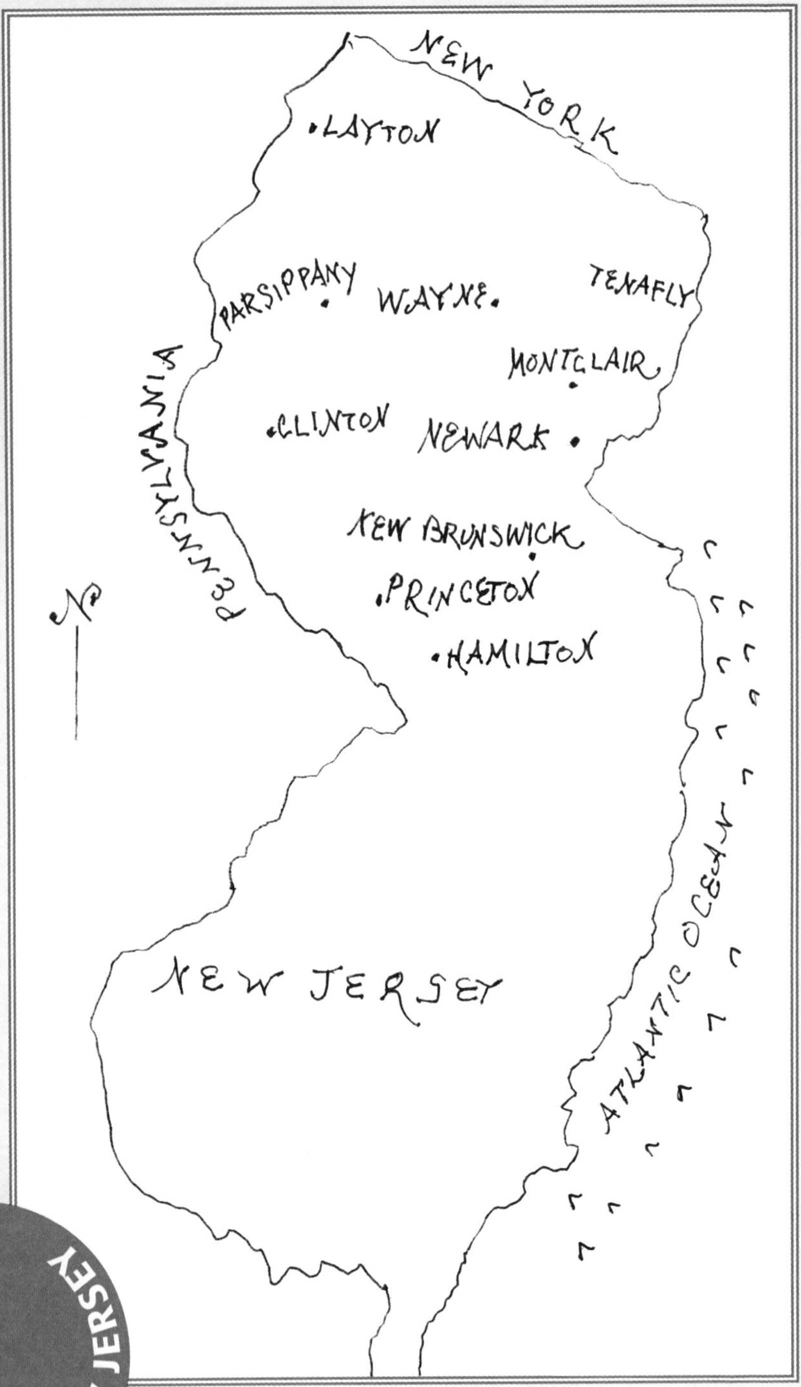

NEW YORK

•LAYTON

PARSIPPANY WAYNE•

TENAFLY

MONTCLAIR•

•CLINTON NEWARK•

NEW BRUNSWICK•

•PRINCETON

•HAMILTON

PENNSYLVANIA

N

NEW JERSEY

ATLANTIC OCEAN

NEW JERSEY

IV. NEW JERSEY
NORTH

68 **An Unusual African Art Experience: The African Art Museum of the SMA Fathers, Tenafly**

DIRECTIONS» By car, from the George Washington Bridge, take the Palisades Parkway north to first exit at Palisades Avenue. Go down the long hill to Engle Street (Englewood) and turn right. Continue past Hudson Street to Bliss Avenue (the first subsequent right) and you'll see the SMA Fathers building on your right.

SMA Fathers, 23 Bliss Avenue, Tenafly (201-894-8611; www.smafathers.org). **H** Daily 8 AM–5 PM. Free admission.

SMA Fathers
23 Bliss Avenue
Tenafly
201-894-8611
www.smafathers.org
/museum

This surprising collection—open and free to the public—is operated by the missionaries of the SMA Fathers, an order of the Catholic Church whose members work primarily in West Africa. Since the order's founding in 1856, they have amassed a fine collection of art and artifacts. This is the only museum in the state devoted entirely to African art. The exhibitions are organized in

Funerary effigy in terra cotta, Akan, Ghana, SMA Museum

a variety of imaginative ways, including by tribe, by usage, by country, and recently in a show called *Values in African Art and Culture*. Some exhibits show Christian subjects rendered in tribal styles.

Although it is not a large collection, it is frequently supplemented by works from private collections.

69 From Egyptian and Roman Artifacts to American Furniture: A Visit to the Newark Museum, Newark

DIRECTIONS » By car, take the New Jersey Turnpike to exit 15 west—Harrison Avenue. Cross bridge to first light, and turn left. Go to the end of the park and turn right on Washington Place. The parking lot is behind the museum building.

The **Newark Museum**, 49 Washington Street, Newark (973-596-6550; www.newarkmuseum.org), is a major art museum, built in the 1890s with a more recent addition by Michael Graves & Associates. ❿ Wednesday–Sunday noon–5 PM. (Closed Monday and Tuesday.) Suggested admission fee. The museum houses some 80 galleries, which include notable collections from foreign and past cultures, including ancient Egypt and Rome; as well as Japanese, Chinese, and Tibetan art and artifacts; sculpture from India; and a large and important collection of American paintings, sculpture, decorative art, and furniture. Of particular note is a panoply of American paintings, ranging from Hudson River School to impressionism to modernist, as well as African American art, including Jacob Lawrence's works. Among the recent shows we enjoyed was a spectacular exhibition called *Patchwork from Folk Art to Fine Art*.

The Ballantine House, a finely furnished brick mansion built in 1885, gives a picture of elegant life in the upper echelons of society.

There is a sculpture garden (the Alice Ransom Dreyfuss Memorial Garden) one block from the museum. Here, in a 1-acre, walled setting, are works from the 1960s and '70s (including George Segal's popular—and real—bronze-coated tollbooth from the Holland Tunnel), as well as pieces by David Smith, James Rosati, and other notable 20th-century sculptors. This is an important, multifaceted collection, and well worth a visit.

NEW JERSEY

70 Aljira, a Center for Contemporary Art, Newark

DIRECTIONS » By car, take I-95 to exit 15, merge onto I-280 west toward Newark/Kearney; exit 15-A/15-B toward NJ 21 north (Belleville/Newark Downtown/Ironbound); left onto Grant Street; left onto Broad Street.

Aljira, a Center for Contemporary Art, 591 Broad Street, Newark (973-622-1600; www.aljira.org), is a visual arts center with ongoing exhibits and educational programs for adults and children, as well as a graphic design studio. Recent featured shows have included one on hip-hop culture and another on African American printmaking. **⏱** Wednesday–Friday noon–6 PM, Saturday 11 AM–4 PM.

Aljira, a Center for Contemporary Art
591 Broad Street
Newark
973-622-1600
www.aljira.org

AND IN ADDITION . . .
Time and Again Galleries, 1416 East Linden Avenue, Linden (908-862-0200), is an auction house that deals in fine arts and antiques from private collections and estates.

Time and Again Galleries
1416 East Linden Avenue
Linden
908-862-0200
www.timeandagain antiques.com

71 Three Centuries of American Art in an Appealing Setting: The Montclair Art Museum, Montclair

DIRECTIONS » Garden State Parkway South: Take exit 151, Watchung Avenue. Make a right at the light onto Watchung Avenue and continue on that road. After the railroad underpass, bear right and follow Watchung until the second light at North Mountain Avenue. Make a left at that light. Proceed on North Mountain Avenue until you cross Bloomfield Avenue. The museum will be on your left.

The unusually nice **Montclair Art Museum**, 3 South Mountain Avenue, Montclair (973-746-5555; www.montclairartmuseum.org), is in a town that was once home to an artists' community; a number of American landscapists lived and painted in Montclair in the 19th century—most notably George Inness. **⏱** Wednesday–Sunday, noon–5 PM. (Closed Monday and Tuesday.) Admission fee; free admission first Thursday evenings 5 PM–9 PM.

In this attractive museum you'll find an outstanding collection of American paintings that covers some three centuries. Major artists of each period are repre-

Montclair Art Museum
3 South Mountain Avenue
Montclair
973-746-5555
www.montclairart museum.org

sented. You can see two notable portraits of George Washington (one by Gilbert Stuart, and another by Charles Willson Peale), and works by Mary Cassatt, Edward Hopper, Thomas Cole, John Singer Sargent, and Robert Henri. An entire gallery is devoted to art by George Inness. More modern examples include paintings by Josef Albers, Stuart Davis, Robert Motherwell, and Andy Warhol. Sculpture ranges from works by Daniel Chester French to George Segal and Louise Nevelson, among many others.

The museum has a well-known print collection and a frequently changing series of exhibitions, in addition to this outstanding selection of American art. There is also a good collection of Native American art.

72 William Paterson University: The Ben Shahn Center for the Visual Arts and Outdoor Sculpture Collection, Wayne

DIRECTIONS » By car, take Route 80 west to Route 23 north. Turn right on Alps Road. Go 2 miles and turn right on Ratzer Road. Go 2 more miles to intersection with Hamburg Turnpike and continue on Ratzer Road; the university is on your left. To reach the Ben Shahn Center, park in Lot 3/4. You can walk to the various sites from here, or if you prefer to drive, to reach the first set of outdoor sculptures, turn at Gate 2 off Ratzer Road. To reach the second set of sculptures, turn at Gate 4 and drive to Lot 7 for parking.

Ben Shahn Center for the Visual Arts and Outdoor Sculpture Collection
William Paterson University of New Jersey
300 Pompton Road
Wayne
973-720-2000
www.wpunj.edu

While it is a rather spread-out sculpture walk, a number of pieces are placed near one another, directly between the **Ben Shahn Center for the Visual Arts and Outdoor Sculpture Collection**, 300 Pompton Road, William Paterson University of New Jersey, Wayne (973-720-2000; www.wpunj.edu), which hosts a variety of art exhibitions, and the Student Center of William Paterson University. ❶ Monday–Friday 10 AM–5 PM. Another outdoor collection is between Gate 2 and Hunziker Hall. The sculpture collection—all abstract shapes and forms—includes many works in geometric and evocative forms. The artists include William Finneran, Rosemarie Castoro, Lyman Kipp, Stephen Antonakos, and Michel Gerard, among others. There are new additions and changing exhibitions both indoors and out. Pick up a map and descriptive brochure at the Ben Shahn Center.

73 The Stickley Museum at Craftsman Farms; Where the Arts and Crafts Aesthetic Took Root in America, Parsippany

DIRECTIONS » By car, from I-80 west take I-287 south to exit 39B. Take Route 10 west for about 3 miles, then turn right onto Manor Lane and watch for the sign to Craftsman Farms. The main entrance is on the right.

The **Stickley Museum at Craftsman Farms** is located at 2352 Route 10 West, in Morris Plains (973-540-1165; www.stickleymuseum.org). 🅗 Thursday–Sunday noon–4 PM. (Closed Monday–Wednesday.) Admission fee. To visit the museum you must take a guided tour, which lasts about one hour. You are welcome to walk around the grounds on your own and visit the gift shop for additional information, as well as for books and objects of relevance to the Arts and Crafts movement.

Stickley Museum at
Craftsman Farms
2352 Route 10 West
Morris Plains
973-540-1165
www.stickleymuseum.org

Once the home of the country's foremost proponent of the Arts and Crafts movement, Craftsmen Farms is an especially interesting place to visit. Gustav Stickley was a furniture designer (his furniture is still in great demand), manufacturer, publisher, philosopher, social critic, and architect.

His originally 650-acre (reduced today to 30 acres) tract of land in rural New Jersey, was, as he described it, his "Garden of Eden." In this lush, wooded area he built his beautifully crafted log house in 1911, and then went on to set up a utopian community that he called Craftsman Farms. Its idea was to further "the simple life," a life devoted to crafts and trades, a life that would value country living.

Following a similar movement in England begun in the 1880s, the American Arts and Crafts movement culminated in the years between 1910 and 1925. Both in England and the USA, emphasis was on simplicity— a reaction to the excesses and overdesign of the Victorian era, in architecture and crafts and garden design. Stickley and his colleagues believed that beauty does not need ornamentation of elaboration. Simplicity and function were the goals, in addition to an organic emphasis on the handmade. The master craftsman was to be both designer and producer, working with his hands, taking pride in his handiwork.

Stickley was able to live by his philosophical principles at Craftsman Farms. Between 1908 and 1914 he designed furniture, lived in his log house, published a journal, oversaw the local farmers who worked his land, and created a school offering programs in agriculture and handicrafts for children.

When you visit Craftsman Farms (only by guided tours), you'll find a log "cabin" (actually a fair-size house), with a great stone chimney, rounded ceiling beams, overhanging eaves, small diamond-paned windows, and wooden columns. The exterior of the house is in what we think of today as quintessential Arts and Crafts style, with its low horizontal lines and rustic simplicity. Its long, sloping roofline and wide overhang makes it seem to be nestling into the earth. In the interior you'll see examples of his wood furniture (now often described as "Mission") set into rooms with dark, simple woodwork.

Now a National Historic Landmark, the property includes a number of other buildings: stone stables, three cottages, and farm structures, all reflecting Stickley's goal of building in harmony with nature, using natural materials, and being constructed by hand.

74 Folk Art and Modern Craft Workshops at Peters Valley Craft Center, Layton

DIRECTIONS» By car, from Route 80 take exit 34B to Route 15 N to Route 206 N; go left onto Route 560 west, straight through the blinking light in the center of the small village of Layton, onto Route 640. After about 2 miles, turn right at the stop sign onto Route 615. Go about 0.5 mile to the entrance of Peters Valley.

Peters Valley Craft Center is located on Route 615 in Layton. It is open daily, year-round, from 11 AM–5 PM. Note that the studios are open to the public only on weekends (Saturday and Sunday) 2 PM–5 PM, during the summer. Guided tours are offered on weekends at 2 PM and leave from the craft store. The Doremus Gallery (973-948-5200; www.petersvalley.org) is open daily during the summer, 9 AM–5 PM, and only on weekdays during the rest of the year.

If you've never watched crafts being made by skilled artisans, or if you are perhaps a would-be artisan yourself, don't miss a trip to this tiny but bustling community. Anyone with an interest in the creative process will find this a fascinating experience. Here, you can watch everything from musical instruments

to weathervanes to horse shoes to wall hangings in process.

Beautifully situated within the Delaware Water Gap National Park Recreation Area, Peters Valley is a one-of-a-kind creative community where its crafts persons live, work, and teach. (They have no objection to visitors watching them work.) It has been in existence for more than 40 years as a nonprofit community whose aim is to promote both traditional and contemporary crafts. It usually has one artisan in each field or discipline: blacksmithing, photography, textiles, fine metals, ceramics, woodworking; each craftsperson is selected to live on-site for one year and is given a studio and an assistant. In the summer, artisans from all over come to teach their techniques to students at every level. There are eight studios (one for each discipline), a craft shop, and an art gallery. Summer weekends bring a bustling and exciting mix—both of artistic and natural beauty, for Peters Valley is situated in one of the most spectacular landscapes around—and is ideal for woodsy hikes.

Begin by picking up a self-guided walking tour at the Craft Store (the first building you see as you arrive, and directly in front of a grand Greek Revival–style house (the photography studio). Across the street is the office; here you can sign up for a guided tour if you wish. Upstairs is the Doremus Gallery, which has three shows each summer (including one devoted to works form the anagama kiln behind the ceramics studio).

If you decide to visit studios without a tour, your itinerary will probably follow the older of the studios on the map. Among our favorites were the one dedicated to "special topics" (such as stained-glass making, or collage, or soap making), the photography studio (workshops dealing with both historic and contemporary techniques and ideas), and silversmithing and metal casting (forging and soldering). You'll see printmaking and ceramics—some 150 workshops are offered each summer season (June 1–August 31), and you can be a casual visitor, or a participant—at any level. There is an annual Craft Fair in late summer. If you prefer a quieter experience, visit in spring or fall.

NORTH

Peters Valley Craft Center
19 Kuhn Road
Layton
www.petersvalley.org

CENTRAL

75 The Hunterdon Art Museum, Clinton

DIRECTIONS» By car, take Route 78 west to exit 15; bear right to Route 173 east; left at Exxon station, and go over the yellow bridge. The museum is in the stone mill on your left.

Hunterdon Art Museum
7 Lower Center Street
Clinton
908-735-8415
www.hunterdon
artmuseum.org

The fine small collection at the **Hunterdon Art Museum**, 7 Lower Center Street, Clinton (908-735-8415; www.hunterdonartmuseum.org), concentrates on prints and drawings and paintings from the 1930s to the present. ☻ Tuesday–Thursday, Saturday, and Sunday 11 AM–5 PM; Friday 11 AM–9 PM. (Closed Monday.) Suggested admission fee. Works exhibited include those by internationally known artists, as well as by younger artists from our region. Among the highlights are prints by Mark di Suvero, Alex Katz, and Philip Guston.

76 A University Art Museum with a Distinctive Collection: The Jane Voorhees Zimmerli Art Museum at Rutgers University, New Brunswick

DIRECTIONS» By car, take the New Jersey Turnpike to exit 9. Follow the signs for "Route 18 north, New Brunswick" for approximately 3 miles. Follow the large overhead green sign that reads "George Street, Rutgers University, exit 1/2 mile." At the exit light (George Street), turn left. Go to the next light at Hamilton Street. The museum is on the corner.

Jane Voorhees Zimmerli Art Museum
71 Hamilton Street
New Brunswick
732-932-7237
www.zimmerlimuseum
.rutgers.edu

The **Jane Voorhees Zimmerli Art Museum**, 71 Hamilton Street, New Brunswick (732-932-7237; www.zimmerlimuseum.rutgers.edu), is home to an interesting and distinctive collection on the campus of Rutgers University. Although the museum began as a small collection, it now includes more than 50,000 works, and also hosts many special exhibits. ☻ September–July: Tuesday–Friday 10 AM–4:30 PM, Saturday and Sunday noon–5 PM. (Closed Monday and entire month of August.) Admission fee; free admission for children under age 18.

You'll find painting, sculpture, and prints (an outstanding Japanese collection). One of the highlights—and most unusual elements—of the museum is the George Riabov Russian art collection, which includes

NEW JERSEY

folk art, stage design, lithographs, and prints—a well-worth-seeing broad view of Russia's nonconformist past.

77 Art to Enhance the Corporate Corridors of Johnson & Johnson, New Brunswick

DIRECTIONS » By car from New York City, take the New Jersey Turnpike to exit 9 to New Brunswick.

Although many large corporations collect art and display it within their buildings, few allow the public at large to enjoy it, too—especially these days with heightened security.

Fortunately, Johnson & Johnson, Inc., the healthcare conglomerate, has a much more public-spirited attitude and welcomes visitors to see some of their art treasures (via conducted tour).

The sleek and spare **Johnson & Johnson International Headquarters**, located at 1 Johnson & Johnson Plaza, in the heart of New Brunswick (www.jnj.com), houses a large collection of contemporary American art. This elegant building complex, designed by I. M. Pei in the early 1980s, is a fairly extensive art "gallery," as well as the home of the conglomerate's headquarters.

The Johnson & Johnson art collection was started in the early 20th century but not formally organized until 1983. Some 1,200 works—prints, gouaches, paintings, photographs, and sculpture—form the collection, from which pieces are selected to adorn offices, hallways, atria, and nooks and crannies. The art is moved around regularly—with means that you will likely see different pieces at different times. To view the art you must take a tour, which will lead you mostly through the common rooms (private offices are usually off-limits). You will see maybe 20 percent of the entire collection. To arrange for a tour, phone the curator, Michael J. Bzdak, at 732-524-3698. Mr. Bzdak will give you directions to the headquarters. Tours last 30 to 40 minutes and are offered preferably during the week.

The parts of the collection that we saw included a wide variety of styles and media. Among them were a number of prints and smaller works by leading contemporary American artists. As you wind your way along circular passageways leading from one "maze" to the next, or through long expanses of corridors, you

CENTRAL

Johnson & Johnson International Headquarters
1 Johnson & Johnson Plaza
New Brunswick
732-524-3698 (tour)
www.jnj.com

will find the collection is eclectic and somewhat unpredictable, but you might well be surprised by some unexpected artistic treat tucked away in an unlikely spot. All of the art is American, with the exception of a Henry Moore reclining *Mother and Child* (1983), also the only outdoor piece. You will find art by Louise Nevelson, George Segal, Jim Dine, Alexander Calder, Jasper Johns, Robert Rauschenberg, and Joseph Cornell, to name only a few.

The tour also includes the various views of the surrounding panorama and of the buildings' lower roofs, punctuated with unmistakably Pei pyramid-shaped skylights. Pei's concept for Johnson & Johnson was to create "a city in a park, a park in a city," which is, in fact, what he accomplished.

In addition, Johnson & Johnson has a gallery, where you can view works by New Jersey artists on themes related to health care and children. Exhibits here are not included in the tour, and you can see these works on your own.

78 A Treasure Trove of Art on Campus: Princeton University, Princeton

DIRECTIONS» By car, take the New Jersey Turnpike to exit 9. Take Route 1 south, then Route 571 west to Princeton. Follow the signs to University Parking.

Princeton University, 1 Nassau Hall, Princeton (609-258-6306 for general information, 609-258-3788 for museum; www.princeton.edu/artmuseum). ♿ The university campus Sculpture Walk and museum are open year-round. Museum: Tuesday, Wednesday, Friday, and Saturday 10 AM–5 PM; Thursday 10 AM–10 PM; Sunday 1 PM–5 PM. (Closed Monday.) Free admission.

This is both an indoor and outdoor artwalk. All over Princeton University's beautiful campus you'll find notable sculptures available for all to see. And in the fine art museum is a notable and exciting collection, also open to the public (as well as for teaching purposes). Pick up a walking map of campus at the information desk at the main gate.

The museum (which offers tours, if you wish) was founded in 1882, and is one of the leading university art museums in the country. It is housed in an imposing building on campus.

Princeton University
1 Nassau Hall
Princeton
609-258-6306
www.princeton
.edu/artmuseum

NEW JERSEY

The museum has a fine collection of art from both Western and Eastern cultures. There are more than 72,000 pieces here, making this an important site for both visitors and students. Among its specialties are Chinese art, Central European modernists (Kandinsky and Nolde, for example), African sculpture, historic Americans paintings, work from the ancient Americas, ancient and Islamic art, a collection of French paintings (including landscapes by Monet), American modernists, and a large collection of prints and drawing by Europeans (Rembrandt, Dürer, Goya) and Americans (Winslow Homer and Georgia O'Keeffe).

This is a wonderful collection, with new additions to be seen frequently. (On our last visit, a series of Asian scroll paintings were a recent and beautiful acquisition.)

But the museum is not the only art sight at Princeton. The campus is home to a spectacular collection of sculptures (almost all of it from the 20th century), and they are set carefully to enhance their beauty. You'll find some 20 works as you walk around.

If you begin your visit at the museum, your first major sculpture to see will be the huge Picasso in front of the museum. *Head of a Woman*, made of cast concrete, was executed by Carl Nesjar (who did many of Picasso's sculptures from maquettes by the master. (It was made for this very site; students had the unusual experiences of watching it being made.)

With map in hand you can walk in any direction from here to see works by your favorite sculptors, or you can return to the campus main gate and follow the tour from there.

First you will come upon a Henry Moore work, *Oval with Points* (which may remind you of an elephant head); it sits elegantly on the campus green. On the pathway behind West College, to your left, are George Rickey's *Two Planes* and *Vertical Horizon II*. The kinetic parts of his sculptures move with the wind and are mesmerizing.

Between Firestone Library and University Chapel is a well-known Jacques Lipchitz work called *Song of the Vowels*, with a cubist harp motif and a soaring bronze construction.

In the lobby of the Firestone Library is an Isamu Noguchi sculpture *White Sun*; made of marble, it is a large irregular open circle.

Back in the outdoor campus, there is another nearby "classic": Louise Nevelson's *Atmosphere and Environment*. Made of COR-TEN steel (measuring 21 feet high and 16 feet long), its geometric forms are in an interlocking pattern of whit, gold, and black.

Abraham and Isaac, in Memory of May 4, 1970, Kent State is George Segal's memorial to the massacre; it is situated between Firestone Library and Dickinson Hall. Note the very realistic look of this work—unusual in this mostly abstract collection.

Inside the Architecture Building, in the stairwell, is a contemporary work by Eduardo Paolozzi, *Marok-Marok-Miosa*. An exponent of England's junk sculpture style, Paolozzi used found objects and combined them in imaginative ways.

Clement Meadmore's minimalist *Upstart 2* (1970), Naum Gabo's *Spheric Theme*, and Masayuki Nagare's *Stone Riddle* can all be seen in the Engineering Quad.

In the center of the campus you'll recognize a work by Alexander Calder: his *Five Disks: One Empty*. Placed in the plaza between Fine Hall and Jadwin Hall, this giant work is a stabile with his iconic cutouts and pointed forms in black steel. Within the Fine Hall Library is a well-known work by Jacob Epstein, a head of Albert Einstein. (As you may know, Einstein was a familiar and beloved figure on this campus for many years, and this statue is appropriately placed in the physics library.)

Just behind Fine Hall is Jadwin Hall; here Antoine Pevsner is represented by a 10-foot-high bronze abstraction called *Construction in the Third and Fourth Dimension*. Pevsner was interested in spacial ambiguity and the idea of infinite continuity; he was active in the constructionist movement in Russia in the 1920s.

Sphere VI is a work by Arnaldo Pomodoro, placed in the Butler College Courtyard. Pomodoro specialized in negative/positive casting, in which he gouged out parts of the surface to give the form a sense of motion from within; he described it as an "expression of interior movement."

David Smith's constructions are always favorites; his *Cubi XII* is no exception. On the lawn of Spellman Hall (not far from the train station) is his exploration of cubism in welded steel, one of a series of 38.

In the heart of the campus is a particularly lovely spot: Prospect Gardens. Here you can rest, enjoy the plantings, and also see Tony Smith's *Moses*, whose angular planes also call to mind the cubist movement with its painted steel and angular forms.

There are more contemporary works to be seen as well. Of particular note is the Richard Serra sculpture adjacent to the Lewis Science Library, a building designed by Frank Gehry. (In fact, within his building is a Gehry sculpture; a most unusual work, it resembles a small building within the giant first-floor space.) The Serra work is a giant walk-through monument of undulating forms.

In addition to the works we have mentioned, look also for art by Gaston Lachaise, Reg Butler, and Kenneth Snelson.

The combination of traditional Gothic architecture amid lovely landscape and modernism (in both architecture and sculpture) is a rare and wonderful one. Don't miss this outing!

79 Contemporary Sculpture in a Bucolic Landscape: Grounds for Sculpture, Hamilton

DIRECTIONS » By car, take the New Jersey Turnpike to exit 7A, then I-195 west to I-295 north, and to exit 65B, Sloan Avenue west. Go 0.2 mile and turn right at first traffic light. Follow the signs for Grounds for Sculpture, turn left onto Klockner Road and turn right at first traffic light; go less than a mile and make the

Carlos Dorrien: *The Nine Muses* (1990–97), Grounds for Sculpture

second left turn onto Sculptors Way, go 0.2 mile. Turn left onto Fairgrounds Road. You'll find Grounds for Sculpture down the road a bit, on your right.

Grounds for Sculpture, 18 Fairgrounds Road, Hamilton (609-586-0616), is a 22-acre sculpture park and museum situated on the former site of the New Jersey State Fair. ♿ Tuesday–Sunday 10 AM–6 PM year-round. (Closed Monday.) Admission fee. Tours are available, though you may take your own self-guided tour (brochures are available at the reception desk).

Here, on a rolling terrain dotted with crab apple trees, dogwood, and weeping beeches are some 170 works of art by some of our best-known sculptors. A walk in and among these gracefully set statues—both realistic and abstract—is a treat not to be missed.

The grounds are picturesque; there is a lotus pond, a woodland gazebo with an observation deck, and a charming arbor of wisteria (visit in late spring), as well as the glass-walled museum with changing exhibitions. Works displayed are both by established and lesser-known artists, both American and international. They vary in size from small to monumental, and are placed harmoniously in natural settings. Some are quite avant-

Grounds for Sculpture
18 Fairgrounds Road
Hamilton
609-586-0616
www.groundsfor
sculpture.org

NEW JERSEY

garde, making this a more unusual sculpture site than many we have visited.

Grounds for Sculpture was created by J. Seward Johnson, a renowned American sculptor of lifelike figures. Here you'll see his witty and charming work of flowers sitting at the edge of a country pond, an homage to (or take-off on) Edouard Manet's iconic painting *Déjeuner sur l'herbe*. We recommend visiting in warmer weather; there is even an elegant terraced restaurant overlooking the grounds.

80 Georgian Court College, Lakewood

DIRECTIONS» By car from the Garden State Parkway, take exit 91 (Route 549) south to Route 88, and go west. The entrance to the college campus is just off North Lake Drive.

Enclosed by high walls, the elegant campus of **Georgian Court College**, 900 Lakewood Avenue Lakewood (732-364-2200; www.georgiancourtcollege. edu), features formal gardens, a magnificent mansion (once the home of financier George Jay Gould) and classical marble sculpture, including the huge Fountain of *Apollo*, by John Massey Rhind, and an imposing lion. **H** Open daytime to visitors. Free admission.

Georgian
Court College
900 Lakewood
Avenue
Lakewood
732-364-2200
www.georgiancourt
college.edu

Lion at Georgian Court College

PHOTO CREDITS

Page i: Eagles and Prey, Christophe Fratin. Photo by Robert L. Harrison. *Page vi: The Shimmering of Heated Air,* Shono Shounsai (1904–1974). Living National Treasure ca. 1958. Courtesy of the Asia Society, the Lloyd Cotsen Collection. Photo by Pat Pollard. *Page vii:* Edward Hopper's boyhood home. Photo by Lucy D. Rosenfeld. *Page viii:* Bridge of Sighs, Yale University. Photo by Margaret Brooks. *Page ix:* Geleda-Yoruba mask, Nigeria. Courtesy of the SMA Museum, Tenafly, New Jersey. Photo by Robert Mates. *Page 7:* Fountain-head figure at Channel Gardens, René Chambellan. Courtesy of Rockefeller Center. Photo by Lucy D. Rosenfeld. *Page 10: Atlas* (1937), Lee Lawrie and René Chambellan. Courtesy of Rockefeller Center. Photo by Lucy D. Rosenfeld. *Page 14: Honey Bear*, Frederick George Richard Roth. Wikimedia, p.d. *Page 15: Alice in Wonderland*, José de Creeft. Wikimedia, p.d. Photo by Robert L. Harrison. *Page 19: Alma Mater* (1904), Daniel Chester French, Columbia University Library. Photo by Magnus Torfason. Wikimedia, p.d. *Page 41:* Japanese flower basket. Courtesy of the Asia Society, the Lloyd Cotsen Collection. Photo by Pat Pollard. *Page 47:* View of the High Line. Photo by Lucy D. Rosenfeld. *Page 57:* Vairapani, Tibet (12th century). Courtesy of the Rubin Museum of Art. *Page 65:* Eldridge Street Synagogue East Window. Photo by the authors. *Page 71: Rector Gate*, R. M. Fischer: Photo by Lucy D. Rosenfeld. *Page 73:* Museum of Jewish Heritage. Photo by Lucy D. Rosenfeld. *Page 74: Korean War Memorial.* Mac Adams. Photo by Lucy D. Rosenfeld. *Page 75: The Immigrants,* Luis Sanguino. Photo by Lucy D. Rosenfeld. *Page 76: Alamo*, Tony Rosenthal. Wikimedia. Photo by Beyond My Ken. *Page 77: Giuseppe Garibaldi* (ca. 1888), Giovanni Turini Photo by Robert L. Harrison. *Page 89:* A New York Public Library lion. Photo by Lucy D. Rosenfeld. *Pages 105 & 107:* St. Ann's Church windows. Photos by the authors. *Page 117:* Sherman Monument, Augustus Saint-Gaudens. Photo by Robert L. Harrison. Page 150: Nassau County Museum gazebo. Photo by Lucy D. Rosenfeld. *Page 151:* Old Westbury Gardens, Photo by Lucy D. Rosenfeld. *Page 157:* SUNY at Stony Brook, The Charles B. Wang Center. Photo by Lucy D. Rosenfeld. *Page 158: Requiem 9/11,* Dan Christoffel. Photo by Robert L. Harrison. Courtesy of Adelphi University. *Page 159:* Installation, Grace Knowlton. Photo by Lucy D. Rosenfeld. Courtesy of Rockland Center for the Arts. *Page 163: Endless Column,* Tal Streeter. Courtesy of Storm King Art Center. Photo by Lucy D. Rosenfeld. *Page 164: Adonai*, Alexander Liberman. Courtesy of Storm King Art Center. Photo by Lucy D. Rosenfeld. *Page 170:* Fountain on the grounds of Kykuit. Photo by Gryffindor. *Page 172: The Crucifixion,* Marc Chagall. Courtesy of Union Church of Pocantico Hills. Photo by Lucy D. Rosenfeld. *Page 174:* Courtesy of the Russel Wright Design Center. Photo by Carol Franklin. *Page 183:* Chuang Yen Monastery. Photo by Lucy D. Rosenfeld. *Page 186: Reclining Woman,* Henry Moore. Courtesy of the Donald M. Kendall Sculpture Gardens at PepsiCo world headquarters. *Page 194:* César Pelli's Malone Center at Yale University. Photo by Margaret Brooks. *Page 199: Screen Sculpture* (1995), David Hayes. Courtesy of the Kouros Gallery. *Page 200: La Construcción* (ca. 1990), Juan Bordes. Courtesy of the Kouros Gallery. *Page 201:* Tin Man, Stephen Cote. Courtesy of the Garden of Ideas. Photo by Lucy D. Rosenfeld. *Page 207:* Funerary effigy, Akan, Ghana. Courtesy of the SMA Museum. Photo by Robert Mates. *Page 218:* Lewis Science Center and Richard Serra sculpture. Courtesy of Princeton University. Photo by Lucy D. Rosenfeld. *Page 220: The Nine Muses* (1990–97), Carlos Dorrien. Granite, 132 x 240 x 360 inches. Courtesy of the Sculpture Foundation, Inc. © Artist/Artist's Estate. On view at Grounds for Sculpture, Hamilton, New Jersey. Photo by David W. Steele. *Page 221:* Georgian Court College lion. Photo by Lucy D. Rosenfeld.

INDEX